Hero of the Crossing

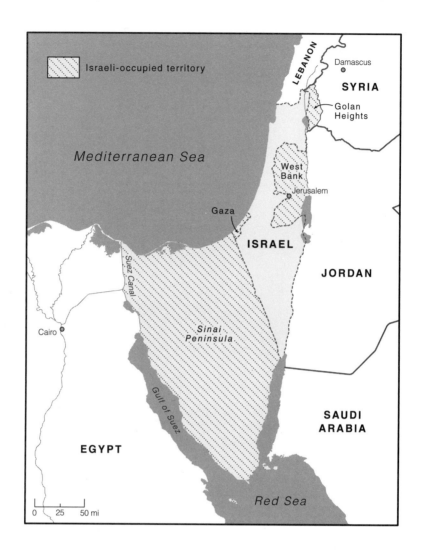

Egypt, Israel, and Syria on the eve of the 1973 War.

HERO OF THE CROSSING

How Anwar Sadat and the
1973 War Changed the World

THOMAS W. LIPPMAN

Potomac Books
An imprint of the University of Nebraska Press

All rights reserved. Potomac Books is an imprint
of the University of Nebraska Press.
Manufactured in the United States of America.

Library of Congress Cataloging-in-Publication Data

Lippman, Thomas W. author.
Hero of the crossing: how Anwar Sadat and the
1973 war changed the world / Thomas W. Lippman.
pages   cm
Includes bibliographical references and index.
ISBN 978–1–61234–702–8 (cloth: alk. paper)
ISBN 978–1–61234–795–0 (epub)
ISBN 978–1–61234–796–7 (mobi)
ISBN 978–1–61234–797–4 (pdf)
1. Sadat, Anwar, 1918–1981. 2. Presidents—Egypt.
3. Israel-Arab War, 1973. 4. Egypt—Politics and
government—1970–1981. I. Title.
DT107.85.L565 2016
956.04'81—dc23
2015033701

Set in Next LT Pro by L. Auten.

Contents

Acknowledgments

This book would have been much more difficult to write, and would have taken far longer, had it not been for the prodigious work of Jonathan Bertman, my research assistant for this project at the Middle East Institute in Washington. I am deeply grateful to him, and to the Institute for making him available.

The relentless researchers of the National Security Archive at George Washington University deserve the gratitude of every author, journalist, and historian whose work benefits from the vast troves of previously classified U.S. government documents that they have unearthed and catalogued. I am grateful to them, and in particular to my daughter-in-law, Autumn Kladder, for their prompt responses to my requests.

I greatly appreciated the help of my wife, Sidney, and my agent, Janet Reid, who read the manuscript and saved me from embarrassing mistakes and omissions. What errors remain are my own.

And finally, I am grateful to the editors of the *Washington Post*, who sent me to Cairo as the newspaper's resident regional correspondent for four crucial years and dispatched me back to the Middle East innumerable times afterward to report on people and events there. They enabled me to roam the Arab world from Morocco to Oman and to talk to Arabs of every school of political and religious thought.

A Note on Arabic Words and Names

There is no universally accepted standard for the transliteration of Arabic words and names into English. The Arabic alphabet contains letters for which there is no English equivalent. The way a particular word or name is written in the Roman alphabet sometimes depends on whether the original transliterator wrote in English or French. In spoken Arabic, the article *al-* or *el-* is elided before some consonants, as in *An-Nahar*, a Lebanese newspaper, or Majlis ash-Shura, the Saudi consultative assembly, and is sometimes transliterated that way, sometimes not.

In this book I have used the transliteration style that has become standard in American print media, with no attempt to reproduce the no-equivalent consonants or glottal stops of the original through orthographic markers, as is done in academic texts. Where an individual's preferred transliteration of his or her name is known, or where an individual's transliterated name is well known in the West, I have deferred to that form, as in Gamal Abdel Nasser. Many men named for the Prophet of Islam transliterate the name as Muhammad, which has become the English standard, but others use different versions. When these are known, I have used them, as in Mohamed Heikal.

In quotations from the writings of others, I have retained the style of the original. Thus, Jeddah may sometimes appear as Jidda, Assad as Asad, Abdul as Abdel, and *sharia*—or Islamic law—as shariah.

Names of individual men usually consist of a given name, a middle name (sometimes a patronymic such as 'bin Abdullah,' or son of Abdullah), and a family name: Muhammad Anwar el-Sadat. In the index, he would be listed by the family name: Sadat, Muhammad Anwar el-. In a name that contains the word Abdul or Abdel, as in Omar Abdel Rahman, Abdul is not a freestanding name: it is a prefix to and part of the name that follows. Abdel Rahman is one name, meaning "servant of the Merciful One," that is, of God. On second reference, and in the index, this person is Abdel Rahman, not just Rahman. (The exception is Abdel Nasser, from whose name the Abdel is usually omitted.)

Introduction

All wars end sooner or later. Shooting stops. Documents are signed. Prisoners are exchanged. Troops and refugees go home. The effects of war, on people and societies, often linger—sometimes permanently. Wars reshape history, geography, and demography. People who lived in one country at the start of hostilities may live in another, without moving, when the war ends and maps are redrawn. Entire communities migrate, or are forced to move, to new locations. Countries are dismantled, as in Yugoslavia, or created, as in Bangladesh and South Sudan. Alliances are dissolved and new ones formed. Shipping routes change. Industries relocate. New patterns of commerce develop.

In the past half century, these phenomena have been on display most dramatically in the Middle East. The Vietnam War and the conflicts ignited by the breakup of Yugoslavia were long and lethal; they killed uncounted numbers of civilians. But their impact was pretty much limited to the regions in which they were fought. Neither had the widespread, long-lasting effect on the world of the Arab-Israeli War of 1973, the October War, even though that conflict itself was confined to a small corner of the world and the fighting ended inconclusively. That war, and the related international politics, resonated far beyond the boundaries of the combatants. It permanently transformed everything from the Cold War balance of power to the global economy to tank warfare doctrine. It is remembered mostly because it eventually made possible the 1979 peace treaty between Egypt and Israel, which altered the strategic balance of the Middle East; but the effects of the war—and of the political decisions that led to it and arose from it—affected more than the combatants in their time. The war provoked a dangerous confrontation between the United States and the Soviet Union that tested, and ultimately reinforced, their bilateral détente. Other decisions related to the October War contributed to the Soviet Union's eventual defeat in the Cold War. War-related policies revolutionized global energy markets, enriching some oil producers beyond their imagination while inflicting long-lasting economic pain on consumer countries. Yet the war and the flawed peace that followed also left unresolved issues that underlie much of the tension that grips the Middle East today.

The architect of that 1973 conflict was Muhammad Anwar el-Sadat, president of Egypt from 1970 to 1981, who defied worldwide incredulity and ridicule to pursue—and eventually achieve—a strategic vision in which only he believed. With the passage of time, the publication of memoirs, and the declassification of mountains of documents by the United States, the Soviet Union, and other countries, we can see that what Sadat did and the way he did it had a profound impact, for better or worse, on the world of today. It could even be argued that the causes of radical extremism in contemporary Islam can be traced to Sadat's policies.

When Sadat became president of Egypt in the autumn of 1970, he gained a prize of dubious value. A proud nation with a seven-thousand-year history, Egypt was in ruins, economically and psychologically, and had no prospect of short-term improvement.

Four wars with Israel, in 1948, 1956, and 1967, and the so-called War of Attrition, the artillery duels of 1969–70, had drained Egypt's treasury. Under the influence of his supporters in Moscow, President Gamal Abdel Nasser had nationalized the entire economy—heavy industry, banks, real estate, department stores, transportation, insurance companies, the cotton market, and the food distribution network. The result was that a country of thirty-five million people had been stripped of incentives to work. Its industries were obsolete, its bureaucracy bloated, its infrastructure deteriorating, its currency worthless outside Egypt. Good-quality consumer goods had disappeared; some popular products were replaced by shoddy substitutes made in Egypt that consumers bought only because there was no alternative; some were obtained through barter with Warsaw Pact nations. (For the first two years I lived there with my family, the only butter available was rancid-tasting stuff made locally from the milk of water buffalo.) The country gave up on maintenance. Telephones didn't work because thieves had stolen the copper wires. No new hospitals had been built in decades. Public spaces in the cities reeked of urine. Farmers still relied on animal power to plow their fields and transport their crops. Donkey carts clogged the streets of Cairo, where the air was so dirty that residents who washed their hair in the shower could see the grit flowing down the drain. The Suez Canal, one of the few principal sources of hard currency, had been closed since Egypt's forces were routed by Israel in the shattering Six-Day War of 1967. The crucial tourism industry had evaporated, large areas of the country were off-limits to foreigners, and the Red Sea beaches were under Israeli control. And the country was deeply in debt to the Soviet Union for the weapons it had been buying to rebuild its armed forces after the disastrous 1967 rout.

In addition, every gain that had been achieved under Nasser, such as delivery of electricity to the villages, had been outstripped by the rapid growth of the population.

Egypt was a broken country, not only physically but spiritually, the morale of its people crushed by the military catastrophe of 1967. That wipeout had shattered morale not just in Egypt but throughout the Arab world. In that brief conflict, Israel seized the part of Jerusalem it did not previously control; the Gaza Strip; the land between the Jordan River and Israel known as the West Bank; Syria's Golan Heights; and all of Egypt's vast Sinai Peninsula. Egypt's air force had been destroyed without leaving the ground. When Nasser died in 1970 Israel remained in control of those areas and there was no prospect that any would be restored to Arab rule. The stalemate was intolerable for all Arabs, but they saw no way out. Arabs live in what is known as a culture of shame, in which fear of disapprobation by family and the public is a powerful element of social behavior; in 1970 they were collectively living in a state of humiliation, shamed by their power-lessness against tiny Israel.

With Moscow's help Nasser had begun to reequip his army and air force, but not to the point where Egypt was a credible match for Israel. The arms supplies only increased Egypt's dependence on the Soviet Union, which was also the principal supplier of Iraq and Syria. Egypt and the United States had broken diplomatic relations in 1967.

In addition to its economic and military plight, Egypt was politi-cally comatose. Nasser ran a police state. He tolerated no dissent, per-mitted no political parties other than his official Arab Socialist Union, and imprisoned opponents. The government owned the newspapers and the television network, which naturally followed his orders. To rebuild his country after inheriting the presidency, Sadat believed it was necessary to exorcise the legacy of Nasser, break the grip of the Soviet Union, and adopt an entirely new strategic line based on part-nership with the United States. To achieve those goals, he was pre-pared to go to war if necessary.

At the time, few people, even among his close advisers, under-stood what he was up to or how far he was prepared to go. All of Sadat's major initiatives and decisions, undertaken at the height of the Cold War, seemed to catch Washington and Moscow by surprise. The same was true of Saudi Arabia's decision to support Egypt dur-ing the 1973 fighting by participating in an oil embargo against the United States. The irony is that the Central Intelligence Agency and a handful of shrewd diplomats predicted many of these developments and assessed them accurately. Their reports, now declassified, show that the leaders of the United States refused to believe what their ana-lysts were reporting because the analyses ran counter to conventional wisdom, while the leaders of the Soviet Union failed to respond to their analysts because what Sadat did could not be reconciled with the Kremlin's inflexible ideology. That same inflexibility also came to undermine Moscow's once-flourishing relations with other Arab countries, in a crucial defeat for the communist side of the Cold War.

Modern history offers many examples of leaders who were little known or lightly regarded when they ascended to power, only to seize the opportunity to leave an indelible mark on their times. Harry S. Truman could be placed in that category, as could Fidel Castro, Pope John XXIII, and Iran's revolutionary leader, Ayatollah Ruhollah Khomeini. Surely the outstanding exemplar was Sadat, who became president of the largest Arab country almost by accident and was a figure of ridicule to many of his countrymen. How little they knew.

As a correspondent for the *Washington Post*, I had the privilege of living in Egypt during four dramatic years of Sadat's presidency and of traveling throughout the region as leaders and organizations struggled to understand what he was up to and figure out how to respond. I knew Sadat, and saw him in action many times. My journalistic colleagues and I chronicled dramatic, unpredictable events as they unfolded; what we could not assess at the time was their long-term strategic, economic, and demographic implications. Compounding this problem, not just for us but for diplomats and negotiators, was the fact that Sadat himself often seemed to make up policy as he went along.

By the time I arrived in Cairo, in 1975, his main strategic objectives had become clear: to restore Egypt's national pride after the military thrashing by Israel in 1967; to forge a peace agreement with Israel that would return to Egypt every square inch of land lost in that conflict; and to construct a strategic alliance with the United States in place of the fruitless partnership with the Soviet Union, which had brought Egypt to ruin in the time of Nasser. We could discern the strategy, but we could never predict the tactics Sadat would adopt in pursuit of it; his tactics were a zigzag through a maze, even to some of his closest advisers. As for what his decisions might mean in the twenty-first century, it is doubtful that Sadat gave it much thought. He certainly did not intend to disrupt the global economic order and set off the greatest transfer of wealth in history from rich nations to poor, but that was one of the consequences of his decision to go to war.

This attempt to assess the long-term implications of those decisions began a few years ago as an intellectual exercise for me and my colleagues at the Middle East Institute in Washington. We were asked to nominate the most important events in the Middle East since the institute was founded in 1946. The most obvious candidates were the creation of Israel in 1948, the war of 1967, and the Iranian revolution of 1979. But in less obvious ways, the 1973 war and its aftermath had, and continue to have, an impact on far more people across a much wider range of the world.

Sadat is not remembered fondly in Egypt. During his eleven years in office, he evolved in Egyptian public perception from clownish light-weight to national hero—the "Hero of the Crossing," he was called after Egyptian troops crossed the Suez Canal at the start of the war—to reviled failure who deserved the assassination that befell him in 1981.

The people of Egypt were shocked when Sadat was assassinated, but not grief-stricken. By the time of his death, he had blackened his own reputation and sullied his manifest accomplishments with his high-handed, one-man rule, the silencing of his critics, and his pharaonic posturing. Inside Egypt he left a legacy of unfulfilled aspirations for prosperity and for freedom. Under his uninspiring successor, Hosni Mubarak, Egypt descended into political and economic torpor that ended only with the upheaval of the "Arab Spring" in 2011. Mubarak, a colorless plodder ridiculed by students as "La Vache Qui Rit" because of his supposed resemblance to the cow on the French cheese label, represented a stylistic reversal from the theatrical Sadat, and he did briefly allow more political freedom. But he insisted on maintaining the "state of emergency" declared after Sadat's death, the basis for the arrest and torture of the politically undesirable that characterized his regime and stoked the rebellion of 2011, and he was no more able to deliver prosperity than Sadat had been.

It is regrettable that Egyptians benefited so little from Sadat's achievements and have so little esteem for his legacy, because he was a game-changing figure in world affairs. His willingness to break with Egypt's futile past and set his country on a new course, his cunning and often improvised initiatives, changed not only the Middle East but the world. The fact that he was a success as a statesman but a failure as a president does not diminish the significance of his lasting impact. History offers many examples of leaders whose careers ended in rejection by their compatriots but whose legacy endured.

Perhaps the best example was Napoleon, who died in lonely exile but in many ways created the France that exists today.

During the political upheaval that transformed Egyptian politics in 2011, Sadat was hardly mentioned by the street protesters or organizers of any faction, except for the radicals who called for abrogation of the peace treaty with Israel. To Egypt's youthful population, Sadat is just a figure from the past whose greatest accomplishment, peace, benefited Israel more than it did Egypt. But the world in which the Cairo mobs were shouting their slogans was a world forged in considerable measure, even if inadvertently, by Sadat. So was the world of the Palestinian guerrillas in Gaza, the world of the Gulf Arabs enjoying their petroleum wealth, and the world of everyone struggling against the dark, violent factions within Islam.

The German philosopher Georg Wilhelm Friedrich Hegel, who developed the idea of the "world historical individual," wrote that "human actions in history produce additional results, beyond their immediate purpose and attainment, beyond their immediate knowledge and desire. They gratify their own interests; but something more is thereby accomplished, which is latent in the action though not present in their consciousness and not included in their design." In Hegel's estimation, "A world-historical individual is not so sober as to adjust his ambition to circumstances; nor is he very considerate. He is devoted, come what may, to one purpose. Therefore such men may treat other great and even sacred interests inconsiderately—a conduct which indeed subjects them to moral reprehension. But so mighty a figure must trample down many an innocent flower, crush to pieces many things in its path." Hegel could have been projecting the life and work of Anwar Sadat.[1]

Chronology of Key Events

1952

July 26   Free Officers military group, led by Gamal
                       Abdel Nasser and including Anwar Sadat,
                       overthrows Egyptian monarchy.

1955

June 1   Soviet Foreign Ministry announces new post-
                       Stalin policy of cooperating with developing
                       nations, regardless of ideology, to spread
                       Soviet influence.

September 27   Czech arms deal to provide first Soviet weapons
                       to Egypt announced.

1956

July 19   United States backs out of agreement to finance
                       Egypt's Aswan Dam project.

July 26   Egypt nationalizes Suez Canal, owned by
                       Britain and France.

October 29–
November 7   Suez War: Israel, backed by Britain and
                       France, attacks Egypt.

1958

February 1	Syria, Egypt merge to form United Arab Republic.
July 14	Revolution in Iraq; monarchy overthrown.

1961

September 28	Coup in Syria; dissolution of United Arab Republic.

1964

May 29	Palestine Liberation Organization created.

1967

June 5–10	Six-Day War: Israel routs armed forces of Egypt, Syria, and Jordan; seizes East Jerusalem, West Bank, Sinai Peninsula, Gaza Strip, Golan Heights.
June 6	Egypt breaks diplomatic relations with United States.
September 1	Arab summit conference in Khartoum adopts "Three No's" policy: no recognition of Israel, no negotiations with Israel, no peace with Israel.
November 22	UN Security Council approves Resolution 242— "land for peace" cornerstone of all future diplomacy on Arab-Israeli conflict.

1969

March	War of Attrition begins: artillery duels, air strikes between Israel and Egypt.

1970

August 7	War of Attrition ends with tenuous cease-fire.
September 17–27	Black September war between Jordan and Palestinian forces; Nasser brokers cease-fire.

September 28	Nasser dies at age fifty-two. Successor is Vice President Anwar Sadat.

1971

May	Sadat outmaneuvers, imprisons pro-Soviet rivals in his Corrective Revolution and becomes uncontested leader.
May 27	Egypt, Soviet Union sign Treaty of Friendship and Cooperation.

1972

April 9	Iraq, Soviet Union sign Treaty of Friendship and Cooperation.
July	Sadat expels Soviet military advisers and air defense crews.

1973

October 6	Biggest, most costly war between Israel and Arabs begins. Egyptian troops cross Suez Canal, Syria attacks on Golan Heights. Israelis, taken by surprise, forced back.
October 17	Oil-producing Arab countries announce 5 percent production cutback, another 5 percent to follow every month unless "international community" compels Israel to withdraw from lands seized in 1967. At same time, largest producers in Persian Gulf area raise prices by 17 percent.
October 18	As war continues, President Nixon announces he will ask Congress for $2.2 billion for military aid to Israel.
October 19	Saudi Arabia imposes complete embargo on oil exports to United States and the Netherlands.

October 22   In agreement between United States and Soviet Union, UN Security Council adopts Resolution 338, calling for cease-fire, direct negotiations, implementation of Resolution 242.

October 24–25   Accusing Israel of cease-fire violations, Soviet Union threatens unilateral intervention. U.S. military forces worldwide placed on nuclear alert. Sadat withdraws appeal for intervention; Soviets back down.

November 4   OPEC meets in Kuwait, agrees on 25 percent production cutback. Libya, Iraq refuse to participate, demanding stronger action.

November 6   Henry A. Kissinger embarks on first round of "shuttle diplomacy," seeking troop disengagement agreements.

November 11   First Israeli-Egyptian disengagement agreement signed at Kilometer 101 on Cairo-Suez road.

December 21   Multinational peace conference convenes in Geneva, ends without result after pro-forma speeches.

1974

February 28   United States and Egypt resume diplomatic relations.

March 18   Arab oil exporters "suspend" embargo.

May 31   Syria and Israel sign disengagement agreement.

July 10   Oil embargo comes to full, final end.

October 26–29   Arab summit conference in Rabat proclaims PLO to be "sole legitimate representative" of Palestinian people in negotiations on self-government.

1975

April 13   Civil war begins in Lebanon.

September 1   In expanded disengagement agreement known as Sinai II, Egypt and Israel pledge to settle differences peacefully.

1976

March 14   Sadat asks parliament to annul friendship treaty with Soviet Union.

November 2   Jimmy Carter elected president of United States.

1977

January 18–19 Devastating riots erupt in Cairo, other cities, in protest over price increases; government withdraws increases.

May 17   Likud Party wins Israeli elections, Menachem Begin becomes prime minister.

November 19   Sadat goes to Jerusalem, sets out peace terms in speech to Israeli parliament.

December 7   Sadat orders Soviet Union, four Warsaw Pact allies to close cultural offices in Egypt.

December 25–26 Begin becomes first Israeli leader to visit Egypt, meets Sadat at Ismailia.

1978

September 5–17 Summoned by President Carter, Sadat and Begin meet at Camp David. Carter persuades them to accept "framework for peace" known as the Camp David Accords.

October 27   Nobel Peace Prize is awarded jointly to Sadat and Begin.

1979

January–February	Islamic revolution in Iran. Shah forced to leave Iran.
March 26	Peace treaty between Israel and Egypt signed.
March 31	Other Arab states impose total economic, diplomatic boycott on Egypt.
June 24	Sadat offers refuge to deposed Shah of Iran, unwanted elsewhere.

1981

October 6	Sadat assassinated at military parade by Islamic extremists who infiltrated armed forces; Hosni Mubarak becomes president.

1 The War of Redemption

The war that could not happen began at 2:00 p.m. on Saturday, October 6, 1973. Egyptian troops crossed the Suez Canal and attacked Israeli positions on the other side, in the Sinai Peninsula, a rocky, arid land that Israel had seized in the 1967 Six-Day War. Two hundred fifty miles to the northeast, on the far side of Israel, Syrian forces struck at Israeli defenses on the Golan Heights, which Syria had lost in the same 1967 conflict. The Arabs, attacking not to invade Israel but to regain their lost lands, had the advantage of nearly total surprise.

In the Muslim world, it was Ramadan, the holy month of fasting, when little of importance happens in the daylight hours. In Israel it was the Sabbath, when most government offices are closed. More than that, it was the day on which Yom Kippur would begin, the Day of Atonement, the most solemn day of the Jewish year. Most Israeli troops were at home with their families, not on the front lines. They went ahead with their preparations for the holy day because they saw no reason not to do so. Despite months of warning and ominous signals, the Israelis and their friends in the United States took it for granted that the Arabs would not start a war because they knew they could not win. Anwar Sadat, the president of Egypt, had contributed to this dismissive assessment by proclaiming 1971 the "Year of Decision" in the Middle East. When nothing happened in that year or the next, Israeli and American officials concluded that Sadat was bluffing and nothing would happen in 1973. This spectacular miscalculation brought the Jewish state to the brink of disaster.

When the war did come, the Israelis were caught off guard and driven back, reeling and panicked. Then they rallied, and reversed the tide. After nearly three weeks of intense fighting that included the biggest tank battles since World War II, Israel prevailed on the battlefield, but in every strategic and political sense, the Arabs won. Israel was victorious but shaken, successful on the battlefield but chastened in its collective soul. The outcome on the ground was not the same as the outcome in history.

For Israel's American allies, that phenomenon was all too familiar. They had experienced it at the height of the Vietnam War, with the Vietcong's Tet Offensive of 1968. After a month of horrifying combat, America forces prevailed. They wiped out most of the Vietcong's cadres, curtailing the Vietcong's ability to fight to such an extent that the indigenous South Vietnamese rebels were no longer a factor in the war; regular units from North Vietnam came down the Ho Chi Minh trail to replace them. Nonetheless, Tet proved to be a decisive political victory for the Vietnamese communists because it turned American opinion against the war, of which the eventual outcome was no longer in doubt.

In the same way, the Middle East war of October 1973 ended in military defeat for Egypt, Syria, and their Arab allies. Had the United States and the Soviet Union not imposed a cease-fire, Israel could have marched virtually unchallenged into Cairo and Damascus. But in a larger sense the man who planned and started that war, Anwar Sadat, achieved virtually all of his objectives, which were more political and psychological than territorial. Sadat, of course, wanted all of Egypt's territory back, but he understood that the land could be regained only through a negotiating process in which Egypt was an equal participant and had the support of the United States, the only country able to put pressure on Israel.

The October War restored the Arab honor shattered in the humiliating defeat of 1967. Sadat forced the United States to take him seriously and commit itself to a comprehensive regional peace settlement; his troops and, to a lesser extent, their Syrian allies, broke down the assumption of Israel and its allies that the Arabs were incompetent in war. Henry A. Kissinger, who as the only person ever to be secretary of state and White House national security adviser at the same time directed American policy throughout the October War, wrote afterward, "Sadat achieved his fundamental objective of shaking belief in Israel's invincibility and Arab impotence, and thus transformed the psychological basis of the negotiating stalemate."[1]

No fighting took place inside Israel itself. The war was fought entirely on Arab soil, on sparsely inhabited territory that Israel had seized in 1967 and the Arabs wanted back—and thus it was that rare modern conflict without civilian casualties. Yet the scope of the combat was vast. Israel and the Arabs—Egypt and Syria, plus token contingents from Iraq, Morocco, and Jordan—threw some eight thousand tanks into the battle, along with combat jets and antiaircraft missiles. In three weeks, twenty-two hundred Israeli soldiers and airmen were killed, equivalent in percentage of population to two hundred thousand Americans. More than eighty-five hundred Arabs died.[2]

As with many great battles of the past, the details of the 1973 fighting matter little now except to military analysts and historians. There is scant reason decades afterward to rehash which unit attacked which outpost on a particular day. Events after the war would demonstrate that while Egypt's battlefield position when the shooting stopped was extremely perilous, in the larger context of the Middle East at the time, the country and its president had greatly improved their standing and their negotiating strength.

Within a few days of the war's outbreak, the U.S. ambassador in Israel, Kenneth Keating, reported that Israelis with whom his staff had been in contact "are saying they must rethink their previous assumption about Arab character, courage, ability to learn modern technology, and capacity for planning, coordination, and keeping of secrets."[3] This had been one of Sadat's objectives: breaking the sense of invincibility that Israel developed after its overwhelming and lightning-fast triumph in 1967.

Many years after the October War, the prominent Israeli columnist and peace advocate Uri Avnery recalled watching news on television with a neighbor in the early days of the combat: "An image appeared on the TV screen: Dozens of Israeli soldiers crouching on the ground, hands over bowed heads, with terrifying Syrian soldiers crouching over them. Never before had we seen Israeli soldiers like this: Dirty, unshaven, obviously frightened, miserable as only prisoners of war can be. There was silence in the room. At that moment the myth of the Israeli superman, of the invincible Israeli soldier, which had dominated our lives for a generation, died. This myth was the ultimate victim of the Yom Kippur war."

When recriminations and finger-pointing among Israel's leaders broke out after the war, Avnery wrote, "their quarrels destroyed the prestige of the military leaders, who until then had been the idols of the public. It has never fully recovered."[4]

Israel and the United States, its ally and protector, should not have been caught flat-footed and out of position when the Arab guns opened up. There had been ample signals for months that war was coming. William P. Rogers, Kissinger's predecessor as secretary of state, had told President Nixon in May 1972 that Sadat might "initiate at least limited military action" because he was "frustrated at the lack of stronger Soviet military and political support, at United States failure to produce any softening of Israel's positions while strengthening Israel militarily, at his own military weakness and at his inability to mobilize the Arab world against Israel and the U.S."[5]

By the following spring, Sadat was making it clear that he felt he had no choice but to go to war. Raymond Close, at the time the Central Intelligence Agency's station chief in Saudi Arabia, recalled that in April 1973, six months before the first shots, he had been "informed by my official Saudi intelligence counterparts that Anwar Sadat had reached his decision to begin preparing for a major assault across the Suez Canal. He had informed King Faisal of this decision in a letter received that day, the 17th of April, 1973. Sadat acknowledged unashamedly in this letter that he did not expect to win a war against Israel, but he explained that only by restoring Arab honor and displaying Arab courage on the battlefield could he capture the attention of Washington and persuade Henry Kissinger to support a peace process."[6] Sadat knew that his putative ally, the Soviet Union,

had no influence with Israel. The United States was the key to persuading—or coercing—Israel to pull out of Arab lands.

"Sadat boldly all but told us what he was going to do and we did
not believe him," Kissinger wrote. "He overwhelmed us with information and let us draw the wrong conclusions. . . . Every Israeli
(and American) analysis before October 1973 agreed that Egypt and
Syria lacked the military capability to regain their territory by force
of arms; hence there would be no war. The Arab armies must lose;
hence they would not attack. The premises were correct. The conclusions were not."[7]

In fact it was not true that "every Israeli (and American) analysis"
at the time agreed that there would be no war. In May, Ray S. Cline
of the State Department's Bureau of Intelligence and Research—who
would have seen Raymond Close's report about Sadat's letter—wrote
a memo saying that his department was "inclined to state the case on
the risk of hostilities for a political purpose with a little more urgency."
Cline said Sadat had decided that "the present situation is both an
affront to his personal self-respect and ruinous of national morale,
dignity, and constructive purpose. For him the key to an escape from
this debilitating situation is the recovery of the Sinai." In the circumstances of the day, Sadat understood that there was no prospect of
regaining Egypt's land through negotiation; therefore, absent some
improbable break in the diplomatic stalemate, he could find it necessary to take "some form of military action which can be sustained
long enough . . . both to activate Washington and Moscow and gal-
vanize the other Arab states, especially the major oil producers, into
anti-American moves."[8] Cline's projection was uncanny in its accuracy, but even a veteran, respected analyst such as he could not break
through the entrenched attitudes of the leadership.

Even on the second day of the war, as the Arabs advanced, Kissinger belittled them: "By tomorrow the Israelis will be reversing the
tide," he told President Nixon. "By Wednesday morning at the latest
Israel will be in Arab territory."[9]

The next day, Monday, when it was clear that Egyptian forces had
crossed the canal in large numbers and were moving eastward, Kiss-

inger reassured the president again that the incursion was doomed. "They'll cut the Egyptians off," he said of the Israelis. "Poor dumb Egyptians getting across the canal and all the bridges will be blown up. They'll cut them all off–30 or 40 thousand of them."

To which Nixon indicated that a decisive Israeli victory might not be desirable: "Just so the Israelis don't get to the point where they say to us, 'We will not settle except on the basis of everything we got,'" the president expostulated. "They can't do that, Henry. They can't do that to us again. They've done it to us for four years but no more."[10] This was the first hint of the deep anger at Israel that would overtake the White House at a later stage of the war. Had he known of this outburst from Nixon at the time, Sadat would have been delighted: changing Washington's attitude was one of his primary war aims.

The Great Intelligence Failure

Even as Nixon and Kissinger spoke on that Monday evening, panic was beginning to wash over Israel, but Washington had still not understood that the Arabs this time were better equipped, better trained, better led, and better motivated than they had been in 1967.

This intelligence debacle was not the result of a lack of information, it was the result of failing to grasp the significance of the plentiful information that was available. Looking back years later, the Central Intelligence Agency concluded that its analysts, like political leaders and policymakers, had failed to evaluate the information correctly, Cline's paper notwithstanding, because of their near-universal belief that no realistic national leader would start a war he knew he could not win. Because it was taken for granted at the time that another war would result in another major defeat for the Arabs, most analysts believed that starting one would be irrational and therefore the Arabs would not do it. The fact that Sadat a year previously had expelled all his Soviet military advisers and trainers because Moscow did not deliver all the weapons it had promised reinforced the conviction in Washington that Egypt was not capable of going to war against Israel. So deeply entrenched was this assumption that it prevented policymakers from understanding what Sadat was trying to accomplish.

Had they recognized that his war was more about attitudes than territory, their response might have been different.

"Sadat had done a brilliant job of misleading the Israelis—and American intelligence," according to the CIA. "By orchestrating a false war scare in May, and then repeating more 'scares' in the form of Egyptian and Syrian troop concentrations opposite Sinai and the Golan, Sadat lulled Israeli watchfulness. Hence Israeli and U.S. intelligence judged the Arab military concentrations in the first week of October to be simply more of the same."[11] According to Sadat, Israeli defense minister Moshe Dayan, asked after the war why Israel had not mobilized in the days before, replied that Sadat "made me do it twice, at a cost of ten million dollars each time. So, when it was the third time round, I thought he wasn't serious, but he tricked me!"[12]

The reason those feints succeeded, the CIA concluded, was that they were assessed through the conviction in Tel Aviv and Washington that Sadat and Syrian president Hafez al-Assad were rational people who would not undertake a suicide mission. "A 'rational actor' model can fail because what seems rational to the analyst—or generally rational in that analyst's culture—may not be rational to the actor in question," CIA historians wrote. "To Sadat and Asad, for example, it may have been irrational to attack Israel on a purely military basis, but it may have been rational to do so to restore Arab prestige or force other countries to intervene and press for a settlement more favorable to the Arab side than if there had been no attack."[13]

That was exactly how Sadat saw it. He knew that Egyptian forces were not going to march into Tel Aviv and compel Israel to surrender, but he believed war was necessary to restore Arab honor and break the debilitating stalemate that was crippling Egypt. He was convinced that Egypt would never recover the land lost in 1967 unless war transformed the international atmosphere. He had expelled the Soviet advisers, even as he sought more and more Soviet weapons, because he believed the Soviets, for their own reasons, did not want another Middle East war and would hamper his preparations. He knew that Egypt and Syria could not achieve a decisive triumph, but he went to war anyway because he had a different definition of victory.

"What literally no one understood beforehand was the mind of the man," Kissinger wrote in his memoirs. "Sadat aimed not for territorial gain but for a crisis that would alter the attitudes into which the parties were then frozen—and thereby open the way for negotiations. The shock would enable both sides, including Egypt, to show a flexibility that was impossible while Israel considered itself militarily supreme and Egypt was paralyzed by humiliation . . . rare is the statesman who at the beginning of a war has so clear a perception of its political objective. Rarer still is the war fought to lay the basis for moderation in its aftermath."[14] Kissinger could not have said the same of Syria's president, Assad, whose war aims were not the same as those of his ostensible ally, Sadat. Assad soon came to feel that Sadat had misled him about his reasons for starting a war from which Syria gained little.

The joint military effort was "flawed from the start," according to Patrick Seale's definitive biography of Assad. "Asad went to war because he believed there could be no satisfactory negotiation with Israel until the Arabs had snatched back at least some of their land," Seale wrote. "Peace-making, he believed, could be a product of war, but not a substitute for it. Sadat went to war because the peace diplomacy he was already conducting, covertly as well as overtly, had faltered. He thought a shock would revive it." Whereas Assad's "was a war of liberation, Sadat's was an essentially political war." This divergence provoked a bitter split between the nominal allies that poisoned negotiations for a cease-fire and all the diplomacy that followed, right up to the Egyptian-Israeli peace treaty of 1979, and even more so after that.

According to Seale, who knew Assad well and reflected his views, this "crucial difference in war aims" did not become clear during prewar planning sessions because "Sadat lied to Asad, deliberately deceiving him about his intentions and leading him to believe that the offensive Egypt would launch would be wider in scope than was ever intended. The deception was not a mere verbal misunderstanding: the Syrians were actually fed false war plans" that exposed Assad to "dangers far greater than those he had anticipated."[15]

The military outcome of the war would probably have been the same even if Sadat and Assad had been on the same wavelength about its objectives. The larger significance of Assad's belief that Sadat misled him was that it ignited the deep feud among the Arab countries that followed the war and hung over all the peace negotiations to come. Arab unity, already undermined by national and tribal rivalries, died even as Arabs were fighting together against their common enemy.[16]

This struggle to define a mutually acceptable outcome to the war also plagued the combatants' patrons, the United States and the Soviet Union. The United States was committed to the survival and security of Israel, but did not want the Arabs, and especially Egypt, to suffer another humiliation similar to that of 1967. Moscow supported the Arabs, but opposed the war because it feared that the expected Arab defeat would further discredit the value of Soviet military aid—its primary tool for winning friends in the developing countries.

Sadat, disenchanted with the Soviets, was already beyond whatever political influence Moscow's weapons might have given it. Regardless of the details of the tank battles and aerial combat, the very fact of the war made it possible for Sadat to negotiate a peace treaty with Israel a few years later. Had Egypt and Syria not gone to war in 1973, any peace agreement would have meant their submission to Israeli terms. Once the Egyptians had crossed the Suez Canal, destroyed the Israeli fortifications known as the Bar-Lev Line, and thrown the Israelis into panicked fear of annihilation, Sadat had achieved his larger purpose, which was to gain equality at the bargaining table and bring the United States into the negotiations. For him, the cease-fire that silenced the guns after three weeks was the beginning of a process, not just the end of a limited conflict. The Arabs fought honorably and well; they forced a frightened Israel to beg for an emergency airlift of military supplies from the United States. After that, almost any outcome of the fighting short of destruction of the Egyptian armed forces would have been acceptable to Sadat.

"We went to war," he said afterward, "after the Big Powers, all the powers, had closed the doors of peace in our faces. We waged war only when the whole world had turned a deaf ear to our calls for peace, which we made in all sincerity. They turned their backs with erroneous ideas that we were weak, and that we were a lifeless corpse, immobile and incapable of mobility for the next fifty years. We went to war, after we had reached a stage which I repeatedly described as 'to be or not to be.'" He said he had told his generals before the shooting started that "it is far nobler for us to die while liberating every inch of our land, [than] in this state of 'no war no peace' which they would have us live in, as humiliated slaves."[17]

Sadat went to war because Egypt—shabby, impoverished, and stewing in humiliation—was desperate for peace, but only on honorable terms. Assad seems to have had a more conventional military objective: retaking the Golan Heights. He did not want peace with Israel for its own sake; this difference in outlook and objective between Egypt and Syria would bedevil peace negotiators for years afterward. Syria never achieved the "psychological breakthrough" trumpeted by Sadat because the cautious Assad lacked Sadat's sophistication. Assad was obsessed with details; Sadat was a big-picture visionary.

"The world after October 1973 is different from what it was before," Sadat wrote in *The October Working Paper*, a political and personal manifesto that he published after the war. "After 1967, Israel became the domineering power in the area. The prevailing belief was that the Arabs could do nothing to alter this reality, and international politics were drawn up according to this concept." As a result of the war, he wrote, "the picture has changed radically and it has become incumbent on all parties to reconsider their policy in the light of the new circumstances which were the outcome of the blood of the war dead, the sacrifices of the heroes, and the military planning and excellent political action which preceded, accompanied and succeeded the battle. . . . With our achievements we can affirm that the Egypt of October is the Egypt of the future."[18]

Sadat's Great-Power Conundrum

When he became president upon the death of Gamal Abdel Nasser in 1970, Sadat took over a country that seemed beyond repair. Egypt was destitute, militarily impotent, and economically dependent on the Soviet Union. The Suez Canal, one of Egypt's biggest sources of foreign currency, had been closed since 1967. Tourism, another mainstay of the economy, had dwindled to a trickle—the beach resorts on the Red Sea had been lost when Israel seized the Sinai, and Americans stayed away because Cairo and Washington were at odds. And the Egyptians, like all Arabs, were in a collective state of despair and humiliation because of the war of 1967, a six-day rout. In that conflict, Israel had blown away its Arab opponents almost without effort and had seized the Golan Heights from Syria, the Sinai Peninsula and Gaza Strip from Egypt, and the West Bank and East Jerusalem from Jordan. To many Arabs—and in particular to King Faisal of Saudi Arabia—the loss of East Jerusalem was the deepest cut of all, because it put the Jewish enemy in control of al-Aqsa Mosque and the Dome of the Rock, monuments holy to all Muslims.

Sadat faced a conundrum. The only way to break out of this morass of dependence and despair was to go to war once again, this time better prepared. He said so many times. But he could not do so until the Soviets had rebuilt Egypt's shattered armed forces. Sadat needed the Soviets and kept importuning them for new supplies of arms right up until the start of the war. But he also mistrusted them and came to believe that Moscow was putting its interest in a relaxation of tensions with the United States, or détente, ahead of Arab interests in the Middle East. Moscow used military assistance as a lever of influence in the region but did not actually want war; Kremlin leaders feared that a new Middle East war would drag the Soviet Union and the United States, backing opposing sides, into a confrontation with each other. These considerations added Moscow's interests to an already complicated picture.

When the war did come, in 1973, the contest unfolded in multiple arenas: on the ground; in the oil fields of the Persian Gulf and North Africa, where Arab rulers backed Egypt and Syria; at the United Nations; and in the Soviet Union and the United States over détente and the protection of their clients. Egypt and Syria started the war, but the cease-fire that ended it, in the form of a UN Security Council resolution, was negotiated between the White House and the Kremlin.

The United States in the 1970s had become a major strategic power in the Middle East almost by default after Britain's withdrawal from its former colonies "East of Suez." Before the October War, however, Washington had little reason to involve itself directly in the standoff between Israel and the Arabs. Despite all the warning signals, the situation did not appear to the Americans to be urgent. On the ground, the front lines were stable. A tenuous cease-fire that had ended the bombing and artillery duels between Israel and Egypt in 1969 and 1970, known as the War of Attrition, was holding. The Arabs, while naturally working to rebuild their shattered armed forces, with Soviet assistance, presented no imminent threat to Israel; moreover, Washington assumed, they were wards of Moscow politically so it would be futile to make overtures to them. The Middle East's oil fields and Gulf shipping lanes were out of harm's way.

From the U.S. perspective, too many fires were raging elsewhere to make room on its agenda for the Middle East. Nixon was engulfed in the metastasizing scandal known as Watergate, which had also ensnared several of the president's senior advisers. Vice President Spiro T. Agnew was about to be indicted on bribery charges arising from his tenure as governor of Maryland; he would resign on October 10, after the war started, as part of a deal with prosecutors to avoid a prison sentence.

And Washington was very busy elsewhere in the world, preoccupied by efforts to enforce a tenuous peace agreement in Vietnam, salvage Cambodia from the advancing Khmer Rouge, build relations with China after Nixon's breakthrough visit there the year before, and pursue the policy of détente with the Soviet Union. Sadat was correct in his belief that the United States and the Soviet Union were committed to détente and thus neither wanted its Middle East clients to start a war that might drag the superpowers into it. To Sadat, détente was part of the problem: in his view the Soviet Union was holding back on military equipment and support because it was more interested in improving relations with the United States than in helping the Arab cause.

Preserving Détente First

One of the first telephone calls Kissinger made when he heard that war was imminent, at 6:40 a.m. Eastern time on October 6, early afternoon in the Middle East, was to Soviet ambassador Anatoly Dobrynin. He told Dobrynin that war seemed to be coming and assured him that the Israelis would not begin it with a preemptive strike.[19] In another call three hours later, he told Dobrynin that the first objective for Washington and Moscow should be "to not have everything we have achieved be destroyed by maniacs on either side."[20] That Kissinger called Dobrynin even before talking to President Nixon, Secretary of Defense James Schlesinger, or Kenneth Keating, the U.S. ambassador to Israel, reflected the importance he placed on relations with Moscow as a primary consideration throughout the war.

In a memo to the president on that first morning, Kissinger wrote more about the Soviets than he did about the war itself. He said he had told Dobrynin that "[i]t was important for our own relationship that this crisis not degenerate into armed conflict," which of course it was doing almost at that moment. Kissinger told Nixon that he had asked Dobrynin to "call Moscow immediately" about the imminent outbreak of fighting and "to ask his government to restrain Syria and Egypt. He promised to do so and has done so."[21]

In another conversation that morning, with White House chief of staff Alexander Haig, Kissinger said, "The open question is, [are the Arabs acting] with Soviet collusion or against Soviet opposition?" The fact that Moscow had evacuated civilians and dependents from Cairo and Damascus two or three days earlier raised suspicion that the Soviets knew what was coming and might even be supporting it. Kissinger said he would propose that the United States and the Soviet Union jointly call for a meeting of the UN Security Council to seek an immediate cease-fire. "This is designed in part to smoke them out," he said. "If they refuse to do it, we have two problems. The first is to get the fighting stopped and the second is the long-term policy."[22]

Soviet leader Leonid Brezhnev himself later assured Kissinger that the Kremlin knew nothing about the war in advance. "On my honor," he said, "I had no discussion with the Arabs, either at that time or any other time, up to the beginning of the October war. I simply saw the situation developing."

"I personally believe it, though there are many in America who do not," Kissinger replied. He suggested that the Soviets "mildly encouraged" the Arabs, but Brezhnev denied even that. With détente on the line, Kissinger had little choice but to accept Brezhnev's word.[23] The imperative of détente hung over his diplomacy throughout the war and his negotiations afterward.

As Kissinger prepared for a crisis meeting on the first afternoon of the war, two members of his staff asked in a memo, "How can we best take advantage of this crisis to reduce Soviet influence in the Middle East?"[24] It was an obvious question, but Kissinger faced an irreconcilable policy conflict: he was trying, as his aides suggested, to undercut Soviet influence in the region, but he was also trying to improve relations with Moscow and pursue détente. This dilemma forced him into many duplicitous conversations with the Kremlin leadership, as when he told Foreign Minister Andrei Gromyko directly that "the United States is not pursuing a policy in the Middle East to negate Soviet influence or reduce Soviet influence, or that is in any way anti-Soviet."[25]

The Two-Front War

War is one of the most confusing and unpredictable of human endeavors. It can take years after shooting stops to figure out exactly what happened at any given place or time in the conflict. The main outlines of the October War were easier to follow than most because the major engagements took place in open terrain, in clear weather, on fronts where there were few civilian inhabitants, but scholars and military analysts still argue about some of the tactics, especially in armor battles.

The Suez Canal represented a clear line of demarcation between the Egyptians, on the west side, and the Israelis, on the east, in the Sinai, Egyptian territory that they had seized in 1967. The canal itself was closed, choked by sunken ships and military debris, and there were no bridges across it. On their side, the Israelis had built up massive berms of sand fifty feet high as a defensive wall, to delay if not block any potential Egyptian crossing. Behind that was the string of fortifications known as the Bar-Lev Line.

When the war started, it took the Egyptians less than three hours to blast away the sand wall with high-pressure hoses. While tanks on the western side of the canal opened fire on Israel's thinly manned positions, small groups of Egyptians crossed the water in boats ferrying bridge-building equipment. Within a few hours, tanks were rolling across, along with antiaircraft guns and antitank weapons.

At the same time, Syria began a large-scale assault on the Golan Heights, with tanks and fighter jets. Now there could no longer be any doubt: an unprepared Israel was caught in a two-front war that presented the gravest threat to the Jewish state since its founding in 1948. The Egyptians sent one hundred thousand troops and a thousand tanks across the canal; on the Golan, thirty-five thousand troops and eight hundred tanks broke through.

"The Israelis apparently did not plan on what to do if attacked by Egypt and Syria simultaneously, what to do if the Egyptians crossed the canal in massive numbers and at many points, or what to do in the event of a military surprise," the CIA's postwar analysis said. "These were all symptoms of the arrogance and tunnel vision of which the Arabs, and not a few Israelis, accuse the pre-October Israeli military command."[26] The Israelis had earned that arrogance in 1967; what they failed to perceive six years later was that the Arabs would go to war to break it down.

"The lack of military preparedness led to catastrophic outcomes," an Israeli scholar later wrote:

Within 24 hours the IDF [Israel Defense Forces] lost the Bar-Lev line along the Suez Canal and about half the territory of the Golan Heights. About two-thirds of the 450-tank force with which Israel started the war had been lost and more than 500 soldiers were killed during this period. This would have been proportional to a loss of 31,000 soldiers in the US in 1973. On the eve of the war,

Israel perceived itself as an unchallenged regional power; less than 24 hours later, Defense Minister [Moshe] Dayan spoke about "the fight for the Third Temple," implying that just as the First Temple was destroyed in 586 BCE and the Second Temple in 70 CE, the third Jewish commonwealth was again under the threat of destruction.[27]

The Bar-Lev Line was no match for the armament unleashed by the Egyptians against its defensive points, which were soon overrun. Worse, according to Chaim Herzog, a retired Israeli general, was that the steel used to build its fortifications had been ripped from a railway across Sinai that the Israelis had captured in 1967, and thus that rail line was not available when the Israelis most needed it to bring up reinforcements.[28]

"Within the first hours," CIA analysts wrote in their extensive postwar assessment, "the Israelis made two costly mistakes. Their experience in the 1967 war led them to believe they could use tanks alone to fight infantry" instead of sending infantry troops to back up the armor units, as conventional tank warfare doctrine would have dictated. "They did not take adequate account of the effect of antitank missiles in the hands of now better-trained, more highly motivated Egyptian troops. The Israelis compounded this error by sending unaccompanied tanks to rescue the isolated garrisons of their canal-side defensive barrier called the Bar Lev Line. When the Israeli tanks attacked alone on 6 and 7 October, they were badly mauled. The low point came on the 8th when an Israeli armored battalion charged into an Egyptian ambush. The unit's tanks were nearly all destroyed or damaged, and the commander was captured. On 6 October Israel had 293 tanks in the whole of Sinai. Approximately half were out of commission within 36 hours."[29]

The Israelis were shocked and frightened, but once their field commanders grasped the full scope of what they were facing, they rallied. Their troops were better trained, and their officers proved much more flexible and adaptable tactically than their Arab counterparts, who were trained by the Soviets and locked into rigid Soviet military doctrine.

By October 10, less than a week into the war, the Israelis had retaken the Golan Heights after fierce fighting and a major tank battle near the town of Kuneitra. They broke through not only the Syrians but also Iraqi units sent to support them. The Israelis bombed Damascus, targeting factories and antiaircraft batteries. The next day a Syrian counterattack failed and Israel's Seventh Brigade crossed into Syrian territory before pausing. With the Golan secured, Israel began shifting troops and planes to the Sinai front. Now under pressure from Syria to intensify the war on the western front to deter Israel from advancing toward Damascus, Egypt committed its armor reserve; seven hundred tanks that had been held back crossed into Sinai.

In the field, Israel appeared to be pulling itself together after the initial shock of the Arab attack, but behind the scenes its leaders were close to panic. According to a narrative by William Burr, who documented and chronicled the war for the National Security Archive in Washington, "Early in the morning of 9 October, the day after the initial counterattack had failed with major losses, Kissinger received a call from a chagrined Simcha Dinitz, the Israeli ambassador, about the 'difficult' position in which his country found itself. At 8:20 a.m., when the two met for a more detailed conversation, Dinitz acknowledged that the Israelis had lost over 400 tanks to the Egyptians and 100 to the Syrians. Egyptian armor and surface-to-air missiles were taking their toll in the air and ground battle and the Israeli cabinet had decided that it had to 'get all equipment and planes by air that we can.' Israel was begging the United States for weapons and ammunition." Kissinger, who had assumed that Israel could reverse its losses without major infusions of aid, was perplexed by the bad news—"Explain to me, how could 400 tanks be lost to the Egyptians?"—and by the troubling diplomatic implications of substantial U.S. wartime assistance. The United States would be taking Israel's side in a war in which Israel itself was not under attack—the land the Arabs were trying to take was their own. In that 8:20 a.m. meeting, Dinitz relayed to Kissinger a request from Prime Minister Golda Meir for a secret meeting with Nixon to plead for military assistance, but Kissinger quickly refused because he feared that overt delivery of U.S.

military aid to Israel while the war was still being fought would reinforce Soviet influence in the Arab world.[30]

Kissinger would soon have to rethink his position on assistance to Israel because at about that time the Soviet Union began a large-scale airlift of weapons to reinforce its Arab clients. At its height, one hundred flights a day took part in this arms shuttle.

While the fighting continued, the United States and Moscow were negotiating over a proposed UN Security Council resolution calling for a cease-fire. At this point, Assad wanted a cease-fire but Sadat, whose forces were still advancing, did not. On October 13, Sadat brushed aside a British proposal that he accept a cease-fire resolution agreed upon by Washington and Moscow—to the dismay of Kissinger, who had been assured by the Soviets that Sadat would accept it. The Arabs "want the Israelis to return to the 1967 borders. That is insane," Kissinger said.[31]

The Israelis were running out of ammunition and their pleas for help were growing more urgent. On October 13, one week into the war, when Sadat rejected the initial cease-fire plan, President Nixon ordered an airlift of weapons and ammunition, code named Operation Nickel Grass. This was a massive and diplomatically tricky operation because none of the countries where American planes could refuel wanted to be publicly associated with it, and the privately owned air charter companies that the Pentagon sought to conduct the airlift declined to participate, forcing the United States to use air force planes with recognizable markings. The U.S. Defense Department, in a half-hearted effort to keep the flights secret, arranged for refueling at a remote Portuguese base in the Azores and scheduled the planes to arrive in Israel at night, but there was no way those planes could land in a gossipy country the size of Israel without being spotted by the news media.

This airlift operation went on for thirty-two days, longer than the war itself.[32] On October 18, after the Israelis had begun to reverse their losses in the Sinai, Nixon officially asked Congress for $2.2 billion in extra money to pay for it. That news outraged Arab oil-producing countries, which responded by imposing an embargo on oil exports to the United States and other countries considered friendly to Israel.

A day after Sadat rejected the initial cease-fire plan, Egyptian forces attacked eastward in the biggest tank battle since World War II. The Egyptians threw everything they had into attacks all along the front, apparently trying to reach passes through the Sinai mountains known as Gidi and Mitla. This time the Israelis held, shredding the Egyptians with missile and artillery fire and turning the tide on the Sinai front. On the night of October 16, Israeli troops in boats—led by the intrepid Major General Ariel Sharon, later prime minister—began to cross the canal onto the west bank to cut off Egyptian forces from behind, as Kissinger had predicted a week earlier that they would do. It was reckless of Sharon to move troops across the canal without armor or artillery support but the Israelis rectified that the next day. They constructed their own bridges across the waterway, enabling their tanks and mechanized infantry units to cross to the Egyptians' rear. The Egyptians responded with heavy artillery fire but did not move troops to thwart this Israeli maneuver.

"The Egyptians were faced with a painful dilemma," CIA analysts wrote in a postwar assessment. "If they withdrew forces from the east side of the canal to cope with the Israeli incursion, they would give up the territory they had started the war to reclaim. If they did not withdraw forces, they ran the risk of losing all the forces deployed on the east side of the canal."[33]

Now the leaders of the United States and the Soviet Union felt even greater urgency to secure a cease-fire; neither wanted to be dragged into direct confrontation with the other to protect its clients in the Middle East, nor did the United States want to see the Arabs routed again. Such an outcome, the Americans feared, would only make them more dependent on the Soviet Union.

In Cairo, on October 19, Soviet Premier Alexei Kosygin met five times with Sadat. The Egyptians professed to make light of the Israeli threat from their rear, either because they misread it or because they were playing it down for morale reasons. But after hearing what Kosygin relayed to the Kremlin, the Soviets understood the "full significance," Chaim Herzog wrote. "The Soviets realized that the entire gamble was at risk and that once again they were in danger of facing a total military Arab collapse."[34] On the evening of the following day, October 20, Soviet ambassador Vladimir Vinogradov delivered to Sadat a message from Brezhnev urging him to accept a cease-fire.

Kissinger Goes to Moscow

In Moscow, Brezhnev was at that moment meeting with Kissinger, who at the Kremlin's invitation had flown in a few hours earlier.

While he was in the air, the Watergate scandal blew up, in what came to be known as the "Saturday Night Massacre." The president ordered Attorney General Elliot Richardson and his deputy, William Ruckelshaus, to fire the special prosecutor in the investigation, Archibald Cox, who was demanding that the White House release tape recordings of secret conversations. They refused, and quit, so it fell to Solicitor General Robert Bork to dismiss Cox.

Kissinger had labored mightily to distance himself from the scandal at the White House. Now, at a crucial point in the war, he and the president he served were at cross purposes. Kissinger did not believe that a comprehensive regional settlement in the Middle East was possible; he wanted to proceed incrementally. Nixon, struggling to save his presidency, believed that a comprehensive peace agreement, forged in cooperation with Moscow, might be the triumph that placed him above his critics and out of the reach of the encircling legal investigation.

On that same infamous Saturday night, October 20, Nixon sent a letter to Kissinger with instructions on what to say to Brezhnev. "I have just written a note to Brezhnev emphasizing to him that you speak with my full authority," the president wrote. Kissinger was flabbergasted—one of his standard negotiating ploys was to tell the Soviets that he would have to take ideas back to the president for approval, and now the president had cut off that path. Even worse, the president told Kissinger, "I now consider a permanent Middle East settlement to be the most important final goal to which we must devote ourselves," and he was prepared to put whatever pressure was necessary on Israel to achieve it. In his discussions with Brezhnev, Kissinger was to "point out to him that if we and he together can be reasonable and achieve a Middle East settlement it will be without question one of the brightest stars in [what] we hope will be a galaxy for peace stemming from the Nixon-Brezhnev relationship. . . . Only the U.S. and the Soviet Union have the power and influence to create the permanent conditions necessary to avoid another war. If we fail, history and the thousands of brave men who die in the next war, as well as their widows and children, will hold us accountable."[35]

Kissinger not only refused to comply with these instructions, he wrote an extraordinary, insubordinate response in which he rejected them as "unacceptable." In a note to his White House deputy, Brent Scowcroft, he said he was "shocked at the tone of the instructions, the poor judgment in the content of the Brezhnev letter, and the failure to let me know in advance that a press statement would be issued." Brezhnev had already used the "full authority" line to deflect some of his arguments, Kissinger said. But beyond that, he said, it was difficult enough to come to agreement on a cease-fire to end the fighting; any grand strategy such as the president sought remained far out of reach. The Soviet Union and the United States were nominal co-chairs of a proposed peace conference to be held at Geneva, but the last thing Kissinger wanted was to make the Soviet Union a full partner in negotiating a region-wide comprehensive peace agreement; he was trying to cut down Moscow's influence in the Middle East, even while telling the Soviets that he had no such intent.[36]

Because both the United States and the Soviet Union wanted it urgently and Sadat was now eager for it, Kissinger and Brezhnev were able to come to terms on a cease-fire. On October 22, the United Nations Security Council, by a 14–0 vote, adopted Resolution 338, calling upon "all parties to the present fighting to cease all firing and terminate all military activity immediately, no later than 12 hours after the moment of the adoption of this decision, in the positions they now occupy."

The resolution also demanded that the parties immediately implement Resolution 242, which had been adopted after the war of 1967.

That was a much broader and more ambitious document calling for a negotiated peace that would guarantee the security of all states in the region, including Israel, an implicit recognition of the Jewish state that the Arabs had uniformly rejected at the time.[37] Syria accepted the new cease-fire only reluctantly, partly because it incorporated 242, but also because Assad was furious at reported Israeli violations of the cease-fire after the Security Council vote. Assad sought to join the Iraqis in a new offensive and held off only because Moscow did not support him. "It can be argued," Kissinger told his diplomats in the region, "that by accepting Resolution 338, the Syrians have at least implicitly accepted Resolution 242, since the latter is part of the former," but that sort of diplomatic nuance was for the future, when and if peace negotiations actually began.[38]

Although Syria backed off from a new offensive, the immediate result of the Security Council action was not an end to all the fighting—it was a last flurry of Israeli battlefield action in Sinai that stoked a deep anger at Israel in Moscow and among most senior officials in Washington, even though Kissinger had given informal consent to it. From Moscow he had sent instructions to his deputy, Scowcroft, to "tell Ambassador Dinitz that in the circumstances we would understand if [the] Israelis felt they required some additional time for military dispositions before [the] cease-fire takes effect."[39] This last burst of action by Israel against Egypt, a country Moscow still thought of as a client, brought the United States and the Soviet Union to the brink of nuclear confrontation. The relationship of trust and admiration between the United States and Israel that had developed since the Suez War of 1956 would not survive the events of the next few days.

With the wink from Kissinger, the Israelis seized upon the twelve-hour window in Resolution 338 to press their advantage. At the time of the Security Council vote, as the CIA's postwar analysis noted, "The Israelis had advanced barely more than halfway to the city of Suez at the south end of the canal. Claiming Egyptian cease-fire violations, the Israelis pressed ahead and cut off the Egyptian Third Army and the city of Suez before accepting the cease-fire. . . . Violations by both sides continued for several days as the Israelis sought to solidify their hold on the west side of the canal and complete their encirclement of Suez and [as] Egyptian Third Army units made several attempts to break out."[40]

The "encirclement of the Egyptian Third Army" meant that some forty-five thousand Egyptian troops were at Israel's mercy, cut off from ammunition, food, and medical care. Now the most urgent task for Kissinger and Brezhnev was to prevent Israel from destroying those trapped Egyptian forces, which it appeared intent on doing despite the cease-fire. The conversations between Kissinger and the Israelis became increasingly rancorous. Sadat's hope of putting distance between the United States and Israel, a critical objective in the war, was about to be fulfilled.

At 10:40 on the morning of October 23, the day after the Security Council resolution, the Soviet diplomat Yuli Vorontsov called Kissinger to read a message from Brezhnev:

> President Sadat has informed us that in the morning on the 23 of October Israeli forces in violation of the decision of the Security Council renewed firing on the West Coast of the Suez Canal and are moving in the southern direction. We would like to underline that Moscow has its own reliable information which proves that this is the fact and that the Israelis apparently decided to widen their bridgehead on the West Coast of the Canal. Thus Israel once again challenges the decision of the Security Council. This is absolutely unacceptable. All this looks like a flagrant deceit on the part of the Israelis. We will express the confidence that the United States will use all the possibilities they have and its authority to bring the Israelis to order.[41]

He offered a proposal, which he said had originated with Sadat, to use UN observer forces to police the cease-fire.

This was a moment of high stakes and high peril. Superpower détente was on the line. The entrapment of the Third Army was forcing Sadat to seek help from the Soviet Union, from which the United States had been encouraging his desire to detach himself. Destruction of the Egyptian force would surely enflame the other Arabs, including many of the world's most important oil exporters, and Soviet influence among them would escalate. President Nixon, who should have been taking charge, was crippled by the Watergate scandal.

The president's initials appeared on a message sent to Brezhnev on the afternoon of the twenty-third, although it was probably written by Kissinger. "I want to assure you," the message sent via the White House–Kremlin "hotline" said, "that we assume full responsibility to bring about a complete end of hostilities on the part of Israel. Our own information would indicate that the responsibility for the violation of the cease-fire belongs to the Egyptian side, but this is not the time to debate that particular issue. We have insisted with Israel that they take immediate steps to cease hostilities, and I urge you to take similar measures with respect to the Egyptian side. You and I have achieved an historic settlement over this past weekend and we will not permit it to be destroyed."[42]

Later that day, the Security Council adopted another resolution, calling on the parties to return to the positions they were in when the original resolution was passed, but violations continued. Another resolution followed the next day, October 24, with the same outcome. That morning, Kissinger warned Ambassador Dinitz that "we cannot make Brezhnev look like a goddamn fool in front of his colleagues," but the Israeli still insisted that it was the Egyptians, trying to break out, who were "attacking" and that Egypt had deployed combat aircraft to support the attempt.[43]

The situation on the ground was nearly out of control. "Even if the major combatants stop shooting," State Department intelligence director Ray S. Cline warned Kissinger that day, "this cease-fire appears much more precarious than its predecessors. With two Egyptian salients east of the Canal and one Israeli salient west of the Canal, in addition to possible Egyptian enclaves inside the Israeli salient, the cease-fire on the Suez front will be extremely difficult to police. Israeli violations of the October 23 cease-fire—and possibly the October 24 cease-fire—appear to have reflected an effort definitively to isolate the Egyptians' southern salient. With their forces on the east bank reportedly running short of supplies, the Egyptians will be under acute pressure to reopen their two main supply lines from the Nile

Delta region to Suez and Isma'iliyyah [Ismailia] through Israeli lines." The United Nations could muster an observer force of only two hundred, Cline said, not nearly enough.[44]

On the afternoon of October 23, according to Kissinger, Sadat had sent an urgent plea to Nixon. He "made the extraordinary proposal that the United States, with which Egypt had not had diplomatic relations for six years, should 'intervene effectively, even if that necessitates the use of forces, in order to guarantee the full implementation of the cease-fire resolution in accordance with the joint U.S.-USSR agreement.'" That is to say, the president of Egypt was asking the United States to take military action against Israel, which of course was out of the question. This request, Kissinger wrote, was "no more tenable than the Israeli desire that we run diplomatic interference while it strangled an Egyptian army trapped *after* the cease-fire." In his view, whether the Third Army was destroyed by direct attack or starved out, the Soviets "could not possibly hold still while a cease-fire they had cosponsored was turned into a trap for a client state."[45]

Rebuffed on that request, Sadat next proposed to the Soviets that they and the United States send a joint military force to police the cease-fire. That idea was acceptable to Moscow, but not to the White House. Kissinger relayed this blunt message from Nixon to Sadat:

I have just learned that a resolution may be introduced into the Security Council this evening urging that outside military forces— including those of the US and USSR—be sent to the Middle East to enforce the cease-fire. I must tell you that if such a resolution is introduced into the Security Council it will be vetoed by the United States for the following reasons:

—It would be impossible to assemble sufficient outside military power to represent an effective counterweight to the indigenous forces now engaged in combat in the Middle East.

—Should the two great nuclear powers be called upon to provide forces, it would introduce an extremely dangerous potential for direct great power rivalry in the area.[46]

The last thing Nixon and Kissinger wanted to do was participate in deploying Soviet ground troops into the Arab-Israeli conflict.

A Nuclear Alert

A few hours later, this crisis would reach its peak on one of the longest, most dangerous nights in American diplomatic history. This was no longer about battered armies throwing a few last punches at each other in a Mideast desert; this was about a potential confrontation between the two nuclear superpowers.

At about 10:00 p.m. on October 24, the most senior military and national security officials of the United States gathered at the White House: Kissinger, Schlesinger, Haig, Scowcroft, CIA director William Colby, and Admiral Thomas Moorer, chairman of the Joint Chiefs of Staff, the nation's highest military officer. President Nixon—against whom the House of Representatives had that day initiated impeachment proceedings—remained upstairs in the family residence, and it is still not entirely certain how much he knew about what was happening.

The topic of discussion was a strongly worded letter from Brezhnev, addressed to Nixon, about violations of the cease-fire.

"Mr. President, I have received your letter in which you inform me that Israel ceased fighting," the Soviet leader wrote. "The facts, however, testify that Israel continues drastically to ignore the cease-fire decision of the Security Council. Thus, it is brazenly challenging both the Soviet Union and the United States since it is our agreement with you which constitutes the basis of the Security Council decision." Brezhnev said that Israel "continues to seize new and new territory [*sic*]. As you know, the Israeli forces have already fought their way into Suez. It is impossible to allow such to continue."

He proposed that the United States and the Soviet Union "urgently dispatch to Egypt Soviet and American military contingents" to enforce the cease-fire. And if Washington said no? "I will say it straight that if you find it impossible to act jointly with us in this matter, we should be faced with the necessity urgently to consider the question of taking appropriate steps unilaterally."[47]

According to Victor Israelyan, a Soviet official who was in the Kremlin at the time, the suggestion that the Soviet Union would, on its own, send ground troops into Egypt to take on the Israelis was the Kremlin's "trump card." The Politburo leaders expected an appropriate response, which in their view would have been an immediate U.S. commitment to force the Israelis to pull back and to allow supplies to reach the besieged Egyptian Third Army.[48]

What they got instead was an order from Admiral Moorer placing U.S. armed forces worldwide, including the nuclear forces, on an elevated state of alert known as DEFCON III, the highest state of alert short of deployment for war. DEFCON II would have readied nuclear weapons for use. The highest possible level, DEFCON I, would be actual war. The Americans thought Brezhnev might be bluffing—as indeed he was, according to Israelyan, because he had already ruled out Soviet military involvement.[49] But the Americans believed it was a bluff they could not risk calling, because they thought Soviet ships and East German troops were already on the move. The longest-range nuclear-capable bombers in the U.S. Air Force were ordered to redeploy from Guam, where they had been based while bombing North Vietnam, to the United States, and two aircraft carrier groups were ordered to sail eastward.[50]

At 5:40 a.m. Washington time the next day, the twenty-fifth, a letter transmitted to Brezhnev in Nixon's name rejected the Soviet demands. "We have no information which would indicate that the cease-fire is now being violated on any significant scale," it said, and the United States was already leaning on Israel to ensure compliance. "In these circumstances we view your suggestion of unilateral action as a matter of gravest concern involving incalculable consequences." The letter proposed instead that the United States and the Soviet Union send small contingents of noncombat forces to "augment the present truce supervisory force." The letter said that the United States, anticipating a favorable reply, would begin taking steps to do that, but reiterated, "We could in no event accept unilateral action," which would "end all we have striven so hard to achieve."[51]

Shortly afterward, the superpowers were reprieved by Sadat, who withdrew his request for joint U.S.-Soviet action and proposed instead an "international force" sponsored by the United Nations, which under UN rules would mean that none of the five permanent members of the Security Council could participate. Without Egyptian support there was virtually no chance that the United Nations would adopt any resolution calling for joint U.S.-Soviet action.

"If the Soviets sent troops it would be unilaterally, without the sanction of either the host country or the UN," Kissinger said in his account of these events. "This would be much easier for us to resist and we were determined to do so. Sadat's action showed—though we could only guess this at the moment—that Sadat was staking his future on American diplomatic support rather than Soviet military pressure."[52] This "guess" was correct; that was exactly what Sadat had decided, even before the war. To him, the war was the lever that would bring the Americans to this realization.

So Brezhnev backed off. That same day, the United States and the Soviet Union joined twelve other Security Council members in passing a resolution calling for the immediate creation of a multinational military force to supervise the cease-fire. No permanent members were to take part, a provision that excluded the Soviets and the Americans. As Kissinger put it, "They played chicken with us and they lost."[53]

Détente survived, and in fact emerged strengthened, according to Nixon, because, despite their confrontation over the cease-fire, the Soviet Union and the United States "now realize that we cannot allow our differences in the Mideast to jeopardize even greater interest that we have, for example in continuing a détente in Europe, in continuing the negotiations which can lead to limitation of nuclear arms and eventually reducing the burden of nuclear arms, and in continuing in other ways that can contribute to the peace of the world. As a matter of fact, I would suggest that with all of the criticism of détente, that without détente we might have had a major conflict in the Middle East. With détente, we avoided it."[54]

The end of the superpower standoff did not resolve the fate of Egypt's Third Army, which was still being strangled by the Israelis. The language and the tone employed by Kissinger and other Americans in pressing Israel to lift this siege reflected the drastic transformation of Israel's standing in Washington. Had Sadat heard these conversations, he would have relished them. The Israelis did not.

On the afternoon of the twenty-sixth, for example, Kissinger warned Ambassador Dinitz that "the Third Army will never surrender no matter what you do and [the Egyptians] will take drastic measures if you continue blockading them." He said the president was preparing to hold a news conference, and "I don't want him to say something you will regret."

It made no difference, Kissinger said, who first violated the cease-fire. "What produces the fighting is that they are desperate." He said that Israel, instead of making the Egyptians try to fight their way out and then complaining that the Egyptians were breaking the cease-fire, should "let them break out and go home," taking their equipment with them.

"We will not open up the pocket and release an army that came to destroy us," Dinitz retorted. "It has never happened in the history of war."

"Also it has never happened that a small country is producing a world war in this manner," Kissinger snapped.[55]

Six hours later, this unpleasant conversation resumed. The Israelis were now talking about allowing nonmilitary supplies to reach the Third Army as part of a larger package, including a prisoner exchange.

"Let me give you the president's reaction in separate parts," Kissinger said. "First he wanted me to make it absolutely clear that we cannot permit the destruction of the Egyptian army under conditions achieved after a cease-fire was reached in part by negotiations in which we participated. Therefore it is an option that does not exist. . . . Secondly, we would like from you no later than 8:00 a.m. tomorrow an answer to the question of non-military supplies to reach the army. If you cannot agree to that, we will have to support in the UN a resolution that will deal with the enforcement of 338 and 339," the second cease-fire resolution. "We have been driven to this reluctantly by your inability to reach a decision." The bottom line, he said, is that "[y]ou will not be permitted to destroy this army."[56]

This back and forth went on for three more days as the Israelis debated with themselves and the Soviets began to question the sincerity of U.S. efforts to bring Israel around.

On the twenty-seventh—after Kissinger had told Golda Meir bluntly, "You are playing with the future of your people. Would you prefer supplies to the Third Army to be sent in by Russian helicopters?"—the Israelis agreed in principle to allow a military delegation to meet with Egyptian counterparts to arrange for a single supply convoy, under the auspices of the United Nations and the International Committee of the Red Cross, to reach the Third Army.[57] The outcome of this was that on the twenty-eighth, Egypt's General Mohamad el-Gamassi and Israel's General Aharon Yariv met at the Kilometer 101 marker on the Cairo-Suez Road, a landmark that would become famous over the next two months as the two sides negotiated a disengagement-of-forces agreement.

This was an encouraging development that indicated a pathway out of the cease-fire crisis, but did not resolve it. The Israelis, according to a brief summary of the generals' meeting that they sent to Washington, said they were there to discuss details of a relief convoy but had no authority beyond that. Israel was still not prepared to stand down entirely; in their report to Washington, the Israelis said that the issue of regular resupply and the stabilization of cease-fire lines "would have to be dealt with at a political level."[58]

The fact that Egyptian and Israeli officers met face-to-face on official business represented a success for Israel. It amounted to de facto recognition by the Arabs, who had always refused to grant it. But Prime Minister Meir made no secret of her bitterness at American pressure that had forced Israel to allow the Third Army to be resupplied. Appearing on the CBS program *Face the Nation* that Sunday, she said of Sadat, "For God's sake, he started a war, our people are killed, his in the thousands are killed, and he has been defeated. And then by political arrangements he is handed a victory and has become, or thinks he has become, a hero in the eyes of the Egyptian people."[59] On that point she was correct: at home, the war had elevated Sadat to the status of national hero, the "Hero of the Crossing."

On the thirtieth, Kissinger discussed proposed terms for the political agreement still required with Egypt's foreign minister, Ismail Fahmy. Basically, it would call for an Israeli pullback to the positions it had held on the twenty-second, the exchange of prisoners, and unrestricted delivery of nonmilitary supplies. If the United States could broker such an agreement and provide a "guarantee" of enforcement, Fahmy said, Egypt was prepared to reestablish diplomatic relations.

"President Sadat wants a first-class ambassador to Cairo," Fahmy said. Kissinger promised to send one.[60]

On that same day, the thirtieth, Kissinger briefed Nixon by telephone about the latest Israeli position. They were offering to let nonmilitary supplies reach the Third Army without having to seek Israeli approval for every convoy, provided the Egyptians release all Israeli prisoners and "open the Straits of the Gulf of Suez from their blockade which they've put on." The problem was that Meir, who was scheduled to come to Washington, had not signed off on this because she wanted more, Kissinger said. "What she wants is for the withdrawal of all Egyptian forces from the east bank of the canal. That's out of the question."

"Nope," Nixon replied. "She cannot get her way this time. Too late. She's going to find a very tough problem when she walks into my office this time. You know what I mean. There is not going to be any of this horsing around anymore. I'll be courteous but she cannot come in and in that arrogant way again and say well, they all withdraw and this and that. She doesn't have the cards anymore, Henry."[61]

On the morning of November 1, Kissinger had breakfast with Meir, who was accompanied by Ambassador Dinitz and General Yariv, fresh from Kilometer 101. It was not a congenial conversation. Invited to begin, Meir wasted no time. "The war was enough, but that we can take. If we live one hundred years, it will be impossible to tell all the impossible acts of heroism of our youngsters. But what we can't take is being told at late hours, 'You have to do this. Take your choice.' Maybe Israel has to do everything Egypt wants. But we have to know what is being planned between the parties. Are there plans for the negotiations? We're responsible to our people," she said.

Kissinger denied that he had forged some secret agreement with the Soviet Union, and insisted he had kept the Israelis fully informed. The real issue, he said, was Israel's performance after the cease fire was declared. According to the State Department's record of the conversation, this exchange ensued:

KISSINGER: It is an unusual situation where an army is trapped after the ceasefire went into effect. There would be no problem with us about the Third Army if you had done it before the ceasefire.

PM MEIR: Why believe the Egyptians? Why is it that everything we say isn't believed? It is an impossible situation.

KISSINGER: It may be, but it's the situation.

PM MEIR: I don't have to take that. Whatever Sadat says is the Bible?

KISSINGER: Not what Sadat says.

Meir argued that there was no point in insisting that Israel return to the lines as they existed on October 22 because nobody really knew where those were. Kissinger's response was that Israel should make them up, agree on them with the Egyptians, and then go there. Once that happened, he said, Israel would get back its prisoners of war. She also wanted an end to the Arab naval blockade at the Bab el Mendeb, at the southern entrance to Red Sea, which was interdicting Israeli shipping. Kissinger said that would follow an Israeli return to the October 22 lines.

PM MEIR: They didn't stop shooting on October 22. What are we supposed to do?

KISSINGER: That's irrelevant. It cuts against you too. If you could live with it on October 22, you can live with it now.

PM MEIR: Why should we live with it?

KISSINGER: There is no sense in debating the issue of justice here. You're only three million. It is not the first time in the history of the Jews that unjust things have happened.

Besides, Kissinger said, with President Nixon's public approval rating down to about 30 percent, it no longer mattered whether he had the support of American Jews. He was going to do what he wanted to do.

Meir said Israel would agree to return to the October 22 lines, or to allow a supply convoy, but not both. Kissinger warned her not to take that position to Nixon, whom she was scheduled to meet two hours later. Wisely, she followed his advice. After Nixon gave her a long lecture about how difficult it was for the United States to stand with Israel when everyone in Europe and Japan was going the other way, and about how Israeli intransigence would only play into the hands of the Soviet Union, she agreed to accept the October 22 lines "in principle," with details to be negotiated by military officers on the ground. Kissinger would press the Egyptians on the rest of the package, such as the prisoners, when he went to Cairo in a few days.[62] The war was over.

A New Era in Tank Warfare

Because of the profound political and strategic issues raised by the war, less attention has been paid to its impact on military thinking and planning, but it was considerable.

Sadat had been trained as a military officer, but military theory was not part of Sadat's plan—he was more interested in political attitudes. Nevertheless, because of the way the war was fought, the engagements of 1973 carried implications for the conduct of future wars on other battlefields, especially for the use of tanks. The massive tank battles in the Sinai were all the more intense because of the relatively small area of combat: on that front the zone of engagement never extended more than fifteen miles on either side of the Suez Canal. Egypt inflicted heavy damage with the Soviet-supplied AT-3 Sagger antitank missile, prompting sober reassessments of armor tactics among military officers and analysts, beginning with Sadat himself.

"The tank battles of our era—the age of rockets and electronic war—have now come to assume gigantic proportions and involve unprecedentedly large numbers of tanks," he wrote. "Before this the tank battle of Kursk, Russia, in World War II was the biggest on record, although no more than 500 tanks took part in it. Whereas in the October 1973 battle, which lasted seventeen days (rather than five years) 3,000 tanks were lost by the two sides. More than 5,000 tanks took part in the fighting."[63]

A few years later, he gave President Jimmy Carter his breakdown of the tank losses. "We didn't lose much in the October War," he said. "Syria lost 1200 tanks in one day, but all of my losses were only 500 tanks . . . 3,000 tanks were lost on all fronts, so Israel and Syria together lost 2,500 tanks."[64]

Donn A. Starry, an American tank officer and military historian, concluded, "The armored battlefields of the Yom Kippur War [as Israel called it] yielded striking lessons about what to expect in first and succeeding battles of the next war."

> First, we learned that the U.S. military should expect modern battlefields to be dense with large numbers of weapons systems whose lethality at extended ranges would surpass previous experience by nearly an order of magnitude. Direct-fire battle space would be expanded several orders of magnitude over that experienced in World War II and Korea. Second, because of numbers and weapons lethality, the direct-fire battle will be intense, resulting in enormous equipment losses in a relatively short time. Significantly, we noted, combined tank losses in the first six critical days of the Yom Kippur War exceeded the total U.S. tank inventory deployed to NATO Europe—including both tanks in units and in war reserves.[65]

CIA analysts, in their postwar assessment, took note of the stark contrast between Egypt's complete failure at tank warfare in 1967 and its relatively successful performance in 1973:

> The major improvement was the willingness of infantrymen to use a new weapon to stand up to attacking tanks. This weapon was the unguided RPG-7 bazooka-type antitank rocket, which filled a gap the 1967 war had shown to exist. In 1967 the Israelis had used their armor, unsupported by infantry, in direct assaults on Egyptian positions. The lack of weapons to defeat the Israeli armor often left the Egyptian infantryman with no choice but to run. In 1973, the

Egyptians deployed the RPG-7 widely and the favored tactic was to set up RPG-7 ambushes in advance of the main Egyptian positions. The Egyptians could thus bring antitank fire to bear on the more vulnerable sides and rear of the Israelis. The tactic worked quite well until the Israelis adopted countertactics.[66]

The Israelis made a tactical mistake by sending their tanks into combat without infantry support in 1973 as they had in 1967. Eventually, another American analyst wrote, Israeli tank commanders learned to spot the points from which the antitank Sagger rockets were being fired and use their tank guns to take them out. Another result was the "creation of tactics, techniques, and procedures (TTP) that integrated infantry in M113 armored personnel carriers to clear out [antitank] positions ahead of tanks." Still another was the development of better-armored tanks, more resistant to antitank fire.[67]

The reason the Israelis had sent their tanks into the battle without infantry support, the Israeli general Chaim Herzog concluded, was that they had drawn the wrong lessons from the easy victory of 1967. They thought they could defeat the Arabs with tanks and air power, and thus infantry—more vulnerable to casualties—could be spared. They did not take the RPG-7 into account.

"The Egyptians realized that with the outbreak of another war their problem was how to neutralize the tank and the plane and how to slow down the process of growth of the IDF's reserve potential," Herzog wrote. "Their reply was a missile umbrella, a concentrated mask of anti-tank weapons and strategic surprise which would force the IDF to react piecemeal. But the Israelis did not construct their forces as a reply to this concept; they ignored it, adopting a fixed concept of their own based on experience in the previous conflict. . . . As a result, while infantry were an integral part of the Egyptian defensive system, Israeli armour stormed enemy positions without infantry and mortars, sometimes in wasteful battles."[68]

In their postwar retrospective, CIA analysts observed that the disastrous Israeli counterattack in the Sinai on October 8 "appears to have been the last attempt to use tanks in the unsupported 1967 style and even then the Israelis may have been drawn in by their initial success. Within four or five days after the beginning of the war, the Israelis were adopting tactics which reduced the threat from Arab antitank weapons to manageable proportions. This adjustment in the midst of combat provides a fair measure of the flexibility of Israeli leadership and the thoroughness of low-level training. . . . It is probably safe to say that no large, modern army will again make the mistake of using unsupported tanks against massed infantry."[69] Indeed, in the decades since the October War, the only conflict in which tanks were deployed in similar large numbers was Operation Desert Storm, the 1991 campaign led by the United States to drive occupying Iraqi forces out of Kuwait. In that war, ground troops moved ahead of the armored units to clear away Iraqi defenses, which had first been softened up by aerial bombardment.[70]

Military analysts go through such "lessons learned" exercises after every war, but for the Israelis the war meant more than that. To have been taken by surprise, to have employed faulty tactics that caused heavy casualties, and to have been forced to plead for American support against an enemy they had considered unworthy, were shocking experiences for them. They ultimately prevailed on the battlefield, but it was no longer possible to feel invincible. That was the start of the psychological transformation of the strategic and diplomatic landscape that Sadat had set out to achieve.

The war represented "the deepest trauma in the nation's history," the Israeli historian Abraham Rabinovich wrote. The country "had lost almost three times as many men per capita in nineteen days as the United States did in Vietnam in close to a decade." The Israeli public was furious about the intelligence debacle that led to those casualties and turned against the country's leaders. A soldier who survived showed up outside Meir's office with a placard that read, "Grandma, your defense minister [Dayan] is a failure and 3,000 of your grandchildren are dead." When Dayan appeared at military funerals, grieving relatives shouted, "Murderer." A commission appointed to investigate blamed military and intelligence officers but absolved Dayan and Meir. That outcome only inflamed the public further, with the result that Meir's government fell: she resigned a week after the report came out, to be replaced by Yitzhak Rabin.[71]

Kissinger, who began his career as a student of international strategy, fully grasped the significance of the war's psychological impact even before the Israelis did. On October 26, before the cease-fire had stabilized, he told a Chinese diplomat that "the Soviet Union has suffered a major strategic defeat, and that's why they tried to bluff us last night. For the third time now its friends have lost most of the equipment the Soviet Union gave them. Even the Arab leaders have had to learn that they can get military equipment from the Soviet Union but if they want to make diplomatic progress they have to deal with us. And since we are not anti-Arab we will help them now make diplomatic progress. So we now have a very good position to reduce the Soviet political influence." There would be "some face-saving things" to make the Soviets feel better, Kissinger said, but the United States "will determine for ourselves what will be done."[72]

The next day Kissinger made a similar presentation to anxious oil executives who feared chaos because of an embargo on exports to the United States imposed by Arab producers angered by U.S. support for Israel during the war.[73] In his best professorial manner, he gave them a summary of the situation that included this assessment of the war's impact on Israel: "We are in a better position for negotiations than at any time since 1948. Although the Israelis have won militarily, they have paid a tremendous price. They have suffered some 7,000 casualties, which would be equivalent to some 300 [thousand] to 400,000 casualties for us. They have found out that rapid spectacular victories are no longer possible and that in any war, they face a war of attrition which they cannot win over time. Our influence over Israel is greater than ever. They cannot go to war again without an open supply line from the U.S. They have to address what security they can now achieve by diplomacy."[74]

That is to say, Israel before the war had no incentive to negotiate with the Arabs. Now it did, knowing in advance that any negotiated agreement would require that it yield at least some territory. Moreover, the corollary of Washington's difficulties with Israel during the cease-fire crisis was an American respect for, and eagerness to work with, President Sadat. From Washington's perspective, the clownish tool of Moscow had emerged as a statesman and potential ally, a shift reflected in a letter Nixon sent to Sadat on December 27, 1973: "Relationships between our two countries have been put on a new basis of cordiality and understanding. . . . I am deeply convinced, Mr. President, that our two nations stand at the threshold of a great turning point in history. We can, if we will, bring a new era of peace and prosperity to all the peoples of the Arab world."[75]

Nixon would not survive in the presidency long enough to undertake that mission, but in terms of the American attitude, this was the "psychological breakthrough" that Sadat had sought. The war had established the foundation of the "land for peace" bargain through which Egypt, now a friend of the United States, and Israel, now more than ever dependent on U.S. support, would be prodded by Washington to come to terms just a few years later.

As for the Arabs, Kissinger told the oil executives, they "have fought with honor. Although they have lost the war, they lost like normal countries; their forces were not routed this time. For their part they must know that they can only get territory from the U.S."[76] In other words, the Arabs must realize now that they can get weapons and rhetorical support from the Soviet Union, but if they wanted to persuade Israel to yield occupied land, they had no choice but to work through Washington. Sadat knew that before the war, which is why he started it—to induce a distracted United States government to throw itself into the difficult task of forging a peace agreement Egypt could live with. He had succeeded beyond his dreams.

"Now," he wrote not long afterward, "We see those on whose doors we knocked, receiving no answer, coming to knock on our door, and those who shrugged whenever we spoke of our problems trying hard to understand us."[77]

Kissinger would not have contested the point. "Deep down," he wrote in his memoirs, "the Israelis knew that while they had won the last battle, they had lost the aura of invincibility. The Arab armies were not destroyed. The Arab nations had not won, but no longer need they quail before Israeli might. Israel, after barely escaping disaster, had prevailed militarily; it ended up with more Arab territory captured than lost. But it was entering an uncertain and lonely future, dependent on a shrinking circle of friends."[78]

Israel, Ambassador Dinitz observed years afterward, "had to face a new situation. Instead of a Middle East divided into two blocs— the Arab countries, basically in the Soviet camp, and Israel and the Persian Gulf on the American side—all of a sudden America had turned, as far as Israel was concerned, from an ally to an arbitrator. This was not easy for Israel to swallow because, all of a sudden, we realized that we were no longer the only children. We are part of a set of interests of the United States that now includes Egypt and to some extent Syria."[79]

The extent to which Sadat's Egypt quickly became part of the U.S. "set of interests" was on display in a memorandum sent to President Jimmy Carter by his national security adviser, Zbigniew Brzezinski, in November 1979, recommending a close, long-term military relationship. "With these decisions, we have the opportunity, and in my view the obligation, to cement a relationship of vital importance to the United States," the memo said. "President Sadat has nowhere else to turn for military assistance. He is in this position by virtue of turning away from the Soviets and moving closer to the United States and Israel—steps of unprecedented benefit to our interests in the Middle East. Our failure to support Sadat militarily at this critical juncture could have disastrous effect on our overall peace effort."[80] Carter agreed with this assessment, approving the shipment of tanks and f-16 combat jets. Such a commitment would have been unimaginable before the October War.

This widening of the American role in the region came at the expense of the Soviet Union. Initially, according to Victor Israelyan, the Kremlin evaluated the war as "a triumph of Soviet foreign policy and diplomacy and a political victory for the Soviet Union." In the view of the Soviet leaders, "they had supported the Arab side even after discouraging the war, they had avoided getting involved militarily, and they had preserved détente." In reality, the Soviet Union's foreign affairs professionals understood that it was a "hollow victory" because of the diminished Soviet position in Egypt. "Sadat's growing contacts with the Americans, only some of which were known to Moscow, proved that Egypt had embarked on an entirely new foreign policy, which was pro-American and anti-Soviet. . . . There was no increase whatsoever in Soviet authority and influence in the area as a result of the war."[81]

His assessment was correct. The era of Soviet ascendancy in the Arab world had ended.

2 The Eclipse of the Soviet Union

Shortly after the death of the Soviet dictator Joseph Stalin in 1953, his successors abandoned one of the central pillars of his international policy and turned a new, friendlier face to the developing world. The Kremlin adopted a new attitude toward countries that were neutral in the Cold War and toward the noncommunist, postcolonial states in what came to be known as the Third World. This new doctrine established an accommodating policy that might be called friendly persuasion. Unlike Stalin, Nikita Khrushchev and his Politburo colleagues could see a path to the spread of Marxism-Leninism by providing economic and military aid to such countries even if they were not communist, and by supporting those countries' objectives at the United Nations and in regional organizations.

In effect, the Soviet leaders put Stalin behind them and returned to V. I. Lenin's policy of solidarity with anticolonial movements everywhere. The Kremlin's strategy was to spread its political and economic influence by making common cause with those seeking to liberate themselves from colonialism and imperialist exploitation, real or imagined, even if these new nationalists and freedom fighters opposed communism as an ideology. Moscow was not abandoning its efforts to export its ideology, it was making a friendlier sales pitch. Whether the proffered solidarity with African, Asian, and Latin American regimes was genuine or feigned was irrelevant; it was the face Moscow showed the world for the rest of the Soviet Union's existence.

This old and now new again policy had first been promoted at a

Moscow-sponsored international congress in Baku, Azerbaijan, in 1920, in the earliest years of the Soviet Union, before Stalin rose to power. A communist historian described the Baku event as "the first attempt to appeal to the exploited and oppressed peoples in the colonial and semi-colonial countries to carry forward their revolutionary struggles under the banner of Marxism and with the support of the workers in Russia and the advanced countries of the world." After Lenin's death that policy had been set aside because of Stalin's errors, the new strategy held: "Stalinism, with its 'theory' of 'socialism in one country', had trampled underfoot the principles fought for by the Communist International under the leadership of Lenin and Trotsky. It was understood that the revolutionary struggles in the different parts of the world were integrally related and that the fate of the Soviet Union itself hinged upon the spread of the revolution worldwide."[1]

At the time of the Baku congress, many Arabs were inclined to think favorably of the Bolshevik government in Moscow because it was the Bolsheviks who, upon coming to power in 1917, had revealed the treachery of France and Britain in the Sykes-Picot Agreement. That was a secret pact signed by France, Britain, and Russia to divide among them Arab lands that would be hived off from the Ottoman Empire after World War I, rather than grant them independence. The Bolsheviks repudiated the agreement and made it public. Stalin's ideological rigidity and suspicious personality then squandered much of the Arab good will generated by that gesture. His death opened a new path to cooperation, and his successors promptly took it. The Middle East soon became a major battleground of what became the Cold War.

The Soviet Union's return to the Baku strategy of promoting worldwide relations with receptive countries regardless of ideology was no secret. The Politburo announced it in the Soviet press as early as 1955. *Pravda* published a statement by the Foreign Ministry that began with a denunciation of "the so-called Baghdad Pact of February 1955," which joined Iraq, Turkey, Pakistan, Iran, and Britain in an anticommunist defense group known as the Central Treaty Organization. This agreement inflamed Arab nationalists such as Egypt's Nasser, who saw it as an instrument of Western imperialism and leftover Ottoman ambitions, and Moscow took the opportunity to show its solidarity with them.

"The situation in the Near and Middle East has recently deteriorated considerably," the Foreign Ministry statement said, "owing to the new attempts by certain Western powers to involve the Near and Middle Eastern countries in military groupings meant to serve as adjuncts to the aggressive North Atlantic bloc," meaning the North Atlantic Treaty Organization (NATO), of which Turkey was a member.

"Actions of this nature and the role which the Western powers are assigning [to] Turkey in the creation of military blocs in the Near and Middle East are giving rise to legitimate fears in Arab countries that Turkey is again striving to dominate them and that their national independence is directly threatened." Noting—correctly—that Britain and the United States had tried to put pressure on Jordan, Syria, and other regional states to join the group, the statement said such tactics "are aimed at the political and economic subjugation of these countries to the imperialist powers, which are trying once again to force the peoples of those countries under the yoke of colonial oppression and exploitation." By contrast, the statement said, "The Soviet state from its very inception has resolutely condemned the imperialist policy of aggression and colonial expression. . . . In international organizations the Soviet government invariably supports all legitimate demands of Near and Middle East countries designed to consolidate their national independence and state sovereignty."

Therefore, it said, "The Soviet government will take a positive attitude toward any steps by the governments of Near and Middle Eastern countries to apply these principles in their relations with the Soviet Union. The Soviet government, supporting the cause of peace, will defend the freedom and independence of Near and Middle Eastern states and oppose interference in their internal affairs."[2]

At the time, Iran and Iraq were hardly models of proletarian socialism—they were monarchies supported by Britain. But they were independent, and in the new Soviet thinking that was sufficient; they could eventually be brought around if Moscow stood with them against imperialism. The immediate target, however, was the country leading the regional opposition to the Baghdad Pact, Egypt.

"By that time," the U.S. State Department veteran John C. Campbell wrote, "it was becoming ever clearer what the Soviet strategy was and that the point of concentration would be Egypt. Until then, Soviet propaganda had been calling Abdel Nasser a fascist dictator who persecuted 'democratic' elements such as the Communists. Suddenly he became a patriot, a national leader fighting for his people's rights against the imperialists."[3] The newly independent Arabs, personified by Nasser, were potentially valuable partners for Moscow even if they were not communists or socialists themselves.

Khrushchev, one historian wrote, "rediscovered Lenin's argument that the peoples of the colonial world represented de facto allies of the proletariat and of the first proletarian state, the Soviet Union," and could contribute to weakening the USSR's enemies. By the end of the 1950s, "the Soviets had become the major supporter of the Arabs in their struggle with Israel and of the radical Arab states against the traditional, conservative monarchies of the region." The Kremlin's decision to provide weapons to Egypt, through what came to be known as the Czech arms deal, and to support construction of the Aswan High Dam after the United States backed out, exemplified Moscow's new opportunism. Those decisions "were among the factors that contributed to the Israeli-British-French decision to seize the Suez Canal and destroy growing Egyptian military capabilities in 1956. But despite the massive defeat of their client's forces, the Soviets emerged from the Suez War of 1956 as a clear winner, since [they] had successfully projected the image of supporter of Egyptian and Arab interests against both Israel and the West," this historian wrote.[4]

By siding with Egypt in the Suez crisis, Moscow overcame the hostility it had generated among Arabs by supporting the creation of Israel in 1948, which it had done in the apparent expectation that the intellectual European Jews who dominated the new nation would be sympathetic to Marxist-Leninist ideology.

Soviet premier Nikolai Bulganin, in a letter to Israeli prime minister David Ben-Gurion during the Suez War, left no doubt about Moscow's revised view of Israel: "All peace-loving mankind indignantly brands the criminal action of the aggressors who have attacked the territorial entity, sovereignty, and independence of the Egyptian state. Disregarding this, the Government of Israel, acting as a tool of foreign imperialist powers, continues the foolhardy adventure, challenging all the peoples of the East who are waging a struggle against colonialism for their freedom and independence, all the peace-loving people of the world." He advised Israel to "come to its senses before it is too late" and informed Ben-Gurion that the Soviet Union was withdrawing its ambassador.[5]

Before the Suez War, Deputy Premier Anastas Mikoyan observed at a Kremlin meeting of the Soviet Communist Party's Central Committee, "We had no access to the Arab countries. English influence had such a hold on the Muslim religion that we had no access there. Three imperialist powers gathered together and decided all the issues of the Near East without us. But when we sold arms to Egypt we bared our teeth to our enemies, and Nasser turned out to be a strong leader, so that now they cannot any longer resolve the issues of the Near East without us. Is this not a realization of the Leninist policy on using the contradictions of the imperialist camp? In the given case we are supporting bourgeois nationalists against the imperialists."[6]

Then in 1958, a coup d'état in Iraq overthrew the pro-Western monarchy that had been the anchor of the Baghdad Pact's anti–Soviet Central Treaty Organization (CENTO). The new regime was oriented toward Moscow. Now Egypt, Syria, and Iraq were all viewed by Moscow as progressive regimes that had broken with Western imperialism and were laying the foundations for socialist political and economic development.

Khrushchev was forthright about this Soviet policy in an interview with the *New York Times*. Nasser and other Arab nationalist leaders were not communists and were not going to become communists, he said, but that was not the point: "They are against colonial slavery and they stand for the consolidation of their political and economic independence. We do not conceal the fact that our sympathies are on the side of the peoples who are fighting for their independence and we are ready to assist them in this struggle." Soviet leaders, he said, "know that you cannot inculcate communism with a bayonet. You cannot send ideas with a machine gun."[7]

The Kremlin's policy switch heralded the beginning of a long period of sustained political and economic investment by the Soviet Union in the Middle East, Asia, Africa, and Latin America, on its own and through proxies such as Cuba and North Vietnam. The Soviet Union's Warsaw Pact satellites, such as Poland and Bulgaria, faithfully followed the Kremlin line. Moscow's true interests, the scholar Adeed Dawisha noted, were "no less 'imperialistic' than those of the United States, Britain, or France" but its rhetoric gave the Arabs the impression that it was a friendly, supportive power.[8]

This was the great global contest of the Cold War: Moscow and its communist allies seeking opportunities to spread their power and influence, opposed by the United States and its allies pursuing a strategy known as "containment." In the Middle East, Nasser's Egypt was the most important arena of that struggle, and the outcome was in doubt until Anwar Sadat decided it by breaking with Moscow.

It took years for policymakers in Washington to grasp the full impact of Sadat's rupture with the Soviet Union. With Sadat's decisive turnabout, the contest for influence in the Arab world had essentially been decided, but that did not become clear immediately; the Soviet Union still appeared menacing and expansionist as it continued its quest elsewhere in the world. Frozen out of Egypt within a few years of Sadat's accession to the presidency, the Soviets struggled to find a comparable showcase partnership, and the Americans continued to regard them as a worldwide threat. When the Soviet Union invaded Afghanistan in December 1979 to shore up a puppet government there that was facing an anti-Soviet tribal insurgency, President Jimmy Carter took it as a threat to the Middle East. In his State of the Union address in January 1980, he proclaimed what came to be known as the Carter Doctrine: "An attempt by any outside force to gain control of the Persian Gulf region will be regarded as an assault on the vital interests of the United States of America, and such an assault will be repelled by any means necessary, including military force." His secretary of state, Cyrus Vance, told Congress that the United States faced a "sustained Soviet challenge, which is both military and political. Their military build-up continues unabated. The Soviet Union has shown a greater willingness to employ that power directly, and through others. In that sense, Afghanistan is a manifestation of a larger problem, evident also in Ethiopia, South Yemen, Southeast Asia and elsewhere."[9] It was revealing that the only Arab country on Vance's 1980 list was the marginal, impoverished South Yemen. One reason the Soviet Union felt compelled to intensify its quest to project its power in Africa, South Asia, and Latin America was that its dominance of the Arab world had been ripped away. Several Arab countries still imported weapons from the Soviet Union, but not ideology.

When Nasser gained power in the Free Officers' coup of 1952, there was virtually no Soviet influence in the Middle East, and Nasser was certainly no communist. One of his first acts after the coup was to send one of his lieutenants to assure U.S. ambassador Jefferson Caffrey that the new government wanted friendly relations with Washington.[10] Not long afterward, however, Dwight Eisenhower became president of the United States and installed as secretary of state a patrician dignitary named John Foster Dulles, who adopted a "with us or against us" policy reminiscent of the inflexible doctrine that the Soviets were just then abandoning.

Dulles would have been better advised to absorb the advice of a National Intelligence Estimate submitted in 1954 by his brother Allen, director of the Central Intelligence Agency. This secret assessment, which summarized the views of the U.S. intelligence community, said that "[o]n the whole, the strength of the Communist movement in the Arab states lies not in the appeal of its ideology but in its ability to relate itself to existing dissatisfactions and adjust its propaganda to exploit nationalism and the grievances of ethnic and religious minorities." Therefore, the intelligence analysis said, "The effectiveness of Communism's attempt to arouse hostility toward the West among non-Communist Arabs would almost certainly decline if relations between the West and the Arab states improve." Such a development "would probably eliminate some of the political appeal of Communist and pro-Soviet propaganda and improve the ability and willingness of Arab governments to attempt to correct the conditions which contribute to Communism's appeal."[11]

Indeed, Nasser would have done business with the Americans if Dulles had not reneged on a commitment to finance construction of the Aswan Dam—which he did after Nasser infuriated him by recognizing the communist government in China—and if the United States had been willing to supply weapons. Dulles, unlike the Soviet leaders, was unwilling to accept as legitimate the so-called Non-Aligned Movement, in which the leaders of such emerging postcolonial countries as Egypt, India, and Indonesia declared themselves politically and ideologically independent of either of the two superpowers. Nasser's nationalization of the Suez Canal in 1956 was not done at the behest or in the interest of the Soviet Union but nonetheless fostered the impression in the West that Egypt had placed itself in Moscow's orbit. That became a self-fulfilling prophecy.

Nasser's Ideology

Nasser was no Castro. He was a nationalist, not a communist, and he aligned his country with Moscow only as a means to an end. But in the fashion of the times, he often adopted the rhetoric of the left— "Socialism, based as it is on justice and the satisfaction of needs, is the road to social freedom. . . . Capitalist experience has gone hand and hand with imperialism"—which was not designed to cultivate the United States of the McCarthy-era 1950s.[12] When Washington stonewalled him, an arrangement with the Soviet Union was the obvious alternative, and Moscow seized the opportunity, taking on the High Dam project and arranging to provide weapons through the façade of its satellite Czechoslovakia. With the agreement to acquire tanks, combat jets, and other weapons in exchange for cotton and rice, Nasser's biographer Robert Stephens noted, "Overnight Nasser's prestige and popularity soared among the Arab public to a height no modern Arab leader had reached before. He was admired for his boldness and for his refusal to submit to an arms control system imposed by the Western Powers which seemed to leave the Arabs at the mercy of the Israeli army. Where other Arab leaders had only talked, he had dared to act."[13]

In the United States, however, the arms deal was greeted with dismay. As Roby C. Barrett put it in a history of the Cold War in the Middle East, "The Czech arms deal dealt a double shock to the Eisenhower administration. In the minds of many in Washington, it irretrievably linked 'non-aligned' and pro-communist policies, but perhaps more importantly, it directly affected U.S.-Soviet relations. Eisenhower believed that at the Geneva Conference [of 1955] he had received an 'understanding' with the Soviet Union about spheres of influence. This 'understanding' included the Middle East in the Western sphere. The Czech arms agreement amounted to a Soviet double-cross and demonstrated that the new leadership in Moscow could not be trusted to abide by any agreements." This American assessment that Nasser was now a tool of a perfidious communist power left the Egyptian leader with no place other than the Soviet Union to turn for support.[14]

Moscow moved quickly to consolidate its new relationship with Egypt. Mohamed Heikal, Egypt's most prominent journalist at that time and Nasser's spokesman and confidant, calculated that in the twelve years between the Aswan Dam commitment and the 1967 war, Soviet nonmilitary aid to Egypt totaled $1.84 billion, which on a per capita basis was fifteen times as much as went to India and twenty times as much as went to China.[15]

By the time of Nasser's death in 1970, Egypt was almost entirely dependent on the Soviet Union and its Warsaw Pact satellites, economically and militarily. The Soviet Union built not only the Aswan High Dam but also the great iron and steel complex at Helwan. Egypt's state automobile factory was built by Poland, at the time a Warsaw Pact member. Egypt's wineries, nationalized by Nasser and producers of the worst wine anywhere around the Mediterranean, had East German winemaking equipment. Moscow bought most of the crucial cotton crop. Much of Egypt's international trade was conducted through barter arrangements with Soviet satellite countries. The Egyptian economy was nationalized from top to bottom: factories, banks, insurance companies, newspapers and television, the flagship airline, food distribution networks, apartment buildings, department stores, all were owned and operated by the state, just as in the USSR.

There were Soviet agents in Egypt's intelligence service. Egyptian newspapers reprinted articles from *Pravda* and *Izvestia*, the Soviet Union's official newspapers. The Soviets provided everything from cultural events—a ballet performance by Galina Ulanova, a poetry reading by Yevtushenko—to the first nuclear reactor, which went online in 1961.

The Soviet Union had nearly fifteen thousand military advisers stationed in Egypt, in addition to naval crews. Egypt's military equipment and combat aircraft were almost entirely Soviet, and Egyptian officers went to the Soviet Union for training. Soviet pilots were in Egypt flying MIG-21s. Except for the American University in Cairo, the United States and American institutions were frozen out of Egypt. The United States did not even have an embassy in Cairo—it had been closed during the 1967 war, and a handful of American diplomats worked in an "interests section," under the flag of Spain.

By the late 1960s, in addition to Egypt, the Soviets were the principal suppliers of weapons to Syria, Iraq, Algeria, South Yemen and, increasingly, Libya, all of which also embraced some variant of the state socialist economic systems espoused by Moscow.

Only South Yemen, then an independent country officially known as the People's Democratic Republic of Yemen, was a fully communist state. The others were not "communist countries" in the sense that East Germany and Cuba were communist. On the contrary, they generally prohibited Communist Party activity, and they had strong differences with Moscow over such issues as the emigration of Soviet Jews to Israel. Nevertheless, on Washington's inflexible Cold War balance sheet, they were clearly on the red side of the ledger—Egypt, by far the biggest Arab country, most of all.

Unlike the United States and Western Europe, the Soviet Union had no need for Middle East oil. It did assist Iraq with development of its fields, but the gains Moscow sought were more ideological and political than economic. In the Egypt of 1970, those gains appeared irreversible. Moscow invested heavily in Egypt, and within less than two decades after the Free Officers' coup, the largest Arab country became the grand prize in Moscow's network of influence among the so-called non-aligned countries of the postcolonial era. Peru, North Vietnam, and Somalia were nice to have, but Egypt mattered far more in the global contest against the democratic West.

Influential, but Unpopular

In spite of all that Moscow had bestowed, many ordinary Egyptians were dissatisfied because the Soviets had not delivered prosperity to the masses or the prize they wanted most, victory over Israel. Besides, many Egyptians told me during the years I lived there, Russians were arrogant, secretive, and parsimonious; ordinary people benefited little from their massive presence. At the sidewalk Pepsi-Cola stand outside the Cairo press center, the vendor complained to me that the Russians were so stingy that two of them would share a single soda. Egyptian merchants and street vendors assumed that the Soviets as white Europeans must be affluent and resented it when they counted every piaster in change.

Within the Egyptian armed forces, "the Soviets were considered coarse louts who did nothing to hide their contempt for Egyptian military prowess," an Arab scholar wrote. "Moreover, the Soviets had taken over Egyptian bases and acted as if they owned them."[16]

Ahmed Fakhr, a general in the Egyptian army at the height of Soviet influence, recalled that "they penetrated every segment of Egypt's society—all the way from folk dance troupes, to military advisers, to theater groups, to the press, but Egyptians called them a society of the third person. One could not talk to a Russian without having somebody along to listen and report. The Soviets trained the Egyptian military, and they improved its knowledge about war and force structure. They were helpful according to the contracts in general, but they were task-oriented rather than knowledge-oriented people. When they were expelled from the country, nobody was sorry, because Egyptians had no real friendship with them. I never went to a house where a Soviet expert lived. I was never able to invite a Soviet expert to my house."[17] The Soviet culture of suspicion, party orthodoxy, and secrecy was incompatible with that of the voluble, gregarious Egyptians.

The Soviets had similar problems with all their Arab allies, but in the case of Egypt Moscow became a victim of its own diplomatic intransigence. The Soviets insisted that any peace settlement in the Middle East be comprehensive—that is, that it include Egypt, Syria, Jordan, and the Palestine Liberation Organization—and that it be accepted by other Arab countries. After the October War Sadat espoused the same objective, but before the war, when Egypt was still under Soviet tutelage, he believed, with good reason, that no such agreement could be achieved under the circumstances of the day. Even if the Soviet Union had supplied all the weapons and aircraft he wanted, that would only extend the negotiating stalemate, leaving the Suez Canal closed and the Sinai in Israeli hands. Moreover, the Soviets, for their own reasons, did not want a war in the Middle East, while Sadat believed war was the only way to restore Egyptian honor.

According to Vadim Kirpitchenko, a senior KGB agent in Egypt during that era, the Soviet Union did not want war between the Arabs and Israel because "the effects of military operations would inevitably damage Soviet foreign policy. Every new Arab defeat in the wars with Israel complicated our relations with the Arab states. Their leaders started to reproach us for supplying imperfect arms and for poor training of Arab armies by the Soviet military advisers and specialists because the advisers themselves allegedly lacked the experience of having waged modern warfare."[18] Sadat of course could see that the Soviets were putting their own interests ahead of Egypt's; he had to break away from Moscow, and the only alternative was the United States, which in Sadat's view was the only country that could exert influence over Israel. Soviet aspirations in the Middle East would not recover from Sadat's defection.

Sadat had visited the United States before becoming president and despite his pro forma anti-American rhetoric he liked what he saw, but his astonishing and abrupt transfer of Egypt's allegiance from Moscow to Washington was not based on ideology. Like his decisions earlier in life to support Germany against Britain and to join the Free Officers in overthrowing the monarchy, it was based on a calculation of how to get what he wanted, for Egypt and for himself. In this he was not fundamentally different from many other Arab leaders of the postcolonial era who, free to choose their external partners, chose those that promised to deliver whatever it was they wanted, without necessarily embracing their value systems. For Saudi Arabia, for example, that meant accepting the unwelcome presence of non-Muslim Americans who brought the capital and technology the kingdom needed to develop its oil industry, but it did not mean accepting American ideas about politics and the organization of society. In Iraq the 1958 coup that overthrew the monarchy so alienated Britain and the United States that the revolutionary regime of Abdel Karim Qassem had little choice but to accept Soviet offers to fill the vacuum, but neither Qassem nor his Baathist successors welcomed communist ideology at home. On the contrary, as the Soviet diplomat Yevgeny Primakov wrote, "The Baathist takeover in Iraq was marked by a wave of bloody reprisals in which thousands of Communist Party members and their sympathizers were slaughtered."[19] Later, under Saddam Hussein, "May 1978 saw the unleashing of a virulent anti-communist campaign: almost every member of the Iraqi Communist Party in the People's Patriotic Front was arrested, all the party's publications were banned, and thirty-one communists accused of setting up party cells in the army were executed."[20]

There were few outright communists in Egypt, and Nasser would not have permitted a Communist Party to function. Like Syria and other countries to which Moscow was armorer and economic supporter, Nasser's Egypt was willing to accept Soviet aid but not communist political activity or ideology. Thus by 1970, when Nasser died and Sadat became president, Moscow's influence in the Middle East was broad but shallow, constructed mostly on hardware rather than software.

Sadat Realigns Egypt

After his break with Moscow had upended the Cold War balance of power in the Middle East, Sadat offered a simple explanation for it: "As long as [the USSR] was fulfilling its commitments, we were on the best of terms. But when it reneged on its obligations I expelled 17,000 Soviet experts in a single week."[21] The reality was much more complicated: Egypt's realignment did not take place overnight, and there was not one single cause, but many. Sadat arrived at his decision through a combination of shrewd analysis, frustration, opportunism, admiration for the United States, and his desire to consolidate his power by ridding Egypt of all vestiges of Nasserism.

Within six weeks of taking office, Sadat began to receive overtures from King Faisal of Saudi Arabia, a fervent anticommunist who had been a rival of Nasser's. Through his brother-in-law Kamal Adham, a prominent international fixer, the king dangled the lure of financial inducements for Egypt if Sadat would cut Soviet influence out of his country. Sadat told Adham that he would move against the Soviet military presence as soon as Israel had carried out at least a token withdrawal from the Sinai, and Adham promised to convey this pledge to Washington.[22]

At the time, in the first months of Sadat's presidency, there were few visible signs that he was about to engineer a seismic shift in the global balance of power; he gave no public indication that he was anything but a loyal ally of the Soviet Union. He had not yet consolidated his power and still faced a challenge from senior political and military officials who were committed to the relationship with Moscow. On February 4, 1971, in a speech to the People's Assembly, he proclaimed that "the Soviet Union, in its attitudes toward us in this crisis, has consolidated one of the major friendships in history and made of it a model and example of world fraternity and unity of the powers averse to imperialism, terrorism and aggression."[23]

The following month he went to Moscow, where, according to Mohamed Heikal, he assured Brezhnev that "our future is tied to the future of the Soviet Union" and that "my real enemy is the U. S.

and western imperialism."[24] He and Soviet president Nikolai Podgorny signed a Treaty of Friendship and Cooperation that seemed to put the seal of permanence on the bilateral relationship. That appearance was deceiving. Sadat was already disillusioned with the Soviets and would come to believe that they deceived him with promises of weapons that they did not deliver.

In that first year after Nasser's death, in addition to the message relayed by Adham, Sadat did give the United States a few signals about his new perspective on the superpowers. He told Elliot Richardson, a cabinet officer who was the highest-ranking American official to attend Nasser's funeral, that he was open to the idea of better relations with Washington. Receiving no response, he sent President Nixon a letter through diplomatic channels restating the message more forcefully: "You would be mistaken to think that we are in the Soviet sphere of influence; we are not within the Soviet sphere of influence nor, for that matter, anybody's sphere of influence." Egypt makes its own decisions, he said, and "if you prove friendly to us we shall be ten times as friendly."[25] In fact, he had come to the conclusion that Egypt's path to dignity and prosperity ran through Washington. To regain its lost land and rise from its economic morass, Egypt needed peace and foreign investment, which only the United States could deliver. The Soviet Union was part of the problem, not part of the solution. Once he reached that point, the days of Soviet supremacy in the Middle East were numbered.

In Sadat's retelling of these events, Nasser himself was turning away from Moscow at the time of his death, which explains his acceptance of an American diplomatic initiative known as the Rogers Plan. Nasser "died of fury because they"—the Soviets—"failed to honor any of their commitments," Sadat said. When he made his first trip to Moscow as president, in March 1971, Sadat recalled, he asked Kremlin leaders why they had not delivered to Nasser the weapons they had promised. "The response of the Soviet leaders," he said, "was that they were ready to fulfill their promise provided we do not use these weapons except by orders from Moscow. I told them that, first of all, I categorically refuse to have orders from Moscow and I officially declared my refusal of these weapons; secondly, no one will make a decision for Egypt except its own people and president."[26]

Yevgeny Primakov, Moscow's leading specialist on the Arab world, later wrote that there were abundant clues at the time that Sadat was planning a shift away from Soviet influence, including analyses by the KGB station in Cairo, but Podgorny and other Kremlin leaders brushed them aside. "It is deeply regrettable that the Kremlin took him at his word" when he professed his commitment to Moscow, Primakov wrote.[27]

Dissatisfied as he was with the Soviet Union, Sadat still needed Moscow's military aid if he was to have any hope of challenging Israel on the battlefield. The United States would not have been receptive if asked for military equipment or training. The friendship treaty was Sadat's instrument for keeping the doors of the Soviet arsenal open. It was intended to placate the Kremlin after Sadat's "Corrective Revolution" of May 1971, in which he consolidated his power by arresting Moscow's chief supporters from the Nasser days, including their main ally, Ali Sabry. Sabry, who had been the head of Nasser's Arab Socialist Union and a strong advocate of the Soviet line, was convicted of treason and sentenced to death, later commuted to life in prison.

G. Norman Anderson, the U.S. State Department's Egypt desk officer at the time of the treaty, said he and a colleague, Walter Smith, were assigned to evaluate the pact's significance. "The two of us put together our analysis and we agreed that we should not overreact to this particular friendship treaty," he recalled. "We didn't think it would have much practical effect. We thought it was mostly a propaganda move. However, our analysis was edited as it moved up the line . . . by the time it ended up, this was a tremendously important treaty."[28]

In the view of officials who far outranked Anderson and Smith, it certainly was important. Their response to the treaty showed that Washington did not yet grasp the strategic transformation upon which Sadat had embarked; most of them took the treaty at face value, seeing it as confirmation of their belief that Egypt was firmly in the Soviet camp.

The bombing and artillery duels known as the "War of Attrition" had ended the year before but the region was still a tinderbox, as had been demonstrated by the recent "Black September" conflict between Jordan and Palestinian guerrillas. Now that Sadat had prevailed in his Corrective Revolution and was indisputably in charge of Egypt, Secretary of State William Rogers, looking for pathways to negotiations, assigned two experienced diplomats to sit down with Sadat to assess the man and his policies. The two, Donald Bergus and Michael Sterner, met with Sadat for ninety minutes on July 17, 1971. According to Bergus's report to Rogers, the treaty with the Soviet Union was the first item on the agenda.

Bergus said he and Sterner told Sadat that he should "know that treaty is the subject of major interest in Washington, that it has raised some questions and has delayed [the] process of deciding how we proceed in days ahead. President Sadat interjected at this point that treaty changed nothing—absolutely nothing—it merely provided formal framework for a relationship which already existed and which we knew all about." When the Americans said that the treaty had raised doubts in Washington about Sadat's desire to pursue diplomatic efforts, he was annoyed.

"Obviously making effort to control some irritation, Sadat said he really did not understand need for further assurances on this point," Bergus reported. "Had he not 'given this assurance in very clear terms' to Bergus during a previous conversation? Yes, he had, but 'there were many people in Israel and some in Washington who were saying that Soviet-Egyptian treaty had fundamentally changed things.'"[29]

This dialogue demonstrated the delicate position in which Sadat found himself at that point, two years before he went to war. He recognized that only the United States, not the Soviet Union, could help him achieve an honorable peace with Israel. He was disenchanted with Moscow and wanted to reposition Egypt as a partner of the United States. But he could not just come out and say that because he still needed Soviet assistance in building up Egypt's armed forces and training its officers—even though, as he told Bergus and Sterner, he found that aid grudging and inadequate: The United States was giving the Israelis "everything they need, but we don't get anything like this from the Russians." He would soon have to deliver a major speech on the anniversary of the 1952 revolution, he said, and would have to say something about the prospects for negotiation. Were the Americans serious about this or not?

At that point the honest answer would have been no. The United States was busy elsewhere in the world, most people in Washington still thought of Egypt as a captive of Moscow—a view reinforced by the treaty—and Israel held the diplomatic and military high ground. President Nixon's National Security adviser, Henry Kissinger, had little use for Secretary Rogers, and the fact that he let Rogers handle the Middle East portfolio showed how low a priority the White House assigned to the region. Sadat communicated frequently with Rogers, on the logical assumption that Rogers, as secretary of state, was in charge of U.S. foreign policy. In truth, Rogers lacked access to, and influence with, the president; Kissinger sometimes intercepted his memos. In any case, the Egyptian-Soviet treaty convinced American officials—other than Rogers, who agreed with Anderson and Smith's assessment—that the treaty enhanced Egypt's ties to Moscow and reflected the true state of that relationship.

Bergus, however, had known Sadat for years and picked up on his dissatisfaction with Moscow. "One thing that struck us about Sadat's comments," he said in a follow-up report, "was his barely disguised criticism of Soviets for not giving him adequate arms to face Israel. His beef seemed to be about quality rather than quantity. Implication was that he thought Soviets had better stuff to give but were holding out on him, whereas U.S. was giving Israel its first-line equipment." From the American perspective, however, Sadat had not yet actually done anything to distance himself from Moscow; on the contrary, he had just signed a new friendship treaty. It would take some substantive gesture to compel the United States to reevaluate. That gesture came a year later, propelled by a rapid sequence of events.

Two weeks after Bergus's reports to Washington, Egypt helped Jaafar Nimeiri, president of Sudan, crush a coup attempt by Sudanese communists. Its leaders were executed, including one who had recently won the Lenin Peace Prize. "The Russians," journalist Mohamed

Heikal observed, "were extremely upset over the bloodbath involv-ing their friends," but they were in no position to break publicly with Sadat, any more than he was with them, because Egypt was crucial to their Third World ambitions.[30]

In October Sadat went once again to Moscow, by now embarrassed as well as frustrated because he had proclaimed 1971 "The Year of Decision" in the conflict with Israel but nothing substantive had hap-pened. According to Sadat's account, corroborated by Heikal, he and Brezhnev had long discussions but he obtained none of the advanced weapons he was seeking.[31] Moreover, Brezhnev badgered him about paying, in hard currency, for the limited flow of weapons Moscow had already supplied. This dialogue was repeated in February 1972.

In May 1972, President Nixon and his entire foreign policy team, including Rogers and Kissinger, went to the Soviet Union for a week, meeting with Brezhnev and others in the Kremlin leadership. At the conclusion of their meetings, the two sides issued an extensive joint communiqué that proclaimed a commitment to better relations, arms control, and bilateral cooperation on a range of issues. On Viet-nam, they basically agreed to disagree. As for the Middle East, the communiqué said, "They reaffirm their support for a peaceful settle-ment in the Middle East in accordance with Security Council Res-olution 242. Noting the significance of constructive cooperation of the parties concerned with the Special Representative of the UN Sec-retary General, Ambassador [Gunnar] Jarring, the US and the USSR confirm their desire to contribute to his mission's success and also declare their readiness to play their part in bringing about a peaceful settlement in the Middle East. In the view of the US and the USSR, the achievement of such a settlement would open prospects for the normalization of the Middle East situation and would permit, in particular, consideration of further steps to bring about a military relaxation in that area."[32]

To Sadat, the language of this document, the goal of "military relaxation," came as a "violent shock," he said, because it meant that the Soviet Union would not help him wage the war with Israel that he believed was necessary. He demanded an explanation from Moscow. None was forthcoming for a month. When the Soviet ambassador did finally deliver a response, on July 8, Sadat found it entirely unsatisfactory; it said nothing about weapons.

"I reject this message you've transmitted to me from the Soviet leaders, both in form and content," he told the ambassador. "It is unacceptable." He gave the Soviet Union a week to withdraw its military advisers—all fifteen thousand to seventeen thousand of them.[33] He took this drastic step, he wrote later, partly because of "the Soviet attitude to me" but mostly because he had concluded that "no war could be fought while Soviet experts worked in Egypt."[34] In Washington, officials were astonished that Sadat asked for no specific reward from the United States for this game-changing decision.

Kissinger told Soviet ambassador Anatoly Dobrynin that the United States was "not aware of these events beforehand." At that time, he said, "[w]e had not yet fully understood their significance. Nor did we know the extent of Soviet withdrawal. In any event, I wanted Dobrynin to know that the President had issued the strictest orders that there would be no U.S. initiatives toward Cairo and that we would not try to gain unilateral advantages." Kissinger's memorandum of this conversation gives no indication that he and Dobrynin discussed any of the implications of Sadat's decision.[35]

To Brezhnev the implications were clear and his response was blunt.

"Speculation aroused by your decision has given encouragement to our enemies who are ignorant of the true nature of Arab-Soviet relations," he wrote to Sadat. "We believe that this weakens our friendship and damages relations between us. It does not conform to the true interests of Egypt. We cannot be indifferent to the policy which has been adopted by the Egyptian government, which is objectively and subjectively contrary to the interests of our two peoples. It is a policy resulting from the intrigues of rightist elements directly or indirectly allied with imperialism to halt Egypt's march along the progressive road and turn it back."[36]

Sadat thought it over for a few weeks. Then, on August 30, he wrote a long letter to his "dear friend" Brezhnev reviewing the entire state of the relationship between Egypt and the Soviet Union, in the interest, he said, of maintaining friendship. The message conveyed by the ambassador, the one he had rejected on the spot, was "disappointing," he wrote to the Soviet leader, because it "confirmed to me that such a method as you adopted in dealing with us—of ignoring our position and the battle we have ahead—followed from a certain mentality from which we have been suffering year after year since the aggression [of 1967], for five years in fact. I have repeatedly tried, over one and a half years, to draw attention to it, to no avail. That is why I have rejected this message, and rejected this method; and now we have to pause—as friends—in order to define our positions frankly."

As a result of the U.S.-USSR communiqué, Sadat told the Soviet leader, "the crisis is 'frozen,' and no means of breaking the deadlock are available. The American claim that the United States, and the United States alone, is capable of finding a solution has been increasingly vindicated. . . . Your message of July 8 completely ignores the measures we had agreed upon and which we believe to be absolutely necessary insofar as they would enable to us to resort to military action, if need be, after the U.S. election." (It was a presidential election year in the United States.) The Soviet Union, Sadat complained, was holding back on weapons while the United States was pouring armaments into Israel. "In view of all these considerations, my decision to terminate the mission of the advisers has been designed to give us a pause—to mark the inevitable end of a certain era and the beginning of another, based on fresh concepts, recalculations, and redefinition of our stands."

Sadat reviewed what he said were examples of weapons Moscow had withheld, or even denied having when the Egyptians knew full well that they did. "Let me tell you frankly, my friend, that I feel our future relations to be seriously threatened," Sadat wrote. He unloaded an extensive list of complaints: The Soviet Union was holding back on weapons while the United States continued to build up Israel. The expelled advisers had taken some military equipment with them, saying the Egyptians were incapable of using it on their own. The Russians had denied some specific weapons requests, such as long-range submarine detection equipment and long-range artillery, saying they did not have such items, when Egypt knew they did. The Kremlin had announced that certain sophisticated weapons had been delivered to Egypt when that was not true.

"You look on us as though we were a backward country, while our officers have had education in your academies," Sadat wrote. "We furthermore follow up developments throughout the world—East and West—which are not any longer secret. Armament is dealt with in books which are circulated throughout the world. When the Soviet advisers were asked about a given item, they either fell silent or replied that the Soviet Union didn't have it while we and everybody else knew that the Soviet Union has everything."

Because of this duplicity, Sadat added, "I feel our future relations to be seriously threatened. And the most dangerous thing about it is the sense of bitterness our people will be left with, in regard to the Soviet Union."

He gave the Kremlin two months, until the end of October 1972, to think it over, to decide once and for all whether to help the Egyptians "liberate our land," and offered to send his prime minister, Aziz Sidki, to Moscow at that time to review the relationship. He expressed hope that Brezhnev would "intervene personally" to rectify the situation and closed with a statement of good feelings, but it was indeed "the end of a certain era."[37]

At a retrospective conference held in Washington twenty-five years later, after the Soviet Union itself had disintegrated, Vadim Kirpitchenko, who was the chief KGB officer in Egypt at the time of the Soviet advisers' expulsion, said Sadat knew that he could not confront Israel or achieve peace solely or even mostly on the basis of alliance with Moscow—he needed the Americans and actually had told Nixon that he would reorient Egyptian policy and get rid of the Soviet military units if the United States helped Egypt regain the Sinai. Nixon responded with interest, according to Kirpitchenko, but said that first the Soviets would have to go. Sadat understood, and began planning the expulsion. As early as 1971, Sadat's first year in office, Kirpitchenko said, the Egyptian government undertook a disinformation campaign aimed at discrediting the Soviets and preparing public opinion for their ouster; the Egyptians even accused Soviet officials of smuggling gold out of the country and had them searched in public when they were flying home. But at the same time, "Sadat continued persistently to demand new arms supplies from the Soviet Union, and these demands did not cease up to the end of hostilities in October 1973," Kirpitchenko said.[38]

Nevertheless, news of the expulsion order came as a surprise to Washington as well as to Moscow, because Sadat was handing the United States what looked like an enormous victory in their Cold War rivalry and was not asking for anything in return, at least not directly. This was a critical pivot point in modern Middle East history, but its full implications did not become clear to Washington until after the October War the following year.

Roger Merrick, watching these developments in the State Department's Bureau of Intelligence, said of the expulsion order, "With this action it immediately became clear that we had to take Sadat more seriously. He had demonstrated his courage and was prepared to take major risks." He noted, correctly, that "Sadat must have been disappointed that it produced no significant changes in U.S. policies."[39] The American view was that Sadat's expulsion of the Soviets, who had been training and equipping Egypt's armed forces and operating its air defenses, did not by itself require Washington to undertake a major new diplomatic initiative in the Middle East because war was even less likely than before. Sadat might be realigning Egypt's position in international relations, but the only thing that had changed on the ground was that Egypt was without its most powerful military partner.

David Hirst and Irene Beeson, British journalists who loathed Sadat and wrote a contemptuous biography of him, reported that most people in Egypt celebrated Sadat's expulsion of the Russians because their country had stood up to a superpower. But they noted that "[t]he elation at home was short-lived. Sadat had 'liberated' Egypt from the Russians, but he still had to liberate it from the Israelis." To do that he needed to maintain the appearance of comity with Moscow.[40]

A few weeks after the expulsion, Dobrynin told Kissinger that

"Sadat had miscalculated. He thought the request to leave would produce negotiations. Instead the Soviet Union had pulled everybody out." When Sadat grasped the implications for Egypt's military preparedness, Dobrynin suggested, "it might turn out that the chapter was not yet closed."[41] He was right, in the sense that Sadat still wanted the Soviet Union to provide advanced weapons and could not close the door entirely. He would not do that until after the October War, which was still more than a year in the future. In the meantime he offered palliative gestures and statements to keep Moscow from cutting him off.

Moscow in fact had good reasons to withhold some of the most advanced weapons Egypt wanted. Kremlin leaders believed that the Egyptians were incompetent fighters and that if they suffered another defeat while deploying the best Moscow had to offer, it would be another costly embarrassment and would devalue Soviet military support in the estimation of national leaders elsewhere. The Kremlin did not want to provoke a confrontation with the United States because of its commitment to détente. And the Soviets knew that Egypt could not afford to pay for such items. Nevertheless, some Soviet leaders feared that Egypt would break away completely, and that other Arab countries would follow, if they were not more forthcoming. Moreover, a spectacular worldwide increase in crude oil prices, which was then just beginning, would enrich some of Egypt's Arab friends, who might be willing to put up some cash to cover the costs of rearming Egypt from other sources if Moscow held out.

According to Heikal, who was privy to all these exchanges between Cairo and Moscow, the Kremlin faction that wanted to do more prevailed, "and so at last Egypt began to receive some of the equipment for which Sadat had been so earnestly pleading and for which he had been waiting so long." The weaponry included "vast quantities" of antiaircraft missiles, tanks, and bridging equipment. The Soviets, Heikal surmised, "realized that, having lost the political battle, they might be able to recoup their losses in the military field."[42]

As he had promised, Sadat sent Prime Minister Sidki to Moscow that autumn. While there he attended a reception at which Premier

Alexei Kosygin delivered a speech that showed how little the Soviet leaders understood, or could acknowledge that they understood, the ideological gap that had developed between Cairo and Moscow. In true Kremlin fashion, rather than addressing the issues forthrightly, Kosygin offered party-line bromides:

> The Soviet Union has one foreign policy and one political line in Middle Eastern affairs. This line lends all kinds of support for the Arab peoples and progressive regimes in the Arab countries in their struggle against Israeli aggression . . . international solidarity with the peoples and governments waging a struggle against imperialism is one of the guiding principles of the Leninist foreign policy of the Soviet Union . . . the Communist Party of the Soviet Union, the Soviet government, and all the peoples of our country stand firmly on the side of Egypt, Syria, Iraq, Algeria and other Arab states in their anti-imperialist struggle.[43]

The Egyptians had heard it all many times. What they wanted was advanced weapons. Now that these had begun to flow—even though the Soviet Union did not want the Arabs to actually go to war—an overt breach between Cairo and Moscow was averted.

Sadat notified the Kremlin that a maritime agreement allowing the Soviet fleet to use Egyptian ports, which was due to expire in March 1973, would be extended for five years. "My object," he wrote, "was to show the Russians that in spite of my decision to expel the Soviet military experts I did not wish to break with them altogether." When Field Marshal Ahmed Ismail Ali went to Moscow in February 1973, he brought back what Sadat called "the biggest arms deal ever to be concluded (either with Nasser or myself)."[44] And this time deliveries were prompt. Sadat said Egypt would have gone to war anyway, but now he had the arsenal to confront Israel on more nearly equal terms. The bilateral relationship between Egypt and the Soviet Union was shaky, but temporarily intact. During the October War itself, Moscow shipped vast quantities of arms to Egypt and its ally, Syria, and intervened diplomatically to enforce a cease-fire that Egypt desperately needed. The war obliged Cairo and Moscow to paper over their differences; Egypt needed Soviet weapons, and the Soviet Union still hoped to salvage a critical relationship. But that was the last hurrah. After the war, As Mohamed Heikal wrote, "nothing would be the same again as far as [Soviet] relations with the Arab world were concerned."[45]

The Ideology Gap

With the signing of friendship treaties with Egypt in 1971 and Iraq in 1972, the Soviet Union appeared to be in an unassailable position in the region. Egypt, Syria, Iraq, and Algeria were one-party states with nationalized economies and Soviet-trained armed forces. Muammar Qaddafi, the brash young upstart who had overthrown the Libyan monarchy in 1969, was increasingly following the same line. They and the Soviets espoused similar policies in international forums and supported each other at the United Nations, often in opposition to the United States. Soviet penetration of national institutions in Arab countries ran deep. But beneath this surface harmony, the Soviets were finding the Arabs to be difficult partners. Aside from South Yemen, which was poor and remote, the Arabs rejected communism and Marxist-Leninist ideology and resisted Soviet political tutelage. The countries other than Egypt where Moscow achieved the greatest influence through military and economic assistance, especially Syria, Iraq, and later Libya, refrained from breaking with Moscow entirely because they valued the Soviet Union as a global counterweight to the imperialists and because they had nowhere else to go. Unlike Sadat, their leaders were not seeking to align themselves with the United States.

Among the Egyptian officers trained in the Soviet Union was Hosni Mubarak, Sadat's vice president and later his successor. He brought back military skill, but not ideology. "As happened with many of the Egyptian officers who had gone to the Soviet Union, it did not result in his becoming pro-Soviet," said H. Freeman Matthews Jr., second-ranking diplomat in the American embassy in the late 1970s. "On the contrary, they came back unhappy with the Soviets because of the treatment they received there. I gather the Soviets tended to look down on them and treat them as a kind of subhuman species."[46]

"The Soviet Union's hopes that it could gradually 'co-opt' the Arab nationalist revolutionaries and sign them up to socialist ideals—as Soviet ideologues interpreted them—turned out to be impracticable, for many reasons, both objective and subjective," observed Yevgeny Primakov. "There was no 'socialist phase' in the postcolonial development of Arab nations. The revolutionary romanticism of the postcolonial era gradually disappeared too. What was left was Arab nationalism, which in effect abandoned revolutionary social reform."[47]

Vasili Mitrokhin, a senior KGB official who defected to the West and brought his files with him, said that despite all the attention and aid Moscow lavished on Egypt, the main object of its regional ambitions, the relationship was never destined to move beyond the exchanges of goods and equipment. "In the Middle East, unlike Latin America, there was no realistic prospect of the emergence of a major Marxist-Leninist regime which would act as a role model for the Arab world and spread revolution throughout the region," he recalled.[48]

The Soviets and their Arab partners sometimes saw the same events in different ways, leading to conflicting policies. Iraq, for example, complained that the Soviet Union was strengthening Israel by allowing Jews to emigrate there, even though Moscow had imposed severe limits on such migration.[49] The Kremlin retorted that Iraq had supplied much more Israeli manpower by forcing its Jews to go there after Israel was created in 1948. The Iraqis complained that the Soviet Union sold oil to European countries for higher prices than it paid Iraq for oil extracted from the Rumaila field, which its technicians helped Iraq to develop.[50] The Syrian government of Hafez Assad intervened in the Lebanese civil war despite a direct public appeal from the Soviet leadership to stay out of it. Both Syria and Iraq, governed by rival wings of the Arab Baath Socialist Party, alternated between accommodating their indigenous communist parties, as Moscow wished, and suppressing them. Iraq's communists were in the end purged from the army and politics in waves of mass executions. In Syria, as Patrick Seale noted, the appearances of comity were deceiving: "The evidence now suggests that, after a brief honeymoon period, the relationship . . . was marked less by complicity, cooperation, and strategic dependence than by false expectation, contradictory ambitions, mutual suspicion, and plain muddle. Their dialogue it seems was largely a dialogue of the deaf. At the end of the day, they were both disappointed."[51]

The gaps between Moscow and its Arab clients were not only political, they were cultural. The gregarious Arabs found Russians to be clannish and arrogant, as well as parsimonious; Soviet officers and diplomats rarely mingled socially with Arab citizens. Arabs who went to the Soviet Union for education or military training were kept isolated from the Soviet people. According to Mohamed Heikal, of the two hundred thousand Arabs who went to the Soviet Union in the 1950s and 1960s, fewer than one hundred married Russian women, while of the fifteen thousand Arabs sent to the United States in the same period, seven thousand, almost half, married Americans. Moreover, the Soviets were culturally tone deaf. The movies they sent were didactic and boring. The libraries they set up in Arab capitals featured Marx and Engels but not Tolstoy or Pushkin. Moscow Radio had Arabic-language broadcasts but few Arabs were interested in them; they preferred Radio Monte Carlo, which broadcast Western popular music, and the BBC's Arabic service, which delivered news untainted by propaganda.[52]

Reassessment in Washington

After the October War, Egypt's strategic position was entirely different from what it had been before. Sadat still wanted Soviet arms, but he no longer needed them for any imminent battle. President Nixon and Henry Kissinger had committed themselves to the pursuit of a comprehensive regional peace agreement, which as Sadat well knew only the Americans could deliver. In theory, the Soviet Union was still essential to regional diplomacy because it was nominal cosponsor, with the United States, of the Geneva Conference that was to be the principal forum for negotiations. In reality, Sadat had little enthusiasm for the Geneva process because it excluded the Palestine Liberation Organization; in October 1974, the Arabs collectively declared the PLO to be the "sole legitimate representative" of the Palestinian people, but Israel refused to negotiate with the PLO in any forum on the grounds that it was a terrorist group. In effect, the war had freed Sadat to reposition Egypt as a partner of the United States. The entire Cold War balance in the Middle East was about to be overturned.

Handed this potential strategic bonanza, the United States was at first slow to respond. Preservation of détente remained an important objective, and the Nixon administration had promised the Soviet Union it would not seek gains in the region at Moscow's expense. In those days the United States and the Soviet Union had a long, complicated agenda that included arms control negotiations, tensions over Berlin, the precarious peace in Vietnam, and development of the Conference on Security and Cooperation in Europe; the Arab-Israeli issue was important, but not controlling.

In addition, Moscow's influence with Assad was essential to regional peace negotiations. Kissinger believed that the Soviet strategy was "to maneuver us into a position where we become the lawyers of Israel and they become the defenders of the Arab point of view." Doing that "forces Sadat back into the radical camp, and therefore interrupts the rapprochement between Sadat and us, which in turn is one of the chief bases of our Middle East policy, and that in turn brings enormous pressures on [King] Faisal [of Saudi Arabia]," the leader of the oil embargo that Arab producers had imposed during the October War.

The only point of unanimity among the Israelis and Arabs, Kissinger said, "is that they don't want the Soviets [to be] part of the negotiation. . . . On the other hand, if we don't find some formula by which the Soviets can at a minimum save face, they have it in their power to make it very tough for any Arab government to settle."[53]

Navigating this diplomatic minefield required caution and patience. Sadat was not an advocate of caution and he did not believe he had time for patience. Having thrown in his lot with the Americans, he expected Washington to deliver a peace agreement that would end Israel's occupation of Arab lands, and he was disappointed when nothing much happened in that arena in 1974, the year after the war. The front lines stabilized after Syria finally signed a military disengagement agreement in June of that year and the oil embargo ended, but the big-picture deal Sadat envisioned remained elusive.

The Geneva peace conference, which was nominally the forum in which such an agreement would be negotiated—under the joint sponsorship of the United Nations, the United States, and the Soviet Union—met for one day in December 1973 and recessed after a few speeches, never to reassemble. President Nixon, who had committed himself to the pursuit of a comprehensive peace agreement, reopened U.S. diplomatic relations with Egypt and went to Egypt and Saudi Arabia in the late spring of 1974, but then was forced by the Watergate scandal to resign. His successor, Gerald Ford, was honest and competent, but had neither the personal inclination nor the political stature to undertake a quest for Middle East peace. Treasury Secretary William E. Simon went to Cairo, but no U.S. aid package was immediately forthcoming. No further Israeli troop withdrawals beyond the cease-fire lines occurred. According to U.S. ambassador Hermann Eilts, the United States, by its inability to make progress on that front, nearly forfeited the opportunity Sadat had presented.

Eilts, who knew Sadat better than any other American, recalled that the Soviets sensed in him a disillusionment with Washington as the indecisive year dragged on. In October they "invited the Egyptian ministers of defense and foreign affairs to Moscow. The Soviets were by then furious, of course, about having been excluded from [the] Sinai I and Golan I [postwar troop disengagement agreements]. They now dangled all kinds of military assistance and economic assistance before the Egyptians. The Egyptian ministers came back with their mouths drooling, but the Russians said, 'not until and unless Brezhnev comes to Cairo in January '75, a few months later, and you Egyptians agree that no further peace talks will take place other than in the Geneva Conference forum.' In other words, scuttle the American unilateral effort and go back to the multinational Geneva conference." According to Eilts, Foreign Minister Ismail Fahmy and the Egyptian military urged Sadat to accept these terms. In addition, he said, public sentiment was against trusting the Americans and no aid had been delivered. The Americans were offering only a new diplomatic shuttle, similar to what Kissinger had undertaken to secure disengagement agreements after the war, and even that they were proposing only because of concerns about a new Soviet role. Eilts said that "the debate lasted about a week as to what the Egyptians would do, and it finally took a letter from President Ford to Sadat saying, 'I'm asking you to continue our unilateral effort, to turn the Soviets down.'" Sadat overruled his advisers and did so, "with grave reservations," Eilts said.[54]

On November 1 Fahmy was in Washington, where he had breakfast with Ford and Kissinger, whom Nixon had appointed secretary of state to succeed Rogers and whom Ford kept on in that post. The official memorandum of their conversation indicates that Ford listened but said nothing as this colloquy occurred:

FAHMI: We need some concrete progress on the Sinai front. This is a must. If Kissinger can do it in not more than two months, that is good. It is necessary. We are working with the extremists, to change the image of the United States. It can be done, but it is tricky and could go either way now.

KISSINGER: Can you make a Sinai move alone?

FAHMI: Sure. Not to a peace. We must proceed slowly. We must get some equipment from the Soviet Union, but I can make it sweeping or just enough to get by.

KISSINGER: You must do what you want, but a sweeping deal would cause an outcry that you are a Soviet stooge. The next move will be tough, because in the Sinai the next move will interrupt a decade of infrastructure. I told the President when he came in that there would be an attack on me and an attempt to split me and the President. But we can't move before November 5 [election day]. You didn't notice, but the President got additional aid to Israel taken out of the Continuing Resolution [spending bill in Congress]—for the first time ever. The next step in the Sinai is much more important than the first, because now there is no logical stopping place.

FAHMI: No one can accuse us of being a Soviet satellite. We get nothing from the Soviet Union now and we need something. But if we get nothing from the Soviet Union and nothing from you, and are asked to make more concessions, my army will think I am foolish. We have to get some equipment, but the issue is whether it will be a lot or a little. If we can get something from you early next year, we can get by with only a little [from the Soviet Union]. The oil people are the biggest political amateurs—nice to us internally but with loudspeakers outside.

KISSINGER [TO FORD]: The reason I arranged this appointment is because I agree with Fahmi's appraisal. I think Sadat is very exposed. Last November he made a big gamble. There is no doubt he is anti-Soviet. But the radicals are using his moves against him, and if he gets no progress for his efforts and no help from us, he is in trouble.

The Soviet Union, Fahmy said, "is pushing for a total solution in order to freeze the situation and make progress impossible. If there is no progress in the next six months we are in bad trouble," because Arab radicals would attack Sadat as a renegade who had turned his back on their longtime patrons in Moscow and delivered Egypt to the West without getting anything substantive in return.[55]

Kissinger was correct in his assessment of the difficulty of negotiating a comprehensive peace. What he did not mention was that Sadat himself had exacerbated the difficulty a few days earlier, at an Arab League summit meeting in Rabat, Morocco. Egypt joined all the other participants in declaring that the Palestinian people had a right to govern themselves and that the Palestine Liberation Organization would be their "sole legitimate representative" in establishing and running a Palestinian government. Given that Israel refused to negotiate with the PLO, this made a comprehensive pact even less likely than before. In addition, it forced King Hussein of Jordan—with whom Israel was willing to negotiate, and who had ruled the West Bank before 1967—to relinquish his claim to represent the Palestinians there. Thus the diplomatic stalemate deepened; Nixon and Brezhnev discussed it at a summit meeting in Moscow a few weeks before Nixon's resignation, but basically restated their positions about representation at Geneva, neither persuading the other.

Hirst and Beeson, the British biographers who believed that Sadat was duplicitous in everything he did, wrote that he signed on to the PLO resolution at the Arab summit because it advanced his secret agenda, which was to achieve a separate peace with Israel.[56] The more likely reason is that he had little choice—refusing to go along would have reinforced the suspicion among the Arabs and his own people that a separate peace was indeed his objective. That suspicion was reinforced in September 1975, when Egypt and Israel signed a second disengagement agreement known as Sinai II.

That pact is little remembered now, but at the time it was a landmark of Middle Eastern diplomacy, the first substantive agreement between Israel and an Arab state. It resulted from, and validated, the U.S. position that Geneva as envisioned by the Soviets was a sterile formula and therefore it was more productive to pursue incremental progress. Sadat had expressed interest in such an arrangement when he met President Ford in early June, presenting the opportunity for Kissinger to broker its terms.[57]

The Sinai II document stated, "The parties hereby undertake not to resort to the threat or use of force or military blockade against each other." Egypt agreed to open the Suez Canal to nonmilitary cargoes bound for Israel. Egypt and Israel agreed to establish within five days a "military working group" to settle such details as access to oil fields in the Sinai. The pact set limits on the number of troops and types of weapons each could maintain in the Sinai, created a buffer zone between them, and accepted deployment of a United Nations force to supervise compliance. Israel and Egypt agreed that "[t]he conflict between them and in the Middle East shall not be resolved by military force but by peaceful means."[58]

Thus Sadat pledged, in effect, that Egypt would not support other Arabs who might attack Israel.[59] Not surprisingly, the agreement set off cries of protest and criticism of Sadat throughout the region. Sinai II also angered the leaders of the Soviet Union, who saw it, correctly, as Egyptian rejection of their position that any agreement had to be comprehensive and as acceptance by Sadat of American preeminence in regional diplomacy. They retaliated by further reducing their arms sales to Egypt, demanding repayment of loans for weapons already delivered, and curtailing Egypt's access to repair service and spare parts.

For Sadat, that was the end of the line—the relationship with the Soviet Union was no longer beneficial to Egypt. It was time to end it. "The Soviets know that their days are numbered in Egypt," Sadat told Ford at a meeting in June 1975. He complained that the Soviets had "given me no military replacements since the October 1974 cease-fire" and "are trying to undermine me and the entire world."[60]

On March 14, 1976, Sadat delivered an interminable speech to the People's Assembly. The speech was broadcast on Cairo Radio but few were listening at the end because it was long past bedtime. Those who stayed with it heard Sadat lay out a detailed list of grievances with Moscow. Knowing full well that Egypt was broke, "[t]he Soviets not only refuse to re-schedule the [military] debts, they are claiming interest on the military debts when, so far, they have not yet settled their debts to America for World War II," he said. "After a year or a year and a half, all the arms I possess in Egypt might be used for scrap iron, since they refuse to supply spare parts. They refuse to overhaul the planes and they refuse everything else."

Turned down by Moscow, Sadat said, he asked India for help in servicing Egypt's combat jets and supplying spare parts; India had been manufacturing MIG-21s and parts for a decade under license from the Soviets. "Their reply," he said, "was that they would seek the permission of the Soviet Union. This took four months. Ten days ago, India replied and said that they regretted but the Soviet Union had said, No. Do not supply spare parts to Egypt and do not overhaul their MIGs."

With the remaining audience now fully alert and the English translator on the radio broadcast, Selim Rizkallah, struggling to keep up, Sadat plunged ahead. "It is obvious that this is an operation of blockade, an economic and military pressure," he said. "Economic pressure because of my economic predicament; military pressure so that after a year or a year and a half, all my arms would become scrap iron, unless I kneel before them. But I kneel only to God the Almighty. In the letters exchanged between us, they always justify their actions by referring to the [1971 friendship] treaty. If this is the Soviet Union's way of respecting the treaty and its provisions, if in the view of its leaders the Soviet Union is free to implement or not to implement its provisions at will, because they have the upper hand, then the treaty becomes mere paper."

To loud cheers, he announced abrogation of the treaty.[61] Moscow's obstinacy on weapons and loans had given Sadat a good reason to do what he had planned to do anyway for more than two years. He had told Kissinger in January 1974 that he would scuttle the treaty, and now it was done.[62] It was the end of an era, in Middle East history and in the Cold War. Two decades after Nasser turned to Moscow for the Aswan Dam help that Dulles had pulled back, Egyptian relations with the superpowers had come full circle.

Rubbing it in, Sadat let it be known soon afterward that China, then the Soviet Union's great communist rival, had supplied the aircraft replacement engines and other spare parts Moscow had barred India from sending. Sadat sent Vice President Mubarak to China on a goodwill visit that received lavish laudatory coverage in the compliant Cairo newspapers, and Egyptian television filled its news broadcasts for days with images of Mubarak getting a warm reception: Mubarak at the Great Wall with Chairman Mao Zedong, Mubarak with students at Peking University, Mubarak glad-handing Chinese crowds. In Moscow, the government newspaper *Izvestia* complained that this new Egyptian-Chinese friendship was directed at Moscow and "against the Interests" of the Soviet people.[63]

An Irreversible Breach

Neither Sadat nor the Soviet leaders acknowledged right away that the breach between them was irreversible; perhaps they did not even recognize it immediately. Throughout the rest of 1976 and up to the time Sadat went to Jerusalem on his quest for peace, in November 1977, both sides made intermittent, half-hearted attempts to patch things up. They signed a new bilateral trade agreement. "It is not in Egypt's interest to have bad relations with the Soviet Union," Mubarak said publicly.[64] But the trajectory had been set and it led only downward.

When Moscow criticized the taboo-breaking Jerusalem venture and encouraged other Arabs to unite in opposition to Sadat's initiative, Sadat responded by ordering the Soviet Union and four of its Warsaw Pact allies to close all their consular and cultural offices outside Cairo. Egypt and the Soviet Union maintained formal diplomatic relations, but by then it was true, as Sadat often said, that "the United States holds 99 percent of the cards in the Middle East."

"Probably no other Third World leader inspired as much loathing in Moscow as Sadat," the Soviet defector Mitrokhin said. "Almost a decade after Sadat's death, [Foreign Minister Andrei] Gromyko could still barely conceal his loathing of him. . . . Underlying Gromyko's cry of rage was his consciousness that the Sadat era had witnessed the complete failure of Soviet policy in Egypt and the loss of the largest military, economic, and political investment Moscow had made in any Third World country."[65]

Well into Jimmy Carter's presidency, the United States and its allies still took Soviet influence and even domination in many Arab countries as a fact of life and used the fear of its further spread as a political tool. Washington's suspicions about Moscow seemed reasonable because even Sadat would still occasionally play the Soviet card. PLO chairman Yasser Arafat told an American academic visiting Beirut in September 1977 that "if there is no real progress toward a peace by a certain date, [Sadat] will pick up the phone and ask me to go to the Russians and tell them he is ready to make a deal." Arafat declared that "there is not an Arab leader who does not envy me my good relations with the Russians—not one of them. They are all glad I have these good relations."[66]

Arafat may have believed what he said, but it did not apply to Sadat. By mid-1977, a few months before Sadat went to Jerusalem, the Central Intelligence Agency, in a paper on the "Soviet Role in the Middle East," said, "The Soviets' economic, military, and political position with the principal Arab states has eroded over the past five years, and shows no sign of improvement. The low state of relations between the USSR and Egypt stands out as an important failure of Soviet foreign policy under General Secretary Brezhnev. Moscow's relations with the radical Arab states—notably Iraq and Libya—have expanded significantly in recent years. This improvement has been based primarily on increasing sales of Soviet arms, and has not resulted in a commensurate increase in Soviet political influence among the Arab radicals."

The CIA analysts said that "four principal factors" accounted for a decline in Soviet influence among the Arabs since the October war: "Egyptian President Sadat's estrangement from the Soviets; the general Arab conviction that only the United States can elicit the Israeli concessions necessary for a peace agreement; Saudi Arabia's support and subsidy of anti-Soviet policies in the area; [and] the Arabs' desire to import Western rather than Soviet technology and equipment." The Soviet Union's economic weakness, the CIA said, rendered it unable "to provide financial assistance on the scale required by the Arab confrontation states," which by then had less need of help from Moscow because they were receiving substantial aid from oil producers that were running huge budget surpluses as prices soared.[67]

In Syria, which had intervened in Lebanon's civil war over Soviet objections, the CIA reported that President Assad "wants to reduce his country's overall dependence on the Soviets and thereby weaken Soviet political leverage in situations—such as occurred in Lebanon—where interests conflict." The analysts said that "Syria is not about to sever its ties with the USSR," but had substantially reduced the Soviet military presence, reflecting "the Syrian military's general dislike and distrust of the Soviets and its dissatisfaction with the quality of Soviet equipment and training. A post-mortem by the Syrians on their performance during the 1973 war showed serious deficiencies in the performance of officers trained by the Soviets, compared with those trained in the West."[68]

The discontent of the Syrians was just one example. The CIA's overall assessment that Soviet political influence among the Arabs was eroding despite its weapons sales was borne out by events in other countries. Somalia, a member of the Arab League, transferred its alliance from Moscow to Washington after the Soviet Union began to support procommunist rebels who had seized power in Ethiopia, Somalia's neighbor and archrival. South Yemen, the only fully communist Arab state, signed a twenty-year friendship and cooperation treaty with the Soviet Union in 1979, but a decade later South Yemen ceased to exist as an independent country: after years of internal power struggles and a drastic reduction in Soviet economic aid, South Yemen merged with the rival north to form a unified, noncommunist Republic of Yemen. Iraq distanced itself from the Soviet Union by stridently opposing any peace agreement between Israel and the Palestinians, an objective that Moscow endorsed, and by supporting a secessionist movement in Eritrea, then part of Moscow's new friend, Ethiopia.

Iraq was going its own way, which was not necessarily Moscow's way. Even before the October War, the French government, which was on good terms with Baghdad, was "convinced that there is growing desire within the Iraqi regime for improved relations with West and [that] Iraq, rather like Algeria, seeks to maintain [a] degree of distance from both major blocs and to pursue [a] policy of greater nonalignment," an American diplomat in Paris reported.[69]

A few months later, the Soviets sent First Secretary Boris Ponomarev of the Central Committee to Iraq for what the senior U.S. diplomat in Baghdad described as a "long overdue effort to mollify GOI [government of Iraq] and lessen impact of policy differences that have developed since October war. Although del[egation] received red carpet treatment and press again began speaking of 'strategic alliance,' differences on Mideast settlement have become too obvious even for Iraq's controlled press to ignore."[70]

Sure enough, over the next few years Iraq asserted its independence of Soviet influence by purchasing large quantities helicopters, fighter aircraft, and antitank missiles from France. Because Iraq was flush with oil money and a good customer for weapons, and because the Soviet Union produced few other products suitable for export, those purchases of French weapons were a nasty blow to the Soviet economy. The strains in the Moscow-Baghdad relationship burst into public view in 1978, when the Baathist government unleashed what Yevgeny Primakov called "a virulent anti-communist campaign." By Primakov's account, "almost every member of the Iraqi Communist

Party in the People's Patriotic Front was arrested, and thirty-one communists accused of setting up party cells in the army were executed."[71]

Those events prompted the U.S. Air Force to commission a study of Soviet-Iraq relations by the RAND Corporation, a foreign policy and military strategy think tank. The study, prepared by a young political scientist named Francis Fukuyama, concluded that "Baghdad's dependence on the Soviet Union has been more apparent than real." Their bilateral cooperation was genuine only in the period of the October War and the disengagement agreements that followed, Fukuyama concluded, and "since 1975, Iraq has again moved away from Moscow because the previous factors of dependence were nearly all removed."[72]

The Soviet Union had been pouring weapons into Iraq while Baghdad was fighting to suppress a secessionist rebellion by Kurds in the north. That rebellion ended in 1975 when Iraq cut a deal with the Shah of Iran, who was strongly anti-Soviet, to halt support for it in exchange for Iraqi border concessions. "I do not approve of the brutal way in which Iran and Iraq disposed of the fate of the Kurds," Kissinger told President Ford, "but it created a situation whereby the Iraqis no longer had such need for the Soviets."[73] The Kremlin could see that as well. So distressed were the Soviets about Iraqi policies, Fukuyama's study said, that Moscow actually imposed an arms embargo after the collapse of the Kurdish rebellion, but "Baghdad was able to resist Soviet pressure by using its oil income to diversify its sources of arms purchases, primarily from France."[74]

If anyone in the Kremlin appreciated the irony of Soviet aid to Iraq in suppressing the Kurdish rebellion, which was exactly the kind of liberation movement the Soviet Union always claimed to support, it was not apparent. In fact, all during the second half of the 1970s, when the Soviets had been thrown out of Egypt and their position was eroding all across the Arab world, Moscow continued to portray itself as the only steadfast friend of oppressed peoples in their struggle against imperialism and Zionism. The Arabs could see that the real Soviet policy was opportunism, as demonstrated in the Kurdish rebellion, in Moscow's embrace of the Mengistu regime in Ethiopia at the expense of

Somalia, and in Moscow's decision to sell weapons to Kuwait, a rich and conservative monarchy, because it needed the cash. Soviet political support remained useful, especially on the question of Palestine, but its influence on individual Arab states continued to erode.

In March 1978, after Sadat had gone to Jerusalem and opened peace negotiations with Israel, a Palestine Liberation Organization delegation headed by Yasser Arafat went to Moscow for extensive conversations with Brezhnev and other senior Kremlin officials. They told Arafat what he wanted to hear. "It was noted," the official Kremlin summary of the meetings said, "that the goal of the policies pursued by the USA and Israel in the Middle East, which have now been joined by Egyptian president Sadat, is to destroy the Front of Resistance against Israeli aggression, while at the same time reinforcing Israeli occupation and leading other Arab countries to follow Egypt on the path of capitulation. That is the very reason why all the constructive gains made earlier in preparation for the Geneva conference have now been erased. The organizers of separate negotiations are sabotaging the collective efforts to resolve this conflict, especially when the latter involve the Soviet Union. They are attempting to dictate the conditions for capitulation to every Arab country individually, while the PLO is being completely shut out of the process." The Soviet Union, Arafat was told, would adhere to its "steadfast line," demanding full Israeli withdrawal from all lands seized in 1967.[75]

It was true that the PLO had been excluded from any negotiations, and the Kremlin leaders may well have believed a lot of their own rhetoric. Whether they believed it, or merely said they believed it to keep their Arab allies on the reservation, it served their purposes well. The Arabs may have been hostile to communism, disillusioned about Soviet economic aid, and resentful of Kremlin arrogance, but they needed the Soviets if they were to have any hope of preventing Egypt's "capitulation" to Israel. Thus Sadat, the man who had sabotaged the Soviets' aspirations for regional dominance by shutting them out of the most important country, inadvertently kept those flickering aspirations alive well into the 1980s by seeking peace with Israel.

And Moscow kept trying to reinforce what little of its influence remained, tightening relations with Libya and Syria and supporting Iraq after Saddam Hussein's foolhardy invasion of Iran in 1980. Nonetheless, as a lengthy CIA assessment of the late 1980s put it, "the fact that the USSR's only Arab clients besides Syria are Libya and South Yemen speaks volumes about the decline of Moscow's influence in the Middle East since the early 1970s."[76] That was largely the work of Anwar Sadat.

After the Soviet Union itself passed into history in 1991, the Russia that remained continued to decline in Arab esteem, partly because of its perceived weakening as a world power and partly because of its war against Muslim separatists in Chechnya, according to Shibley Telhami of the University of Maryland (where his title is Anwar Sadat Professor.) Telhami has made a career of extensive public opinion surveys across the Arab world, from Morocco to the United Arab Emirates. Each year he asks respondents, "In a world where there is only one power, which of the following countries would you prefer to be that superpower?" The options in recent surveys were Britain, the United States, Pakistan, France, Russia, Germany, and China. In 2011 the leader was China, at 23 percent, followed by Germany, at 15. Russia was the choice of 12 percent; only 7 percent picked the United States. Separately, Telhami's researchers asked respondents to "name the two countries that you think pose the biggest threat to you." They chose Israel, at 70 percent, and the United States, at 63.

The Arabs did not follow Sadat when he made peace with Israel. It seems they also did not follow him when he embraced Israel's biggest supporter, the United States. They had no love for the Soviet Union, but that did not mean they wanted to swap the influence of one superpower for another. "The biggest single factor in these answers," Telhami wrote, "is the long-standing concern about an unchecked U.S. role in the region."[77]

Treaties of friendship between Arab countries and an ambitious Soviet Union that counterbalanced American power have faded into memory, artifacts from a distant past; the superpower stirring resentment by throwing its weight around in the Arab world today is the United States.

3 Oil Goes to War

At the beginning of the 1970s, the price of crude oil was $2.24 per barrel. At the start of the 1980s, it was $36.83.[1] That surge in the base price of a commodity that everyone needed produced the greatest transfer of wealth in history from the industrial West to the developing world. It brought about a transformation of industrial operations around the globe, stimulated scientists and engineers to find new sources of energy, and changed the way political leaders thought about oil and about the stability of the global oil market.

The flood of oil money fueled the imperial ambitions and extravagance of the Shah of Iran, inspiring the revolution that overthrew him just a few years later; it also provided the money that enabled Iran and Iraq, major oil exporting states, to fight a fruitless eight-year war against each other in the 1980s. The Niagara of cash that poured into Saudi Arabia enabled the Saudis to undertake a massive worldwide effort starting in 1980 to spread their conservative, xenophobic brand of Islam across the Muslim world. The new wealth prompted millions of residents in the oil states to migrate from rural communities to the big cities, where the money was; and it induced millions of workers from South Asia and Egypt, which had little oil, to migrate to the Arab principalities of the Gulf, which needed cheap labor. At the same time, oil-dependent countries in the developing world were driven deeper into poverty and backwardness.

The oil revolution was propelled to triumph by the 1973 war, but it did not start with the war; it started with the 1969 coup in Libya that brought to power to the young radical Muammar Qaddafi, who was determined to nationalize his country's petroleum resources and drive the price upward. His zeal soon inspired many of his fellow Arab leaders. By the early 1970s, the traditional relationship between producers and consumers was doomed as nationalistic new leaders demanded more control of their countries' resources; the October War accelerated the demise of the old order.

When Arab oil producers cut off exports to consumer countries that supported Israel during the conflict, they seized control of a crucial trade in an indispensable commodity from the international oil companies that had previously dictated the terms. Long afterward, it became clear that there were many leaks in the embargo and that the total amount of oil produced worldwide while it was in effect decreased by only a small amount, probably 7 percent at most.[2] The United States actually imported more oil in 1973, the year when the embargo was imposed, than it had the year before, and imports rose again in 1974, when the embargo was in place until the spring.[3] But at the time, panic set in among buyers. Major consuming countries, rather than unite in their mutual interest, began competing with each other for what they thought would be scarce supplies. What had been a controlled market deteriorated into a free-for-all as oil went on the auction block.

As Henry Kissinger put it in his memoirs, "Never before in history has a group of such relatively weak nations been able to impose with so little protest such a dramatic change in the way of life of the overwhelming majority of the rest of mankind."[4]

President Nixon laid it out starkly in an address to the nation on November 7, 1973, as the implications of the embargo became clear. "By the end of this month," he said, "more than two million barrels a day of oil we expected to import into the United States will no longer be available. We must, therefore, face up to a very stark fact: we are heading toward the most acute shortages of oil since World War II." He said Americans, by far the world's biggest oil consumers, "must now set upon a new course. In the short run, this course means that we must use less energy—that means less heat, less electricity, less gasoline. In the long run it means that we must develop new sources of energy which will give us the capacity to meet our needs without relying on any foreign nation."

The president accurately predicted what was coming: "The immediate shortage will affect the lives of each and every one of us. In our factories, our cars, our homes, our offices, we will have to use less fuel than we are accustomed to using."[5] That was just the beginning.

The Bad Old Days

Before the 1970s, the international oil market was largely controlled by the major American and European companies that found, transported, and refined the product—the giant corporations known collectively as the "Seven Sisters." In the standard arrangement, a company such as Chevron or Royal Dutch Shell, or a partnership group of companies, signed a long-term agreement with a producer nation that gave it exclusive access to that country's petroleum resources. In signing such an agreement, the host country yielded control of its most precious asset to a foreign corporation, in exchange for a share of the proceeds. Prices, and the amount of oil to be lifted, or produced, in each country were set by the companies. In Kuwait, for example, the concession was held by a partnership of the old Gulf Oil Company and the Anglo-Iranian Oil Company, now BP. In Saudi Arabia, it was held by the Arabian-American Oil Company, or ARAMCO, a consortium of Chevron, Exxon, Texaco, and Mobil.

The first great challenge to this system came from Iran. During a period of political turmoil in 1951, the parliament—overriding the objections of a weak, young Shah—passed a resolution nationalizing the oil industry and installed a charismatic populist politician, Mohammed Mossadegh, as prime minister. His assignment was to carry out the takeover. Anglo-Iranian held the concession in Iran, and Mossadegh was a dedicated enemy of the giant company, which he and many of his countrymen regarded as an arrogant relic of British imperialism. Mossadegh was frail and bald, and sometimes received visitors in his pajamas, but he was a skillful politician and a crafty negotiator—in French, his preferred language.

Mossadegh alarmed political leaders in London and Washington by forming a tactical alliance with Iran's communist party, Tudeh, but their greater concern was that the oil takeover threatened the Western-dominated international economic order and might set a dangerous example for other countries where nationalist sentiment was on the rise. What if some upstart in Egypt decided to go after the Suez Canal?

The British attempted to negotiate some compromise in Iran, but Mossadegh was implacable. The British contemplated military action, but quickly grasped that it would be folly. They warned of economic retaliation. Mossadegh's response was to order the last British employees of Anglo-Iranian out of the country. With their departure, Britain lost control one of its largest foreign assets, but it was a Pyrrhic victory for Iran: once all the British workers were gone, Britain imposed a boycott on Iranian oil and threatened to sue shippers or refiners who acquired it. Iranian oil exports virtually ceased. Production fell from 660,000 barrels a day in 1950 to 22,000 a day in 1952.[6]

Washington feared that the resulting economic chaos in Iran would strengthen the communists. With the British discredited, American diplomats labored in vain throughout 1952 to craft some arrangement that would bring Iranian oil back into the market and at the same time placate Mossadegh and his allies, but he rejected every offer. Meanwhile, his country was broke and increasingly violent, and he enraged the powerful Shia religious establishment with increasingly autocratic behavior. As the Soviet presence in Tehran increased, Washington and London agreed that Mossadegh had to go. In August of 1953 he was ousted and arrested, in a coup that is widely believed to have been orchestrated by the Central Intelligence Agency.[7] The Shah, who had taken refuge in Rome, was restored to power and returned to Iran in triumph. The United States, eager to see oil exports from Iran resume and to stabilize the country to thwart the communists, assembled a group of seven international companies to resume Iranian production, in partnership with the Iranian National Oil Company. As a legal matter Iran owned its oil, but the industry was once again in the hands of foreign operators.

Thus the crisis passed, but the seed of revolution had been planted. Nationalist sentiment rose in the producing countries as the oil majors reduced prices without negotiation. From Venezuela to Indonesia, the producer countries were inspired by the nationalistic fervor and independent spirit of Egypt's Nasser; Egypt had little oil, but just as the British had feared, Nasser did indeed nationalize the most important foreign-owned asset within his reach, the Suez Canal. In September 1960, five of the most important oil-producing countries—Venezuela, Iran, Iraq, Kuwait, and Saudi Arabia—announced the formation of the Organization of Petroleum Exporting Countries, known as OPEC, through which they would cooperatively seek more favorable arrangements with the oil companies.[8] Other major producers such as Algeria and Nigeria soon joined the group. When Britain, the longtime colonial steward of the sheikhdoms on the Arab side of the Persian Gulf, withdrew from that region in 1971, Kuwait and the others became independent countries, free to join OPEC. The era of oil company domination was coming to a close; its formal dissolution awaited only the rise of some new nationalist firebrand who would succeed where Mossadegh had failed. That man had already appeared on the scene in the person of Muammar Qaddafi, who seized power in Libya in 1969, when he was twenty-seven years old.

By that time, as Daniel Yergin wrote in his monumental history of the oil business, the producing countries had come to believe that the traditional concession contracts "were already a thing of the past, holdovers from the defunct age of colonialism and imperialism, wholly inappropriate to the new age of decolonization, self-determination, and nationalism. Those countries did not want to be mere tax collectors. It was not only a question of garnering more of the rents. For the exporters, the greater question was sovereignty over their own natural resources. Everything else could be measured against that perspective."[9]

Qaddafi wasted little time. In January 1970, his military government demanded an unheard-of price increase of forty-three cents per barrel from each of the foreign countries operating in Libya, beginning with Esso, as Exxon is still known outside the United States. But Esso had oil resources in other countries and refused Libya's demand. The next target was Occidental Petroleum, which had no oil assets anywhere else and was therefore cornered in Libya. After intense negotiations, Occidental yielded: Libya got a thirty-cent price increase and its share of the profits rose from 50 percent to 55.

The headstrong Qaddafi soon went much further, nationalizing a majority share of all the foreign oil operations in Libya. By that time, he was no longer an outlier. Spurred by the Libyan example, OPEC began to demand similar outcomes in other countries and to seek substantial price increases across the board.

Before Qaddafi, the worldwide oil market was stable because supply exceeded demand. Even the United States, by far the largest consumer, had unused production capacity, and the government set prices at a level higher than the world market price to discourage exports. Qaddafi put an abrupt end to this comfortable state of affairs.

The thirty-three months from the beginning of 1971 to the start of the October War were a time of intense, sometimes frantic negotiations between the oil states and the companies that produced their product. The companies agreed to adopt a joint strategy; those based in the United States received a waiver of antitrust laws from the Justice Department, which allowed them to plan and act as a group. Still, for all their maneuvering, the trend was clear and inexorable: the producer countries were wresting the initiative from the oil companies. Acting in concert, sometimes after long arguments among themselves, the OPEC states kept pushing prices upward and extracting a greater share of the profits. The revenue of producer countries rose rapidly because prices were going up and so was their share of the take. On June 1, 1972, Iraq, controlled by the radical nationalist Baath Party, seized the last remaining assets of the Iraq Petroleum Company, one of the oldest European-American concessions in the Middle East, and there was nothing any European or American could do about it. Venezuela announced that all foreign company assets would be nationalized as concessions expired; its negotiations with Exxon and Shell were now about compensation for the seized facilities, not about whether nationalization would occur. Saudi Arabia, always cautious and conservative, was reluctant to nationalize ARAMCO by unilateral decision because the kingdom valued its relationship with the United States for other reasons. Nevertheless, its flamboyant oil minister, Ahmed Zaki Yamani, proclaimed, "There is a worldwide trend toward nationalization and Saudis cannot stand against it alone. The industry should realize this and come to terms so that they can save as much as possible under the circumstances."[10] Rather than seizing ARAMCO outright, the Saudis bought it bit by bit over several years, at negotiated prices. Americans continued to operate the oil fields and terminals under contract, but the government owned the operation, and within a few years most of the senior executives were Saudis.[11]

OPEC and the October War

In September 1973, OPEC members, meeting in Vienna, demanded revisions in their favor of agreements on ownership-sharing and on taxes that they had forced on the Western oil companies during the preceding two years. They scheduled another meeting for October 8 to present these new terms to the companies.

In that environment, the October War added fuel to the fire, so to speak, for OPEC's Arab members. OPEC as an organization never involved itself in the war because major members such as Venezuela, Nigeria, and Indonesia, were not parties to the Arab-Israeli struggle, and because Iran at that time had good relations with Israel. Had the war not occurred, Saudi Arabia, the most important exporter, would have exercised price restraint within OPEC and maintained its longstanding policy of keeping oil and politics separate. But when war came, pitting Arabs against Israel, the Saudis bowed to intense pressure from the other Arab producers and joined them in cutting off exports to the United States and parts of Europe. Whether eagerly or reluctantly, OPEC's Arab members decided they had no choice but to support their Egyptian and Syrian compatriots. It was time to deploy the so-called oil weapon. (Non-OPEC producers such as Mexico were not involved in any of these discussions but they were happy bystanders because in a global market they benefited from the OPEC price increases.)

Another Middle East Surprise

Like the October War itself, the Arab oil embargo came as an unpleasant surprise to political leaders and policymakers in the consuming countries. Just as they had assumed that the Arabs would not fight because they could not win, they assumed that Arab oil producers would not deploy the "oil weapon" because oil revenue was the mainstay of their economies. And even if radical states such as Iraq and Libya did take the self-destructive step of cutting oil exports, the impact would be manageable so long as Saudi Arabia remained reliable. These assumptions were invalid.

As with the war, there was ample warning that trouble was coming, including unmistakable signals from Saudi Arabia, the industry giant and presumably a friend and ally of the United States. And as with the war, the warnings went largely unheeded.

In April, Yamani met with Kissinger in Washington to fill him in on Saudi thinking. Saudi Arabia, he said, was producing more oil than it needed to finance its budget, mostly to benefit the industrial West, but was not seeing appropriate gestures of gratitude in the form of Middle East policy changes. The United States' complete support for Israel had "embarrassed" Saudi Arabia before the other Arabs, he said, because the kingdom was vulnerable to their criticism that Saudi Arabia was a tool of the West and was doing nothing in the face of Israeli intransigence.

"Dr. Kissinger asked whether Minister Yamani had any specific ideas," according to the official U.S. memorandum of this conversation. "Minister Yamani said that the most important issue to be dealt with is a settlement of the Arab-Israeli problem."[12]

There were many similar conversations in the months before the war, according to Alfred L. "Roy" Atherton, a senior Middle East official in the State Department and later ambassador to Egypt. Washington, he said, was hearing from Arab countries, "and in particular from Saudi Arabia, that the situation with continued Israeli occupation, a humiliation of the Arabs, could not go on indefinitely, that this was intolerable from an Arab point of view. And that was when we first began to get hints out of the Arab world that they might be compelled to put a squeeze on oil supplies to the West. So there was some foreshadowing of what became, within the year, the Arab oil embargo. But again, there was a tendency in Washington to discount both the possibility that the Egyptians would start a war that threatened Israel's control and that the oil-producing countries would really seriously go through with this. The reasoning was they would hurt themselves as much as anybody else by cutting off sales of oil to the West."[13]

That was not the view from Kuwait. There, on January 6, 1973, the parliament unanimously adopted a fire-breathing resolution calling on all Arab countries to "freeze all existing oil agreements with Western companies the moment the armed struggle against the Zionist enemy is re-launched." The ruling emir, Sheikh Sabah al-Salim al-Sabah, promptly announced that he would do exactly that: "When the hour comes, we will use our oil weapon against Israel. That is our irrevocable position."[14]

That sort of radical Arab rhetoric put the Saudis in an especially delicate position. Ever since the famous meeting between President Franklin D. Roosevelt and King Abdul Aziz al-Saud in 1945, they had tied their security and their economic development to the United States. But they also saw themselves as leaders of the Arabs and of all Muslims, positions that would be difficult to maintain if Washington continued to tolerate Israel's occupation of Arab lands or supported Israel in a war. Moreover, Saudi Arabia was taking in more money than it could possibly spend and could easily afford a temporary reduction in exports. On the other hand, all Saudi oil was produced and transported by ARAMCO, and the Saudis did not desire to jeopardize that relationship. They did not have the human resources or technical skills needed to run the oil fields and processing plants on their own. Their position was that oil commerce should not be politicized, but King Faisal could see that such a development might be inevitable unless Washington took some action to assuage Arab grievances. If he could get his point across to the United States, an oil crisis might be averted.

Ray Close, the CIA station chief in Saudi Arabia at the time, recalled that "starting in late 1972 . . . King Faisal began warning President Nixon that other Arab states, led by Iraq and Libya, were beginning to put pressure on him to join them in utilizing what became known as the oil weapon against the United States unless the Nixon Administration took a more active interest in resolving the Palestine question. These warnings were earnest, and they were urgent, but we ignored them."[15]

Close said that Faisal "never gave up" the effort to get his view across to the United States, and the record bears that out. The king sent letters, gave interviews, and dispatched envoys to Washington throughout the summer before the war. Saudi Arabia was taking in more money than it could spend, he said, and had nothing to lose by keeping the oil in ground for a while instead of exporting it.[16]

In August, Yamani, the Saudi oil minister, delivered a blunt message to Mike Ameen, ARAMCO's representative in Riyadh: "Mike, I want you go back and tell people there is going to be war and there is no way he [Faisal] can't use the oil weapon if the Arab League calls for it." Later the same day, Ameen heard it from Faisal himself: The King "was feeling pressure from Arabs who continued to accuse him of being 'with the Americans.' He had told us a number of times that it was getting harder and harder to be friends with the United States. We are America's friends, we have told them that policy has to change to keep our friendship. He looked very tired and very old." Ameen relayed the message to Washington, just as many other oil-industry executives were doing at that time.[17]

Faisal's warnings went unheeded, in the sense that they had no effect on U.S. policy in the Middle East. On September 2, the *Washington Post* published on its front page a story by its well-informed Middle East correspondent, Jim Hoagland, saying that Sadat had made a secret trip to Riyadh and received a pledge from Faisal to start withholding oil shipments by the end of the year if there was no change in U.S. Middle East policy.[18] An adjacent story reported that Qaddafi had expropriated 51 percent of the assets of foreign oil companies operating in Libya.

Still, there was no apparent shift in U.S. Middle East policy, which was anchored in support for Israel. The White House had indeed been anticipating an energy crisis for some time but not because of Faisal or the prospect of a war in the Middle East, a possibility that Washington did not take seriously. U.S. officials assumed that Saudi Arabia would not cut off oil shipments because it was a longstanding friend and Cold War ally, and besides, all the wells, pipelines, and shipping terminals there were owned by Americans. President Nixon was worried less about the Middle East specifically than he was about the worldwide implications of the OPEC revolution.

On March 8, 1973, he instructed Kissinger, his national security adviser, to send a "National Security Study Memorandum" to the secretaries of state, defense, and treasury, and to the director of central intelligence. It ordered them to produce within five weeks "a study of the national security implications of world energy supply and distribution" and to "propose alternative policies to deal with problems that are identified." The memorandum presciently said the study "should consider, for example, alternative means of reducing the effects of boycotts by producer nations, other cut-offs, or reductions in foreign supplies."[19]

Among the topics to be addressed were "the foreign policy and national security implications of the consortium of oil-producing nations (OPEC), and the potential role of the Soviet Union as a troublemaker or a market balancer in the event of an oil supply disruption."[20]

As that directive showed, Nixon fully grasped the strategic and economic implications of the worldwide oil revolution, and when the embargo came, he would move swiftly to minimize its impact on the United States and its allies. For Kissinger, who admitted he knew little about the oil business, the embargo at first was only an irritating nuisance that complicated his delicate negotiations with the Soviet Union, Egypt, and Israel. Even though the price of oil increased by 72 percent between 1970 and September 1973, he regarded the developments in OPEC as "commercial disputes" in which the United States government should not be involved.[21] He was soon to understand otherwise.

On October 17, the twelfth day of the war, Kissinger met in Washington with senior national security and military advisers, known collectively as the Washington Special Actions Group, for a review of the situation in the Middle East. When the conversation turned to oil, Kissinger informed them that "[w]e don't expect an oil cut-off now" because of what he had heard from some Arab foreign ministers that morning: "Did you see the Saudi foreign minister come out like a good little boy and say they had very fruitful talks with us?"[22]

Perhaps the foreign ministers had indeed been conciliatory, but they were not in charge of their countries' oil policies. On that same day, the oil ministers of the six biggest producers in the Persian Gulf, including Iran, announced a 17 percent price increase, saying it had nothing to do with the war—which was what they had to say, given Iran's close ties to Israel. Later that day OPEC's Arab members announced that they were cutting production by 5 percent immediately and would cut another 5 percent every month until the "international community" compelled Israel to withdraw from all the Arab territory it had seized in the 1967 war. Saudi Arabia, the biggest exporter, endorsed that decision, but King Faisal was still reluctant to cut off all exports to countries supporting Israel, as Libya and Iraq were demanding.

Then, the very next day, October 18, Nixon announced that he would ask Congress for $2.2 billion in new military aid to Israel. That was too much even for Faisal; a day later he announced that the kingdom would cease all exports to the United States and to the Netherlands, the major trans-shipment point for oil in Europe. The chief of the royal *diwan*, or court, told U.S. ambassador James E. Akins that the king was "as furious as he had ever seen him" about the president's move and had taken "particular umbrage at what he considered to be the difference between [the] reassuring tone of various communications he had received from USG [U.S. government] and [the] U.S. announcement of an 'incredible' amount of aid."[23]

The king made clear to ARAMCO that it would have to comply with the embargo on shipments to the country of its shareholders, the United States, or face immediate nationalization. That directive turned a major American-owned corporation into an instrument of attack against U.S. policy by a foreign government. "There was no doubt about this," ARAMCO chief executive Frank Jungers said afterward. "We did it in lieu of being nationalized. We had no choice."[24]

Within a few days after Faisal's decision, the full Arab embargo was in place. That was the end of an international order that had prevailed in the petroleum business for decades and had assured the industrialized West of abundant cheap supplies.

Other Arab producers adopted the same position as the Saudis about oil sales to the United States and the Netherlands and added a few other countries as targets. One of them was Portugal, punished for allowing an air base in the Azores to be used as a refueling station for the U.S. airlift to Israel.

For Portugal, the embargo's impact was minimal because it still controlled Angola, its oil-producing colony in southern Africa. Elsewhere the reaction was confusion, fear, and even panic, not just over potential supply shortages but over the continuing rapid escalation of the price. Seizing the opportunity presented by the embargo, OPEC dropped an economic bomb on the world: meeting in Tehran on December 23, the group raised the base price of a barrel of oil from $5.12 to $11.65.

"It is now obvious," Kissinger wrote in his memoirs, "that the decision was one of the pivotal events in the history of this century. . . . Within forty-eight hours the oil bill for the United States, Canada, Western Europe, and Japan had increased by $40 billion a year. It was a colossal blow to their balance of payments, economic growth, employment, price stability, and social cohesion. The Tehran decision also cost the developing countries more than the entire foreign aid programs extended to them by the industrial democracies."[25] As Andrew Scott Cooper noted in his narrative of these events, the decision meant that "the price of oil had risen 470 percent in the space of twelve months and that the economic wealth of OPEC members had rocketed by the then astronomical sum of $112 billion—an amount that represented the largest single transfer of wealth in history."[26] The increases in the following year would be even greater.

The London-based International Institute for Strategic Studies, in its annual review of world events, observed in January 1974 that the oil revolution produced changes in the world power structure that were "drastic, not only by recent standards but even in some respects by those of two centuries since the Industrial Revolution . . . this was the first time that major industrial states had to bow to pressure from pre-industrial ones." The Arabs' collective action, the institute said, "was by far the biggest extension of the world's effective political arena since the Chinese Revolution" in 1949.[27]

Before the war, the international oil market was of marginal interest to Washington's foreign policy establishment. The State Department had an Office of Fuels and Energy, but it was a tiny backwater in the Foggy Bottom bureaucracy. William B. Whitman, who was assigned to it in 1972, recalled that "oil was just not of any interest to the State Department" outside of the bilateral relationship with Saudi Arabia. "Oil was not a problem, and it was cheap," he said. "I've forgotten exactly what we did—we went to meetings," to discuss such topics as how to "keep cheap foreign crude out of the United States." The director of that office was "a brilliant and fascinating man named Jim Akins, and Jim was probably one of the two people in the department who knew anything about oil."[28]

Akins, who was soon to become ambassador to Saudi Arabia, certainly understood the potential for the producers to disrupt the market. In a celebrated article in *Foreign Affairs* in April 1973, he virtually predicted what was soon to happen. The Arabs could not simply shut down their oil fields, he wrote, because they needed the money. "Rather, the usual Arab political threat is to deny oil to the Arabs' enemies, while supplies would continue to their friends," which turned out to be exactly what they did six months later during the war.[29] By the time the war started, Akins was in his ambassadorial post, a position that made him a central player in the embargo drama. Unfortunately, Kissinger and Akins disliked each other intensely; they disagreed on policy and on tactics, and their personalities clashed. Given the importance of Saudi Arabia during the embargo, it complicated Kissinger's life for the Saudis to be receiving different messages from the U.S. ambassador than they were getting from him. He fired Akins after less than two years in the kingdom, and Akins was bitter about it for the rest of his life.

At the start of the embargo, Kissinger was more concerned with the diplomatic and strategic impact than the economic. He was trying to stop the war and negotiate some sort of settlement; now the Arabs were demanding an outcome he could not deliver, Israel's withdrawal to its boundaries of 1967. Virtually all Israelis believed that the boundaries between Israel and its neighbors that existed before the 1967 war were indefensible and posed an unacceptable security risk; no Israeli government, however dovish in outlook, would ever agree to a return to those lines.

Kissinger's petro-diplomacy was complicated by the fact that he was playing in multiple arenas at the same time, and it was difficult to balance American economic interests with American strategic interests. Kissinger wanted to stop the price escalation, but he did not want to undercut the Shah of Iran, an ally—and a friend of Israel—who was using the money to build up his armed forces with American weapons. Iran supplied more than half of Israel's oil. Kissinger was trying to strengthen Pakistan and its prime minister, Zulfikar Ali Bhutto, but Pakistan was being crushed by the cost of energy. At the same time, Kissinger was trying to preserve détente with the Soviet Union, complete implementation of the agreement that ended the Vietnam War, steer U.S. policy through the treacherous waters of domestic politics, and keep his distance from the scandals in which the president was entangled. On October 10, Vice President Spiro T. Agnew resigned over a bribery scandal from his time as governor of Maryland. On October 13, the U.S. Supreme Court ordered President Nixon to turn over tape recordings of White House conversations. And then came the "Saturday Night Massacre," while Kissinger was in Moscow negotiating with Brezhnev. In that atmosphere, as the war continued, the Arab embargo was a complication Kissinger had not anticipated, engineered by people he could not control, generating responses that he found dangerous and counterproductive.

He was furious at four groups of people: the Arab oil producers, of whom he said it was "ridiculous that the civilized world is held up by eight million savages";[30] American oil company executives (egged on by Akins) who were lobbying for a retreat from full U.S. support for Israel; European allies and Japan, which were distancing themselves from Israel and seeking bilateral deals with oil-producing countries; and Pentagon officials, led by Defense Secretary James Schlesinger, who were advocating military action.

Kissinger knew from the early days of the war that Schlesinger had an itchy trigger finger. American interests in the Middle East were in jeopardy, Schlesinger had told him on October 10, even before the oil embargo was in place, and the United States might face a choice "between occupation or letting them go down the drain."

"Occupation of whom?" Kissinger replied.

"That remains to be seen—it can be partial."

"But which country are we occupying?"

"That's one of the things we'd like to talk about."

"Who's we?"

"Me," Schlesinger said.[31]

Kissinger then changed the subject, but he blew up two weeks later when White House chief of staff Alexander Haig told him that Schlesinger was talking about sending U.S. Marines to seize oil fields. Schlesinger is "insane," he said. "I do not think we can survive with those fellows there at Defense. They are crazy."[32]

Among the allies, he was especially perturbed by the British and French, who he said were "behaving like complete shits" as they distanced themselves from U.S. policy in the Middle East.[33] In fact, the behavior of the Europeans was predictable, and the CIA had predicted it earlier: "There is very little the West Europeans can do in the near term to get their oil deliveries back to strength," the agency concluded. "They will, of course, continue to distance themselves from Washington's present Middle Eastern policy—in speeches, in UN votes, and in the denial of overflight and refueling rights for U.S. military aircraft. But no European leader expects such behavior to cause Washington to rethink its position or entirely to save Europe from the effects of the oil embargo." What the Europeans wanted, the CIA correctly said, was to sanitize themselves in the eyes of the Arabs by backing away from support for Israel.[34]

The allies had reason to be apprehensive, because Saudi Arabia was telling them in blunt language what was expected of them. Yamani told the Japanese, for example, that "they can escape a 14–15 percent cut in Saudi oil shipments only by cutting diplomatic or economic relations with Israel, selling arms to Arab states or lobbying intensively with the United States on behalf of a settlement of the Mideast conflict in accordance with the U.N. resolutions."[35] Similar warnings were coming from other Arab producers.

As for the American oil executives, Kissinger took nine of them to the woodshed, including the chief executives of ARAMCO partners Exxon, Mobil, and Texaco, at a meeting in his State Department conference room on October 26, almost as soon as the cease-fire in the Middle East finally took full effect.

He objected in particular to public statements that oil executives had been making, advocating that the United States distance itself from Israel. "One thing I want to say about the immediate situation," he told them, "is that it does nobody any good to raise doubts about American foreign policy among those who are already jittery about it. . . . Some comments I have seen made by oil company executives are an unmitigated disaster. It is bad enough to seek to curry favor with the oil states but when this undermines our diplomatic efforts it is intolerable."[36]

Kissinger, like everyone else, was sailing in uncharted waters, in which carefully crafted policies and meticulously negotiated agreements were swamped by consumer panic. Improvising as the oil crisis reshaped the global economy, he even tried to take advantage of it to cement the enduring objective of détente with the Soviet Union: he instructed his staff to negotiate an arrangement by which the United States would acquire Soviet oil in exchange for American grain.[37] This "barrels for bushels" deal was never completed, mostly because the U.S. side insisted on a substantial price discount, which the Soviets refused to grant, but also because the oil issue had become enmeshed in the larger geopolitical struggle for ideological influence in the developing world. The United States wanted the arrangement to have maximum publicity, as a message to OPEC that other oil sources were available; the Soviets wanted to keep it quiet so as not to be perceived as undercutting the very Arab countries they were trying to cultivate.

As the oil industry analyst Edward Morse wrote in an extensive retrospective on the oil crisis, "It enabled oil exporters, all of which were themselves nonaligned developing nations, to gain the support of virtually the entire Third World in a battle for the redistribution of wealth from industrialized to developing countries. Individual exporters—especially the richer Arab countries with small populations and ample reserves—discovered, under the prodding of Venezuela, that they needed to band together to wield influence over the industrialized world. Thus, the politics of resource nationalism were integral to the politics of the so-called New International Economic Order, a Third World movement whose aim was to correct the perceived structural inequities inherent in the global balance of power."[38]

President Nixon, to his credit, had perceived that some sort of energy crisis was inevitable because, as he told the country on November 7, "our deeper energy problems come not from war but from peace and abundance. We are running out of energy today because our economy has grown enormously and because in prosperity what were once considered luxuries are now considered necessities," such as air conditioning. "As a result, the average American will consume as much energy in the next seven days as most other people in the world will consume in a year." The president said it was urgent for Americans to recognize that they would have to use energy more wisely and invest in new energy sources for the long term.[39] He was correct, but in those dramatic months, the focus of consumers and Congress was on the immediate crisis, which seemed to affect everyone.

Crisis Grips the World

In January 1974, listeners to shortwave radio around the world picked up an appeal for help from Pitcairn Island, the tiny, remote British colony in the South Pacific where the mutineers of HMS *Bounty* led by Fletcher Christian had found refuge in 1789. They heard the voice of Tom Christian, great-great-great grandson of Fletcher, pleading for fuel to keep the little community running.[40] That was just one dramatic indication of the impact and the reach of the oil embargo. The total amount of oil coming out of the world's wells had diminished relatively little since the previous summer, but soaring prices, hoarding, and substantial disruption of shipping patterns threw the market into chaos. With winter approaching, the demand for heating oil was cresting just as supplies were being reduced. The disruption was enhanced by unwise government responses, such as Nixon's imposition of price controls on domestic crude oil, which had the perverse effect of stimulating demand.

"I remember, my wife and I were in the car, and there was a bulletin that the president was imposing wage and price controls, and putting together this price commission and this wage commission. It was so un-Republican and un-free market that it was stunning," Frank Zarb, Nixon's energy policy director, recalled. "All I could think of at that time was that conditions must be so bad that people like [Treasury Secretary] George Schultz would be supporting this kind of a move. In any case, whatever reasoning, they did it, and I thought—and I, today, think it was probably the single most important mistake in the Nixon government."[41] (In Canada, where no price controls or allocations were imposed, the market sorted itself out and no gas lines developed.)

The October War itself was receding into history, but the oil crisis cascaded. Fishing fleets were beached. Cargo vessels reduced their sailings, causing random shortages of basic goods: in Osaka, Japan, a woman died in a stampede for toilet paper. The owner of a brothel near Reno, Nevada, ordered thermostats turned down from seventy-five degrees to sixty-eight and instructed the women to wear pantsuits instead of bikinis. Lights on the Golden Gate Bridge were extinguished, and those on the National Christmas Tree at the White House were never turned on. Citrus farmers in California were unable to get fuel for the smudge pots that protected their crops from frost. On the stock market, share prices of automobile and truck manufacturers plummeted as auto sales fell 21 percent from a year earlier. Truckloads of gasoline were hijacked. Tennis players in Virginia canceled matches rather than drive to the courts. Fistfights broke out at filling stations. Massachusetts General Hospital stopped changing bed linens every day.[42]

Airline flights were cut back as the price of jet fuel soared from eleven cents a gallon just before the war to thirty-five cents a year later. A cartoon by Bill Mauldin showed the captain of a jetliner passing the hat among the passengers: "Thank you, sir, thank you, ma'am . . . looks as if we can buy enough fuel for the next leg."[43]

Newsweek, analyzing a worldwide surge in inflation, reported that the quadrupling of oil prices virtually overnight was one cause but not the only one. "The oil producers' cartel was bad enough," the magazine said. "But the situation grew worse when other less-developed countries rich in raw materials decided to imitate the Arab success with cartels of their own. Price-fixing arrangements popped up among producers of bauxite, phosphate, copper, tin, coffee, and bananas," sending prices up as much as 600 percent.[44]

Bicycle sales surged in Italy. The Netherlands banned private auto trips on weekends. France and Italy banned Sunday driving. In Britain, where a nationwide strike by coal miners crippled industry and further increased the demand for oil, Prime Minister Edward Heath cut the work week to three days.

Sadat said in his memoirs that the American people were not the targets of the embargo, and he claimed that "the moment we felt that the oil embargo had started to hit the American citizen, it was lifted."[45] That was not true. Throughout that winter, news outlets in the United States, Europe, and Asia overflowed with accounts of shortages, hardships, disputes over access to gasoline, and even violence, all of which appeared to strengthen the hands of the Arab producers.

Oil was used throughout the world primarily as a transportation fuel, not as a fuel for the generation of electricity, but governments and private businesses alike reacted as if all forms of energy were suddenly in short supply, ordering lighting and television broadcasts cut back to conserve electricity.

The day after the OPEC meeting in Tehran, the Central Intelligence

Agency, noting that the United States received only about 9 percent of its oil from Arab producers, predicted that even if all of them declared a total embargo, "[t]he effect on the United States would be relatively small."[46] In terms of raw numbers, the agency was correct, but its analysts failed to foresee the consumer panic, political posturing, false information, and shipping disruptions that would greatly magnify the embargo's impact on Americans.

To conserve fuel, President Nixon ordered that a nationwide speed limit be set at fifty-five miles per hour. Congress approved construction of the Trans-Alaska Pipeline, to develop the oil resources of Alaska's North Slope. It also authorized the president to allocate the oil that was available, which he promptly did, ordering that more supplies be refined into heating oil, less for vehicle fuel, and directing that gasoline stations be closed from 9:00 p.m. Saturday to midnight Sunday. He authorized the printing of ration coupons, to be used as a last resort.

For the limited amount of oil that was sold on the short-term or spot market, as opposed to long-term contracts, prices soared in bidding wars as cargoes were put up for auction. In December, an Iranian shipment went for $17 a barrel, nearly three times the posted price. A few days later, traders were shocked when Nigeria offered oil on the spot market at an incredible $22.60 per barrel.

Then, at an OPEC meeting in December, Iran and Saudi Arabia, by prearrangement, called for a new price that would guarantee each producing country a minimum cut of $7 per barrel; the posted price would be set to produce that result. For the benchmark crude, Saudi Arabian light, the price was set at $11.65 a barrel.[47]

A few weeks after that move by OPEC, the CIA's Office of Economic Research projected that "[i]ncreased prices will mean a $70 billion increase in the Free World oil bill in 1974, if world oil exports approximate the 1973 level, as seems likely." The United States would to some extent be shielded from this impact because of its own production, but Western Europe and Japan would face potentially crushing burdens. At the same time, the CIA said, "soaring payments for oil threaten a massive loss of purchasing power in the developing countries, equivalent to about 3% of GNP in Western Europe and Japan. Unless expansionary measures are taken, all face severely reduced rates of economic growth—perhaps even declining output—and increased unemployment."[48]

Because this overnight escalation of a commodity in universal use ignited worldwide inflation, the oil-producing countries, suddenly wealthy, were paying ever-higher prices to import consumer goods and industrial equipment they could not previously afford; the surge in prices for these goods—which they had largely caused—meant that they needed ever more revenue to pay for them, which in turn drove the price of oil upward still further.

"In those days there was also the fear that the Arabs were going to buy this country," the State Department's Whitman recalled. "People would do projections of what the Arabs would do, they would buy London, they would buy all the real estate in New York, people would project out exponential growth in their oil receipts which would show them [the Arabs] owning the world in 1990 or something like that."[49]

In his State of the Union address on January 30, 1974, President Nixon said, "In all of the 186 State of the Union messages delivered from this place, in our history this is the first in which the one priority, the first priority, is energy."

He told the nation that he had already sent to Congress a "comprehensive special message" asking for quick enactment of legislation to permit additional limits on consumption, authorize temporary waivers of the Clean Air Act, impose a "windfall profits tax" on oil companies, create federal government agencies to regulate energy-dependent industries and the energy market, and undertake research into new sources of power. Thus did the upheaval in the oil market bring a Republican president to propose a new tax, new government regulations, and the creation of new government agencies.

"Let us do everything we can to avoid gasoline rationing in the United States of America," the president said. To that end, he said he could announce that "an urgent meeting will be called in the near future" to consider lifting the oil embargo. He had hoped and expected to be able to announce that Saudi Arabia, at least, was actually end-ing the embargo, but to his frustration, and that of Kissinger, King Faisal was still holding out, more than two months after the shoot-ing had stopped. The king had said he would keep the embargo in place until there was a disengagement agreement between Israel and Syria parallel to the first disengagement agreement between Israel and Egypt. This demand represented a substantial retreat from his previous position, which was that the embargo would remain until Israel withdrew from all the territories it seized in 1967, but it was still beyond Kissinger's ability meet the king's conditions immediately.

Sadat understood Kissinger's argument that the United States regarded the embargo as blackmail, and he wanted to be responsive to direct entreaties from Nixon.[50] He promised the Americans that he would ask Faisal to agree to end the embargo in time for Nixon to announce it in his State of the Union speech. When that did not happen, Kissinger made his displeasure clear in a letter to Sadat on February 4, 1974.

"As I know you are aware," he wrote, "President Nixon and I have appreciated your efforts to be helpful in bringing about an end to the oil embargo against the United States, and we also understand the problems you have faced in your contacts with other Arab states. We have received with increasing encouragement assurances from you personally and from your advisors of the expectation that there will be a speedy end" to the embargo. Now, however, Kissinger said he was "deeply disturbed" at the news from Saudi Arabia. "I am sure you will understand it when I say that in these circumstances we cannot continue the role that you and I have so carefully and exhaustively talked about."[51] That "role" was to make a full-scale commitment, using all the military, diplomatic, and economic leverage the United States could wield, to bring about a comprehensive settlement that would satisfy the Arabs.

Nixon told the Saudis, "I am the first president since Eisenhower who has no commitment to the Jews and I will not be swayed. I didn't do enough in the first term but I am determined now that the Mid-dle East be settled. . . . What I want you to know is that I have made a commitment. We will work out a permanent settlement as quickly as possible." The president said he knew it would be difficult and could make no promises about the status of Jerusalem, but he added that "the full prestige of my office is dedicated to that."[52] As soon as the embargo ended, he said, he would dedicate himself to this mission.

Unfortunately for the Arabs, the "full prestige" of Nixon's office was vaporizing in the Watergate scandal, but the very fact that he said such things was evidence of Sadat's political success, even if his armies had not won the war. Not only had he gotten the Americans to take him seriously and give him their attention, he and his Arab supporters who withheld their oil had extracted a pledge from the president of the United States to forge a regional settlement, whether the Israelis liked it or not.

King Faisal wrote to Nixon a few days later to say that he greatly appreciated the president's commitment but he still could not comply with the request to lift the embargo. "The other Arabs would not go along with us and we are associated with our Arab brethren in a resolution from which it would be difficult to deviate," he wrote. "It is difficult to convince them to lift the ban if no agreement is signed for the disengagement of forces on the Syrian front."[53] Not until May 31 was such an agreement signed; the embargo was fully and formally lifted shortly afterward. It did not achieve its original stated objective, a full Israeli withdrawal from the lands occupied in 1967, but in other ways it was a strategic success for the Arabs, who demonstrated a unity and cohesion they often proclaimed but rarely achieved, and forced the Western powers to treat them with new respect and deference.

The Start of a New Era

If the Arabs harbored any lingering resentment toward the United States after the war, it was not much in evidence by that summer of 1974. On the contrary, once the oil embargo was lifted, the United States began a new era of engagement and friendship with the Arabs, especially Egypt and Saudi Arabia, beyond even what Sadat had envisioned. Its most visible manifestation was a triumphal tour of Egypt,

Jordan, Saudi Arabia, and even Syria on which Nixon embarked on June 12. His presidency was crumbling and two months later he would resign in disgrace, but in the Middle East he received a grand welcome.

The United States and Egypt restored diplomatic relations. Washington began economic assistance on a massive scale. The United States and allied navies reopened the Suez Canal, clearing it of unexploded ordnance, sunken barges and ships, and other rubble of war, and sweeping its banks of mines and fortifications. While in Cairo, Nixon announced that the United States would provide Egypt with nuclear technology for the generation of electricity.

With Saudi Arabia the new relationship was more subtle, but it formed the foundation of the intimate military, security, and economic ties that link the kingdom with the United States today. When King Faisal deployed the "oil weapon," he changed the political equation between Washington and Riyadh; the United States was no longer the benevolent big brother.

The new reality was on display when Kissinger, visiting Saudi Arabia in October 1974, put on an appalling display of sycophancy in a long meeting with Faisal. He told the king that Gerald Ford, Nixon's successor, wanted to fulfill Nixon's commitment to help the Arabs extract a satisfactory settlement from Israel but "we are experiencing a mass attack by Communists and Zionists." The king, who equated Zionists with communists, remarked that their "normal procedure everywhere in the world is to fish in troubled waters and stir them to make them even muddier," to which Kissinger replied, "I am under strong attack by the Zionists but I can easily overcome it."

After Kissinger described at some length the state of play on the diplomatic front, Faisal complained that Israeli prime minister Yitzhak Rabin had said after a visit to Washington "that the U.S. government promised it would support Israel in whatever it did."

"That statement is absolutely untrue," Kissinger responded. "We gave Israel no blank check. I am bound to say that some of the statements made by Prime Minister Rabin are signs of extreme weakness. What he said was so baldly untrue that it shows he is clearly unstable." And when the subject turned to the price of oil, Kissinger offered this: "Saudi Arabia has pursued an enlightened policy and one to which we will pay public tribute."[54]

The oil price surge reversed the economic balance between the United States and Saudi Arabia. In 1973, the value of U.S. imports from the kingdom exceeded the value of exports to it for the first time. By 1977, U.S. exports to the kingdom were $3.575 billion, while imports— almost entirely crude oil—were $65.36 billion.[55] Nixon, distracted though he may have been as his presidency unraveled, could see this coming. He recognized that Saudi Arabia now would have far more money and far more regional influence than previously. Bypassing Kissinger's State Department, he approved a program designed by William Simon, who succeeded George P. Schultz as treasury secretary in May 1974, to engage the Saudis at every level of government and recapture as much of that oil money as possible for the United States. The instrument of this new relationship was a unique institution known as the U.S.-Saudi Arabian Joint Economic Commission, or JECOR.

Its objectives were listed in a joint statement from the two countries: "Its purposes will be to promote programs of industrialization, trade, manpower training, agriculture, and science and technology." In effect, the United States undertook to teach the Saudis, at their expense, how to run a modern country and a modern economy. Over the next several years, thousands of American government workers, civil servants, were deployed directly into their counterpart agencies in Saudi Arabia, where they helped the Saudis with everything from taking a census to creating the country's first national park to finding internships for Saudi doctors in U.S. hospitals. This program was managed by the Treasury Department, not by State or any aid agency, and functioned outside the authority of the U.S. embassy.

"In 1974 the Saudis had billions of dollars and high expectations but no real government," said Charles Schotta, a Treasury official who was coordinator of the commission. He said the Saudis were in a hurry to build a functioning state, as opposed to the loose organizations of princes and sheikhs of the old days, and they wanted to follow American models, so the Treasury Department took on that assignment. This unique and intimate relationship lasted twenty-five years, until the end of Bill Clinton's presidency, by which time the Saudis no longer needed it. It was little known to the American public because the Saudis paid for it—channeling oil revenue back to the United States through contracts with U.S. firms hired by JECOR—and thus there was no congressional oversight because no appropriated funds were required. This enterprise had an enduring outcome in that every government agency and major business in Saudi Arabia today has senior staff members who worked with and were schooled by Americans.[56]

The Chaos Subsides

The oil embargo finally ended in the late spring of 1974 and the chaos that it had brought to the global oil market and the neighborhood filling station subsided. The price surges that it stimulated remained, however, as did the worldwide economic upheaval that resulted. Drafting an energy policy speech for President Ford in January 1975, Frank Zarb wrote,

> Even today, with the embargo and many of its attendant problems fading in time and memory, our energy situation provides little cause for comfort. Domestic demand will continue to grow, though more slowly than in the past. Domestic petroleum production will continue to decline. The gap between supply and demand will continue to be filled by imports, which already have surpassed pre-embargo levels. Thus we will rely more and more on insecure foreign sources, which have quadrupled petroleum prices over the past year and which probably can maintain today's exorbitant prices—at the growing peril of the international economic system. . . . Overseas, we see many industrialized nations—many of our traditional friends and allies with limited or virtually nonexistent domestic energy sources—accumulating staggering deficits because of these exorbitant oil prices. We hear dire warnings of their bankruptcy and imminent economic collapse.

The producer states, he warned, faced "monetary chaos" as surpluses mounted, and undeveloped countries are "bending to the breaking point" and could face "the tragic spectacle of starvation."[57]

A year later, the government's National Energy Outlook for 1976, the last prepared by Zarb, reported, "Today, the United States spends about $37 billion, or $125 per person, for imported oil [annually] as compared to $3 billion, or $15 per person, in 1970."[58] Zarb could not have foreseen the sudden price declines of the 1980s or the oil and gas production boom that would come to the United States starting in about 2010; despite those market upheavals, the overall forecast of the 1975 speech draft, while excessively apocalyptic, was generally borne out by events.

The revolution that transformed the industry's balance of power triumphed totally. Today no oil-producing country cedes control of its resources to foreign companies or allows its profits or taxes to be dictated by foreign powers. The business is run by state-owned corporations such as the Iranian National Oil Company, Saudi Aramco, and Pemex in Mexico. These state entities may negotiate contracts or enter into partnerships with international companies such as Exxon or BP, but whether they do so is up to them, not to any foreigners.

The governments of the industrialized consumer countries, which Kissinger had criticized for their "every man for himself" responses to the oil crisis, soon came to their collective senses and recognized the need to organize to insulate themselves against future disruptions. In a speech in London on December 12, 1973, with the embargo in full force and OPEC galloping ahead on prices, Kissinger called for a "massive effort to provide producers an incentive to increase their supply, to encourage consumers to use existing supplies more rationally, and to develop alternate energy sources." He proposed creation of an international Energy Action Group to ensure supplies at reasonable cost through technology research, conservation, and production incentives. The European response was cautiously positive to the idea of institutionalizing international cooperation among consumers, if not to the specific structure proposed by Kissinger.[59]

The result of the long negotiations that followed was the creation, in November 1974, of the International Energy Agency (IEA). The charter members were Austria, Belgium, Canada, Denmark, West Germany, Ireland, Italy, Japan, Luxemburg, the Netherlands, Spain,

Sweden, Switzerland, Turkey, the United Kingdom, and the United States. It now has twenty-eight members, including all the major industrial powers except China, which has applied to join, and Russia. Each member country is required to maintain a petroleum reserve equivalent to at least ninety days of imports.

The group assigned itself these tasks:

(i) Development of a common level of emergency self-sufficiency in oil supplies;

(ii) Establishment of common demand restraint measures in an emergency;

(iii) Establishment and implementation of measures for the allocation of available oil in time of emergency;

(iv) Development of a system of information on the international oil market and a framework for consultation with international oil companies;

(v) Development and implementation of a long-term co-operation programme to reduce dependence on imported oil, including: conservation of energy, development of alternative sources of energy, energy research and development, and supply of natural and enriched uranium;

(vi) Promotion of co-operative relations with oil-producing countries and with other oil consuming countries, particularly those of the developing world.[60]

This represents the energy equivalent of a mutual defense treaty, each signatory pledging to help the others in a crisis. At the time, members of Kissinger's staff cautioned that any such multinational effort should be packaged in such a way that the producer nations would not see it as a consumer cabal directed against them, which, as Kissinger said, is what it really was.

"We have said it a hundred times [that it was not targeted at producer countries] and it's bullshit," he said. "Excuse me for using that language. It is of course designed to create a united front. That's the only purpose of a consumer meeting. . . . The purpose is to create a consumer group that improves the bargaining position of the consumers." If the consumer states could not organize themselves, "then we really are in the condition of Greek cities facing Macedonia or Rome."[61]

The most tangible accomplishment of this agency has been the ninety-day reserve rule. Each country has sought to meet this requirement in its own way; in the United States, Congress created a Strategic Petroleum Reserve, operated by the Department of Energy, which was itself created in the aftermath of the embargo. The Reserve consists of about seven hundred million barrels of crude oil owned by the federal government and stored in salt caverns around the Gulf of Mexico coast, mostly in Louisiana. That is more like a sixty-day supply than ninety, but Congress cut off funding for additional purchases during the recession that began in 2007, and now there is little incentive to provide additional money as domestic production surges. During 2014, as the price of crude oil dropped from more than one hundred dollars to below sixty dollars a barrel, a few voices called for seizing the opportunity to fill the Reserve at a discount, but Congress did nothing.

Another achievement of the IEA is international transparency about supply and consumption. During the embargo, consumer panic was exacerbated by a lack of information about how much oil was actually available and where it was, because the oil companies considered the data proprietary. Prominent politicians suggested that the oil companies were taking advantage of the embargo and holding loaded tankers at sea to boost prices and profits. The cover headline of *Time* on January 21, 1974, was, "Energy Crunch: Real or Phony?"

Now under IEA rules, member countries are required to obtain such information and share it with the others. In the United States, the government agency charged with collecting and distributing up-to-date, accurate information about all forms of energy and fuel is the Energy Information Administration, created by Congress in the Department of Energy Organization Act of 1977. The EIA is perhaps the least politicized agency in Washington; the accuracy of its data is rarely challenged.

The Drive for Fuel Efficiency

At the time of the embargo, there were hundreds of millions of people in the world—Chinese peasants, African herdsmen, remote tribes in the Amazon—who never used any petroleum products and were affected only on the rare occasions when they purchased manufactured goods at the new, inflated prices caused by the higher cost of oil. For everyone else, the embargo and the price surge ignited far-reaching and permanent shifts in behavior and in consumption patterns.

Motor vehicles were reengineered to make them lighter and more fuel efficient. Congress in 1975 created what are known as CAFE standards, for Corporate Average Fuel Economy, empowering the Environmental Protection Agency to mandate greater fuel efficiency in vehicle fleets and to levy a "gas guzzler" tax on cars that do not meet the requirements. The European Union has set similar targets.

So effective have the CAFE standards been that by 2015 the Federal Highway Trust Fund, supported by a tax on gasoline set at a flat rate per gallon instead of a percentage of the price, was running out of money. The tax rate stayed the same for years but gasoline use declined so much that the fund could no longer meet highway construction and maintenance needs.

Meanwhile, industries worldwide retooled their factories so they were more energy efficient and could switch from one fuel to another as needed. In the United States, the amount of energy consumed per dollar of factory output declined by about 50 percent from the early 1970s to 1985.[62] In 1973, oil accounted for 48 percent of all energy consumed worldwide. By 2013 that figure was about 34 percent.[63]

In the United States today, oil is almost entirely a transportation fuel; very little is burned to generate electricity, except in Hawaii. That was true before the oil revolution, but much less so: at that time oil was used to create nearly 17 percent of all electricity generated in the United States.[64] The vulnerability of the fossil fuel supply demonstrated by the embargo sparked a quest for other sources of energy across the board.

One sign of this trend was a surge in orders for the construction of nuclear power plants. Another was the creation by Congress, in 1980, of the Synthetic Fuels Corporation, or SYNFUELS, a federal program to subsidize the development of liquid energy sources other than oil. This independent organization was authorized to spend up to $88 billion on its mandated goal, the production of at least five hundred thousand barrels of crude oil equivalent per day of synthetic fuels from domestic sources by 1987 and at least two million barrels per day by 1992. For reasons of domestic politics, including President Reagan's aversion to government participation in business, and economic reality—an unexpected decline in oil prices in the mid-1980s undercut the rationale for subsidizing expensive alternatives—only $960 million was spent and only four projects built, but some of the technologies that were developed in those projects are now in common use.[65]

One of the most durable effects of the oil crisis was harder to quantify: a transformation of consumer attitudes, especially in the United States. This was the land of the big car and the open road, a country where the cramped, transit-dependent cities of the Northeast seemed obsolete as Americans flocked to Houston and Phoenix and Los Angeles, sprawling urban agglomerations built on the automobile, where school systems operated fleets of buses and parking was a more urgent concern than air quality. Suddenly, all those attitudes, and the assumption of cheap gasoline on which they were built, were called into question. Just as the October War itself had transformed the psychological balance in the Middle East, the oil crisis transformed consumer thinking in the West. As President Ford said in an address to the nation five months after he succeeded Nixon, Americans were astonished to find that they were "no longer in control of their own national destiny when that destiny depends on uncertain foreign fuels at high prices fixed by others."[66]

Muscle cars and big chrome bumpers were history. In just five years, from 1978 to 1983, annual petroleum use per capita in the United States dropped 23 percent from a peak of thirty-one barrels; total petroleum consumption declined by 19 percent, even though the population grew.[67] The oil price surge impelled oil companies to search for new supplies in new countries, and at the same time, it impelled users of petroleum to restrain their use. The result has been a world oil market more or less in balance since the late 1980s, at prices high enough to encourage production and investment and yet low enough to enable consumers to keep buying. When the war known as Operation Desert Storm took Iraq and Kuwait completely out of the export market in 1991, there was no consumer panic comparable to that during the embargo because the market was transparent, strategic reserves were in place, and new resources far from the zone of conflict were coming on line.

Lessons for the Oil Producers

The oil producers learned lessons, too. They learned, as the oil experts Joseph Stanislaw and Daniel Yergin wrote in a twentieth-anniversary essay, that "they needed the importers as much as the importers needed them."[68] They watched in alarm as consumers switched to other fuels, industries shifted to natural gas, motor vehicles grew lighter and more efficient, and governments encouraged the development of alternatives to oil. They saw countries that were not members of OPEC developing new oil fields in remote regions where oil had previously been too expensive to extract; in effect, the producers who drove prices up so sharply in the 1970s stimulated competitors to themselves, resulting in additional production that soon began to send prices back down.

In a prescient memorandum to Kissinger on June 5, 1974, Harold H. Saunders and Charles Cooper, senior members of the White House staff, said, "Over time, the Saudis stand to lose if prices are kept too high. The Saudis must consider how much oil in the ground will be worth in coming decades, and it won't be worth very much if high short-run prices lead to production and consumption adjustments in the U.S. and other industrial countries which greatly diminish the future market for Saudi oil. Because of their vast oil reserves, they are more vulnerable to a loss of their market in the 1980s and 1990s than to overly rapid dissipation of their reserves." They were correct, as the Saudis soon realized. The cornerstone of Saudi pricing policy for two decades now has been to seek a balance between the kingdom's revenue needs and the ability or willingness of consumers to keep buying oil, which is the source of about 90 percent of the kingdom's national income. The Saudis are not worried about running out of oil, at least for the next several decades; they are worried about running out of customers if prices rise beyond what the market will bear. The SYNFUELS Corporation is remembered with ridicule in the United States, if it is remembered at all, but the Saudis regard it as a potential threat to them that they do not wish to see exhumed. When world oil prices, now set by the market, dropped sharply in the autumn of 2014, the Saudis were untroubled. They could afford the decline in revenue, and they believed that the price decline would discourage others from investing in new technologies that might undercut long-term demand for crude.

The push by consumers, manufacturers, and governments in the oil-consuming countries to reduce consumption and develop alternate fuels such as ethanol and biodiesel taught the Saudis and other oil-producing states—including Russia—lasting lessons: Do not push prices so high that consumers stop buying. Invest in refineries and filling stations in consuming countries to lock in market share. And get out in front of the development of other energy sources so that when the inevitable switch does come, we, the oil exporters, will not be left in the dark.

The need to maintain market share, to keep the oil exports flowing in the face of competition from other fuels and other energy companies, is the reason big producers have sought captive markets. It is why motorists in Italy can purchase gasoline at a chain of filling stations known as Q8–that is, Kuwait—and Americans call fill up at Lukoil, a Russian-owned brand. It is the reason Venezuela owns Citgo. It is the reason why Saudi Arabia, in partnership with Royal Dutch Shell, owns gasoline stations all across the southern United States, and why Saudi Arabia has financed the construction of refineries in China, where oil demand is growing. And it is why Saudi Arabia is investing heavily in solar energy technology.

"There is nothing wrong with diversifying energy sources and developing renewable sources," the longtime Saudi oil minister Ali al-Naimi told an American audience in 2010. "Even we in Saudi Arabia, despite our large hydrocarbon resources, are embarking on developing our own renewable potential through solar energy. Our concern, however, is about these changing policies and their unpredictable nature, as well as the risk in setting strict timetables and targets to develop sources that are still in their infancy or face too many sustainability obstacles, which might divert needed resources from the already viable ones," namely oil. He was telling consuming countries—whom the Saudis refer to as their "partners" in maintaining a balance between price and demand—not to be stampeded by concerns about climate change into making premature commitments to alternative energy sources. There is plenty of oil still to be found, he said, and for your own good you should keep investing in that even as you attempt to diversify.[69]

The exporting countries briefly seized control of the world oil market in the early 1970s, but they are not in full control today—no one is. New exporters such as Vietnam and Sudan entered the market, competing for customers, and even the radicals in opec stopped demanding ever-higher prices because they saw that doing so only encouraged this trend. The days of price controls and import restrictions are long gone; oil is now traded on open exchanges in London and New York, where "Wall Street refiners" bid prices up or down, sometimes without regard to actual supply-and-demand conditions. opec producers can influence prices by raising or lowering their production ceiling, but not to the extent that they did in the unprepared markets of the 1970s. The rising cost of finding and producing oil has forced countries that nationalized their industries, such as Iraq and Mexico, to reopen their fields to foreign investment, but the terms of those investments are negotiated, not dictated by international oil companies

None of that entered Sadat's mind as Egypt went to war in 1973, and there is not much evidence that King Faisal understood the potential long-term implications of his decision to take part in the embargo. Their objective was to persuade the United States to put pressure on Israel to withdraw from the occupied territories. It is one of the ironies of modern Middle East history that the oil embargo had many far-reaching outcomes, but not the one its architects sought. East Jerusalem, the Golan Heights of Syria, and the West Bank remain under Israeli control.

4 Stranger in a Strange Land

The road from war to peace was treacherous and bumpy. Navigating it was all the more difficult because the travelers were not headed for the same destination. By the end of 1974, it was clear that Egypt and Israel wanted peace, but they had divergent definitions of it; Syria wanted to follow a different route altogether. Sadat believed that the war would make the Israelis more receptive to a negotiated settlement, but he was wrong. Frightened, angry, and suspicious, they were more inclined to hunker down.

Sadat sought an agreement that would restore all of Sinai to Egypt and end Israeli rule over the Palestinians of the West Bank, Gaza, and East Jerusalem. He also declared that whatever Palestinian entity emerged after Israel pulled out of the West Bank would have to be linked administratively to Jordan, a position that the other Arabs collectively rejected. The Arab League summit resolution of October 1974 that declared the Palestine Liberation Organization to be the "sole legitimate representative" of the Palestinians effectively stripped Jordan of its responsibility for the West Bank. Egypt had voted for that resolution; now it undercut Sadat's negotiating strategy.

Israel sought acceptance of its legitimacy and of its permanent place on the map of the Middle East, but it also wanted arrangements on the ground that would ensure its security—against a possible recidivist Egypt under some successor to Sadat, and against its other Arab neighbors, who remained hostile.

Syria was nominally willing to make peace, but only on terms acceptable to all Arab states, which Israel would have to accept in advance. In reality, there were no such terms, because some Arab regimes refused to recognize or legitimize Israel in any way, and none would accept continued Israeli control of Arab East Jerusalem, so Syria never became an active participant in negotiations.

For Israel, it was true then as it is today that any peace agreement would require it to trade the tangible—land on which it could place settlers and troops—for the intangible, namely peace and recognition. The October War had achieved the "psychological breakthrough" that Sadat sought in the sense that it shattered Israel's feeling of unquestionable military superiority, but the corollary was that it also increased Israel's suspicion and mistrust of the Arabs. Yes, Sadat said he wanted peace, but in Israel's view an all-out military attack had been a strange way to demonstrate peaceful intentions.

Caught in the middle was the United States, which by the mid-1970s was the only outside power that mattered. Nominally, the Soviet Union was still in the game as cosponsor of the Geneva Conference that was supposed to be the forum for negotiations, but only the Americans had influence over Israel and the trust of Anwar Sadat. Arabs and Israelis agreed that the superpowers would have to shepherd whatever negotiations might be conducted, but the United States and the Soviet Union held conflicting views about how to proceed.

Before the October War, and for some time after it, the United States, the Soviet Union, Israel, Egypt, Syria, and some of the other Arab countries were nominally committed to collective negotiations for a region-wide settlement of the entire Arab-Israel conflict, to be conducted in Geneva under the auspices of the United Nations. In December 1973, about six weeks after the war, UN Secretary-General Kurt Waldheim actually convened such a gathering. Predictably, it was a fiasco. The following terse account is from the Israelis, but it is not disputed by the other parties:

> The Geneva Conference was held in December 1973. It was a multinational forum headed by the United States and the Soviet Union, and sponsored by the United Nations, as an attempted summit for

peace in the Middle East. The conference was convened on the basis of the United Nations Security Council's Resolution 338, which called for "negotiations (to) start between the parties concerned under appropriate auspices aimed at establishing a just and durable peace in the Middle East." Egypt and Jordan set conditions for their participation, asking for the participation of other countries as mediators so that they would not have to converse directly with Israel. Their participation was regarded in official terms as the sole means to achieve Israel's withdrawal from the territories occupied during the Six Day War.

Israel refused to negotiate with the Syrians before they made public the list of Israeli soldiers taken as prisoners during the Yom Kippur War, and allowed the Red Cross to visit them. Syria refused to participate in the conference altogether.

The Arab countries participating had asked that France and Britain take part in the conference, but Israel and the superpowers refused. A Palestinian representation was not admitted to the opening session, but there were intentions to integrate them into later talks.

The opening session of the conference was held on December 1st 1973. The conference was headed by Secretary General of the United Nations Kurt Waldheim together with the Foreign Ministers of both superpowers. The delegations sat at separate tables, due to the Jordanian and Egyptian demand not to share one with the Israeli delegation, and a vacant table was left for the missing Syrian delegation. Opening speeches were given by representatives of the United Nations, the United States, the Soviet Union, Israel, Egypt, and Jordan and were held in the presence of the media.

Further meetings of the conference were postponed to allow Israel to carry out proper elections procedures for the Eighth Knesset (held on December 31st). An Egyptian-Israeli military committee began meeting in Geneva on December 26th to discuss the Separation of Forces Agreement. The continued negotiations were later mediated by American Secretary of State Henry Kissinger.

The Geneva Conference was not resumed after December 1973,

despite the urging of Arab and European countries that felt that it was the proper framework to achieve peace in the Middle East.[1]

Given the positions of the intended participants, Geneva was never going to be a workable forum for achieving peace, but the reconvening of such a gathering remained the stated objective of the United States, the Soviet Union, and the parties in the region. Fruitless haggling over how such a conference might be structured and who should participate would consume hundreds of hours of diplomats' time in the ensuing three years.

Sadat grew increasingly frustrated as peace failed to materialize. He was naïve in believing that because of the October War the Israelis would suddenly see some light that they had missed previously and walk out of the Sinai Peninsula because it was the right thing to do. Sadat was by nature not much interested in details. He never fully grasped the fact that for Israel, a detail here or there could be a life-or-death issue. There had been an Egypt for as long as there had been recorded history; Egypt's existence was not in question. Israel had a different perspective.

After the Geneva Fiasco

The embarrassing failure at Geneva did not put an end to Henry Kissinger's efforts to broker a peace agreement—it simply refocused them onto ad hoc, limited, and bilateral agreements, rather than on a comprehensive settlement. Even though the stated U.S. objective was to get everyone back to Geneva, Kissinger understood that a comprehensive settlement was out of reach, so he adopted the incremental approach that he had always preferred anyway.

His famous "shuttle diplomacy" produced limited "disengagement agreements" between Israel and Egypt, and between Israel and Syria. The Syria agreement, signed on May 31, 1974, specified the lines separating the rival armies on the Golan Heights and delegated a United Nations observer force to police them. Syrian civilians who had lived in the area were allowed to return. The text specified that "[t]his agreement is not a peace agreement. It is a step toward a just and durable peace on the basis of Security Council Resolution 338, dated October 22, 1973."[2] That was the cease-fire resolution cited in the Israeli account of the Geneva meeting, the resolution that had provoked the nuclear face-off between the United States and the Soviet Union in the last hours of the October War. In addition to ordering a cease-fire, 338 called on the warring countries to begin immediate negotiations to "implement Security Council Resolution 242 (1967) in all of its parts."[3] Resolution 242, which even today provides the theoretical framework upon which negotiations between Israel and the Arabs would be based, stipulated the "inadmissibility of the acquisition of territory by war" and recognized "the sovereignty, territorial integrity and political independence of every State in the area and their right to live in peace within secure and recognized boundaries free from threats or acts of force." It also called for "withdrawal of Israeli armed forces from territories occupied in the recent conflict."[4] Those territories were the Sinai Peninsula, which belonged to Egypt; the Gaza strip, which had been under Egyptian control but which Egypt did not claim; Syria's Golan Heights; and East Jerusalem and the West Bank, which from 1948 to 1967 had been part of Jordan.

Resolution 242 was the foundation of all the "land for peace" negotiations that would follow, but it was a shaky foundation because of the way it was worded. It specified that Israel must withdraw from "territories," but it did not say "all territories" or even "the territories." It did not specify any of them by name, and Israel argued that it did not necessarily apply to all of them, or to any of them in its entirety. To the Israelis, 242 would never apply to East Jerusalem, which included the Old City and holy sites of Judaism, Christianity, and Islam. Israel annexed East Jerusalem after capturing it in 1967 and declared it the eternal capital of the Jewish state, a decision that has never been recognized by the Arabs or by most other countries, including the United States, which even now maintains its embassy in Tel Aviv.

A Google search in 2014 for "meaning of resolution 242" produced 28,700 results, including many argumentative essays over the significance of the missing definite article or the lack of the word

"all" before the word "territories" or whether the use of "des terri-
toires occupés" in the UN's French text did mean all territories, not
just some. Israel's position has always been that because Resolution
242 did not specify "all territories" it therefore did not require withdrawal from "all territories." The Arab position, naturally, was that
if "acquisition of territory by war" is impermissible, as the resolution
states, then the resolution obviously meant "all territories." Israel's
response to that argument was that Jerusalem and the West Bank,
the lands it called "Judea and Samaria," were not conquered territory acquired by force—they were historically Jewish lands that had
reverted to their rightful owners. Kissinger is said to have called the
wording of 242 an example of "constructive ambiguity," defined in
the Palgrave Macmillan Dictionary of Diplomacy as "the deliberate
use of ambiguous language on a sensitive issue in order to advance
some political purpose."

The first disengagement agreement between Israel and Egypt was
a straightforward arrangement requiring Israel to pull back its forces
that had crossed to the west side of the Suez Canal during the war. A
second agreement, known as Sinai II, signed on September 4, 1975,
went much further. It created a buffer zone between Israeli and Egyptian forces in the Sinai, to be enforced by the United Nations; set limits on the number of troops either could maintain in the area; and
restored Egyptian access to oil fields at Abu Rudeis. (Israel had been
using the Abu Rudeis oil itself since 1967, and a guaranteed replacement for that supply later became a sticking point in peace treaty
negotiations.) Egypt and Israel agreed in Sinai II that "the conflict
between them and in the Middle East shall not be resolved by military force but by peaceful means." The agreement said it was "a significant step" toward a peace agreement to be negotiated on the basis
of Resolution 338. In a preview of hard-line Arab responses to all of
Sadat's peace initiatives to come, Libyan officials and state-controlled
news media referred to Sinai II as "the Egyptian capitulatory agreement with the racist Zionist enemy." Iraq and Syria issued similar
vituperative assessments.

The three disengagement agreements, one between Israel and Syria, two between Israel and Egypt, stabilized the situation on the ground, but then the machinery of diplomacy more or less came to a halt by the end of 1975, much to Sadat's chagrin. The United States was less active in diplomacy because 1976 was a presidential election year. For Americans, the most pressing issue in the Middle East was the price of oil. At the same time, the Arabs other than Egypt were preoccupied with the civil war in Lebanon. Fitful efforts to undertake Arab-Israeli peace negotiations bogged down in fundamental disagreements over how to proceed. Officially, the goal was still to get all the interested parties to Geneva. That being the case, Syria and the Palestinians would have to participate in the negotiations. Who would represent the Palestinians if not the PLO?

President Assad of Syria and PLO chairman Yasser Arafat were suspicious—with good reason—that Sadat would work out a separate, bilateral peace that would leave them stranded. They sought to protect themselves against that eventuality by insisting upon a single, unified Arab delegation to the proposed Geneva talks, including official representatives of the PLO. The Soviet Union supported them on that point. Israel refused to accept those terms because it would not negotiate with the PLO or any known members of it. And the United States had promised Israel at the time of Sinai II that it would "not recognize or negotiate with the Palestine Liberation Organization so long as the Palestine Liberation Organization does not recognize Israel's right to exist and does not accept United Nations Security Council Resolutions 242 and 338."[5]

The Arabs offered a compromise in which Palestinians who were not prominent members of the PLO but were authorized to speak for it would be its representatives, an innovative idea Israel eventually accepted. "We will not look at their credentials," Moshe Dayan, who became foreign minister in 1977, told President Jimmy Carter, who was elected in 1976 and took office in January 1977.[6] A larger problem was that Sadat rejected the idea of a single delegation; he understood that if all the Arabs negotiated as a team, nothing would ever happen because each Arab party would have effective veto power. On that, at least, the Israelis agreed with Sadat. "A multilateral negotiation is a recipe for failure," Prime Minister Yitzhak Rabin told Carter when they met in March 1977.[7]

William B. Quandt, a member of the American negotiating team throughout this period who wrote a detailed narrative of it, said that Geneva "was to be the umbrella under which Sadat and [the Israelis] could move forward at whatever pace they could sustain, pulling in their wake, if possible, Jordan, the Palestinians, and perhaps even the Syrians. The problem was that the umbrella could not be raised until the most skeptical of the parties, the Syrians and the Palestinians, were satisfied. Insofar as they thought Geneva would be little more than a figleaf for another separate Egyptian-Israeli agreement—a Sinai III—they had little reason to go along. Yet if their demands for a virtual veto over Egyptian moves were accepted, no progress could be made in negotiations."[8]

The Soviets wanted one conference that would produce a comprehensive regional resolution; the American strategy was to negotiate one issue at a time, one country at a time, because it was impossible to obtain agreement all at once on such thorny issues as borders, the return of Palestinian refugees, the status of Jerusalem, and security guarantees for Israel. "If we lump all these things together, and if our ability to produce gets linked to a big, sweeping program, we are licked," Kissinger said.[9] After Kissinger departed the scene with the end of Gerald Ford's presidency, Carter and his secretary of state, Cyrus R. Vance, came to share his opinion about negotiations. They suggested that after an initial pro forma meeting of all delegations, country-by-country working groups could negotiate separately. The Israelis accepted that proposition; they agreed that there was no reason the Palestinians should be involved in negotiations about the Golan Heights, for example, or the Syrians about Gaza. But when it came to the West Bank, Israel's position was that it had seized that land from Jordan and therefore it would negotiate only with Jordan over its future. The Arabs had rejected that position at their Rabat summit.

Another obstacle was the insistence of the Soviet Union on participating in all negotiations.

A State Department "briefing paper" prepared for Kissinger in advance of an April 1974 meeting with Foreign Minister Gromyko said the Soviet position was that "[t]he Soviet Union is co-chairman of the peace process, including disengagement negotiations," while the U.S. position was that "a direct Soviet role at present would bring out the worst of Israeli suspicions and Syrian truculence." But the United States could not simply exclude Moscow from the process: détente was still an important consideration. The United States needed Moscow's help in yet another way: restraining Palestinian guerrillas, known as *fedayeen*, from staging terrorist attacks on Israel.

Another issue that defied agreement was the definition of "secure and recognized boundaries," as called for in Resolution 242. The Israelis said that they would need to adjust the boundaries that had existed before the 1967 war, to maintain troops in the Jordan Valley and security outposts in the Sinai, and to impose restrictions on Arab armaments. The Arabs said that in the era of missiles, the entire concept of secure borders was "nothing but a fantasy," as Sadat put it, a pretext for holding on to Arab lands that Israel was required by 242 to give up. Carter had suggested the possibility of border adjustments, but Sadat and other Arabs said the only way for Israel to guarantee its security was to make peace with its neighbors. The "secure borders" argument, Sadat said, had been "blown away by the wind" when the most secure borders Israel could have had, the Suez Canal and the Bar-Lev Line, were breached in a few hours in the October War.[10]

This diplomatic miasma hovered over the region for many months while Sadat, who was impatient and was beginning to fear that the perceived triumph of the October War would go unrewarded, chafed over the haggling. In going to war, he had had the initiative; now in seeking peace, he was dependent on the cooperation of others who were not necessarily on the same frequency. Then events in 1977 changed the situation in unexpected and dramatic ways. As has often been the case in the modern Middle East, unforeseen developments overpowered plans and strategies and forced leaders to make adjustments on the fly.

The Dramas of 1977

The inauguration of Jimmy Carter as president in January 1977 put an end to the Kissinger era of Middle East diplomacy. Carter's secretary of state, Cyrus Vance, was a much more cautious and conventional diplomatic thinker than Kissinger. Carter's national security adviser, Zbigniew Brzezinski, was steeped in European affairs and the Cold War struggle, but was less knowledgeable about the Middle East. All three faced a steep learning curve.

As Carter was taking the oath of office, massive riots were raging in Cairo and other Egyptian cities over a decision by Sadat's government, under pressure from the International Monetary Fund, to raise prices of basic commodities and services. Essentials such as sugar and cooking oil had long been subsidized by the state, but the subsidies were bankrupting Egypt; in order to secure a financing package from the IMF, the government was required to reduce some of them. Sadat and his cabinet failed to alert the impoverished citizenry that the price increases were coming or to conduct a political effort in advance to secure popular acquiescence. The result was that Egypt's urban masses awoke one morning to learn from the newspapers that the prices of life's necessities, including bus fares, had soared overnight.

Their esteem for the Hero of the Crossing did not survive this clumsy effort to reduce the country's budget deficit at their expense. They took to the streets for three days of destructive riots in which at least forty-two people died. The government rescinded the price increases, but that left the country's economic crisis unresolved. To Sadat, the riots, which he called "the uprising of the thieves," made it all the more urgent to extricate Egypt from war and focus on economic development.

When Vance went to Egypt the following month, his Egyptian counterpart, Foreign Minister Ismail Fahmy, told him specifically that economic conditions were forcing Egypt's hand. "Egypt does not wish to spend money on arms; it has problems of obtaining enough food and a population explosion that will result in 70–75 million in the year 2000," he said. (The population at the time was about 40 million.) "This is why Egypt wants peace, not at any price, but a just peace and it is ready to take the necessary measures."[11]

Later that evening, when Vance met the Egyptian president, Sadat told him that the time had come for the United States to lead an all-out effort to settle the Arab-Israeli conflict once and for all. "For more than 25 years," he said, "the Arabs and Israelis had no confidence in each other and needed someone to come between them in whom both could have confidence. They both now have full confidence in the U.S. and in President Carter. All was now ready for the process to continue," and Geneva was the appropriate forum. Only the United States, he said, could make it happen: "Without the help of the U.S. for agreement on the broad outlines of a settlement, there would be no positive results in Geneva and it would have no point. The Soviets would simply auctioneer and play the most extremist role."[12]

President Carter said from the beginning of his term that he was committed to achieving regional peace and would work as hard as necessary, but neither he nor Sadat fully grasped, at that early moment of Carter's involvement, how difficult it would be to achieve that goal.

On March 16, Carter—in office less than two months and still a neophyte in Middle East affairs—waded into the subject at a "Town Meeting," in Clinton, Massachusetts. Regional peace, he said, would have to include three elements. First was recognition by Israel's Arab neighbors of its right to exist and to live in peace, with borders open to trade and tourism. The second, which he said was "very, very important and very, very difficult," was the "establishment of permanent borders for Israel." This was a reference to the fact that because Israel's neighbors never recognized its existence and the territories captured in 1967 were in dispute, Israel's boundaries and borders had never been legally established. "And the third ultimate requirement for peace," Carter said, "is to deal with the Palestinian problem. . . . There has to be a homeland for the Palestinian refugees who have suffered for many, many years."[13]

In diplomatic terms, this was a bombshell. For years Israel had refused to acknowledge the existence of any "Palestinian problem," insisting that the people of the West Bank had been citizens of Jordan before 1967, the land had been captured from Jordan, and therefore the territory's future could be negotiated only with Jordan. Out of the blue, the president of the United States had not only recognized that there was a "Palestinian problem" but committed himself to dealing with it. The Arabs were electrified by this diplomatic bonanza. The Israelis were dismayed. And Carter's own advisers, who had not been alerted to what the president would say, were taken aback.

Bill Quandt surmised that Carter "deliberately ventured into public diplomacy in the hope of shaking things up and accelerating the negotiating process. As a newcomer to international politics, he was impatient with fine diplomatic distinctions, with the taboos surrounding certain 'buzzwords,' and with the unimaginative and repetitive nature of many of the discussions of the topic. As a politician, he also seemed to recognize that his power to influence events would be greatest in his first year. Thus, in a pattern typical of a new incumbent of the Oval Office, he was impatient to get on with the task."[14]

A few weeks later, Yitzhak Rabin resigned as Israeli prime minister, and elections were set for May 17, 1977. American analysts and pretty much everyone else outside Israel expected that the Labor Alliance, the party of Rabin, Golda Meir, and all their predecessors, would win enough seats in the Knesset to retain the premiership, and that Shimon Peres would emerge as prime minister. Instead, Labor was ousted by the Likud Alliance, headed by Menachem Begin, who became prime minister. This was a political and strategic upheaval that transformed the negotiating landscape.

Begin was a small, gnomish man with thick eyeglasses whose appearance gave no hint of his background. He was a dedicated Zionist who believed in "Eretz Israel," an expanded "greater Israel," and was prepared to fight for it, literally. He had been a fighter since his youth in Poland, where he had joined the Free Polish Army against the occupying Germans during World War II. After the war, in British-ruled Palestine, he joined the underground army known as Irgun Tzva'i Le'umi, a radical organization that split with the mainstream Zionists headed by David Ben-Gurion to engage in guerrilla warfare against the British authorities, including a bomb attack on British headquarters in Jerusalem's King David Hotel. After Israel became an independent country in 1948, Begin served for many years in the Knesset, or Parliament, where he led the opposition to the ruling Labor Party.[15]

The Israeli historian Avi Schlaim wrote that Begin, who lost his parents and a brother in the Holocaust, "saw the world as a profoundly antisemitic, extremely hostile, and highly dangerous environment. He perceived Arab hostility as an extension of the antisemitism that had resulted in the annihilation of European Jewry. Throughout his political career Begin had demonstrated hostility toward the Arabs." According to Schlaim, Begin reached into the ranks of the Labor Party to select Moshe Dayan as foreign minister because Labor was perceived as taking less of a hard line and Begin was trying to soften the image he knew the outside world had of him, as "an extremist, a fanatic, and a warmonger."[16] In peace negotiations, however, Dayan— his reputation permanently tarnished by the October War—turned out to be nearly as implacable as his boss, if less pugnacious.

Begin exhibited a more formal public personality than had his predecessors, and a greater appreciation for ceremony; he wore suits and ties, abandoning the open-collar tradition of Israeli political life. He was polite, courteous, and gracious to visitors; Brzezinski found him to be "a very engaging and attractive person." But he was also a fierce and tenacious negotiator who took offense at any perceived slight to himself, to Israel, or to Jews. After reading one letter Begin sent him, Samuel Lewis, Carter's ambassador to Israel, described it as "vintage Begin: argumentative, sanctimonious, insensitive, and plaintive—in short, Begin at his worst."[17]

Trained as a lawyer, Begin was a bulldog about details, unlike Sadat, who was bored by them. This trait would give Begin a major advantage in their peace negotiations. Sadat's advisers pleaded that all documents and agreements be shown to them before he signed because they feared, with good reason, that his inattention to detail would prove costly.

Begin rose to power as head of Herut, a small right-wing party that was one of five opposition groups that united as Likud to challenge Labor's longstanding supremacy. Likud's platform in the 1977 election campaign said it would "place its aspirations for peace at the top of its priorities," attend the Geneva Conference, and invite Israel's neighbors to join in direct negotiations. (For the Israelis, face-to-face negotiations with the Arabs were an end in themselves, because they would imply recognition of the Jewish state and acknowledge its legitimacy.) But despite its declaration of peaceful intent, the platform also said that under a Likud government, Israel would keep the West Bank, which Begin always referred to as "Judea and Samaria": "(a) The right of the Jewish people to the land of Israel is eternal and indisputable and is linked with the right to security and peace; therefore, Judea and Samaria will not be handed to any foreign administration; between the Sea and the Jordan [River] there will be only Israeli sovereignty; (b) A plan which relinquishes parts of western Eretz Israel undermines our right to the country, unavoidably leads to the establishment of a 'Palestinian State,' jeopardizes the security of the Jewish population, endangers the existence of the State of Israel, and frustrates any prospect of peace."

That is to say, Begin and his government did not subscribe to the "land for peace" formula that underlay Resolution 242: Sinai might be negotiable, but for reasons of security, ideology, and religion, the West Bank would and should be part of Israel. Begin's predecessor, Rabin, had told Vance in February that once peace had been achieved, Israel would be "ready for territorial compromise in all sectors." Begin and Likud offered no such promise. Indeed, the Likud platform asserted the right and the duty to establish Jewish settlements in "all parts of the land of Israel" and said it would call upon Israel's people, and upon Jews in the diaspora, to "take on the task of inhabiting and cultivating the wasteland, while taking care not to dispossess anyone."[18] The use of the word "wasteland" displayed Begin's contempt for the Arabs, whose olive and citrus groves and peaceful communities of white stone houses hardly fit the term "wasteland."

The Likud platform said nothing about the Sinai Peninsula, which was indisputably part of Egypt. This omission signaled that Begin was willing to give it up because Israel had no historic or biblical claim to it, while maintaining Israel's presence in the other occupied lands.

In the end that was the formula he managed to extract from Sadat in the peace treaty of 1979. Egypt reclaimed all its lost land, but the West Bank remained under de facto Israeli rule, just as it is today under another Likud prime minister, Benjamin Netanyahu.

On July 19, 1977, Begin traveled to Washington for his first meetings with President Carter. At the White House he began, as he often did, with a history lesson: a long discourse about the history of Arab hostility to, and attacks on, Jews in the Holy Land, attacks that as he correctly noted long predated the occupation of Arab territory in 1967. Whatever else came of peace negotiations, Begin said, Israel would never return to the de facto borders as they existed before the 1967 war because to do so would put Israel in mortal danger.

"There was a time in our history when men could not defend their women and children and we will never let this happen again," he said. "And that would be the situation if we went back to the 1967 lines. The maximum width of our country would only be twenty miles. We would lose the chance for peace because the Arabs would look at the map and would conclude that they could push us to the sea. Please excuse my emotions. Our concept of national security is not based on aggrandizement or expansion. But our fathers and mothers got killed only because they were Jews and we do not want this for our children."[19] He was referring to the fact that before 1967, large parts of Israel were within easy range of Arab artillery, and the main road from Jerusalem to Tel Aviv and the Mediterranean coast skirted Arab-held territory.

"It should have been obvious to Carter and his colleagues," Bill Quandt observed, "that Begin was absolutely serious about his commitment to retaining control over Judea and Samaria, as he always insisted on calling them." Carter and his advisers "took longer to realize that Begin was also a superb politician, carefully calculating his moves, with a masterly sense of timing and a remarkable capacity for brinkmanship. They took even longer to recognize that Begin's views on Judea and Samaria were rock hard, not subject to the normal bargaining expected of most politicians."[20]

According to Quandt, Brzezinski did perceive that Begin was dug in, and suggested that the way to ease him toward greater flexibility was to persuade Sadat and other Arab leaders to meet him more than halfway by offering "a very forthcoming position on normalization."[21] This was a reference to the vast gap between the two sides on the timing and extent of diplomatic and economic relations. The Israeli position on "normalization" was that a peace agreement should be accompanied by the immediate establishment of diplomatic relations, an end to the Arab economic boycott of Israel, free trade, and open borders; Israel and its Arab neighbors would be like the countries of Western Europe. The Arab position was that such immediate arrangements would be politically impossible. The Arabs wanted to phase in normal relations over several years, as Israel withdrew in increments from the occupied territories.

Sadat Was Malleable

Brzezinski's proposal offered a hint of the pattern that would develop over the next two years. The Americans thought, correctly, that Sadat was malleable and Begin was not and thus it would be more productive to put pressure on the Egyptians. Carter and his team ran through many hours of angry conversation with the Israelis—at one point, Dayan said of Carter, "those on my side of the table saw cold hostility in his blue eyes."[22] But the Americans also understood that Sadat needed peace more than Begin needed it and therefore could more easily be persuaded to move.

Sadat perceived this American attitude and came to resent it. He complained that the United States "seems to consider him to be line of least resistance whenever Israelis take a hard stance."[23]

In his public statements, and in most of his official talks with the American team, Sadat insisted that he would never accept a bilateral peace agreement between Egypt and Israel that would restore the Sinai to Egypt while leaving Israel in place as the occupier of other Arab lands. But in reality the Americans put that possible outcome on the table even before the start of direct negotiations between Sadat and Begin. Secretary Vance reported to Carter that at a meeting with Sadat in early August 1977, "I then asked what he envisioned if the other parties, Syria, Jordan, et al., could not reach agreement. Was he prepared to make a separate peace with Israel? He replied emphatically, yes. He said he was prepared to meet separately with Begin and you and sign a peace 'treaty.'"[24] Sadat would never admit this in public; on the contrary, he insisted to the day of his death that the treaty Israel eventually signed—with Egypt and only Egypt—was not a separate peace.

The Israelis sensed the same vulnerability in Sadat's position that Vance had detected. A month after Vance's conversation with Sadat, Brzezinski told Carter that "the priority of Israel's policy now seems to be to make a fairly attractive offer to Egypt in order to tempt Sadat into a separate deal. This would allow Israel to put off movement on the Syrian front and to avoid the Palestinian–West Bank issues altogether."[25]

Vance's meeting with Sadat was part of an endless summer of fruitless disputes about how to proceed. These were negotiations about negotiating, arguments of stupefying legalistic tedium about who would participate, under what circumstances, and what the agenda would be. Would there be a single Arab delegation, or several? If single, would there then be "working groups" for specific country-by-country issues? What would Israel accept on the subject of Palestinian refugees? Who would speak for the Palestinians? Would Jordan participate? Would Syria? What would be the role of the Soviet Union? Should there be agreement beforehand on a "declaration of principles"? Would the specific language of Resolution 242 be the basic reference point, or would it be somehow modified? Would Geneva be the forum for the hard work of negotiating, or the site of a ceremonial event, at which agreements already reached would be signed? If Israel were somehow to agree to pull out of the West Bank, who should take over there now that Jordan had been stripped of its claim?

The United States, Israel, and the Palestinians haggled about PLO acceptance of 242 and whether that would be sufficient to gain the PLO a seat at Geneva. PLO leader Yasser Arafat told the Americans—through intermediaries, of course, since the United States would not talk to the PLO directly—that his public statements and PLO policies constituted de facto acceptance of 242, but he would not come right out and say it because factions within his own group were opposed to doing so. Landrum Bolling, a Quaker educator who served Carter as an unofficial emissary to Arafat that year, reported after long hours of conversation with the PLO leader in Beirut in September that "[p]art of Arafat's problem relates to the 'strange and wonderful' nature of the PLO itself. It is a holding company of divergent and irreconcilable revolutionary movements," including radical hard-liners who wanted no acceptance of Israel on any terms.[26]

Meanwhile, the Israelis continued to expand their settlements in the occupied territories, Syria and Israel both intervened in the Lebanese civil war, which distracted their attention, and Sadat grew increasingly disillusioned as he saw the prospects for the peace he needed slipping away.

On September 21, 1977, Carter and Vance met with Dayan in Washington. The president began the discussion by summarizing the issues before them as they tried to set the terms for Geneva. He rolled out the diplomatic equivalent of a Rube Goldberg machine:

> The question of how the parties should be represented in a unified or in separate delegations is complicated by Israel's preference for strict bilateral talks. Our hope is that we can find a solution to accommodate all parties. I have not yet talked to the Syrians or the Jordanians, but I hope that there could be a unified Arab delegation at Geneva, with Palestinian or PLO representatives in the delegation, only excluding visible PLO leaders like Arafat. Others would be OK. There would be opening sessions where we would commit ourselves, along with the Soviets, to stick with the negotiating process and to offer our mediating services. The other parties would make public statements. Then the negotiations would break up into separate groups, in accord with the desire of Egypt and Israel. There would be an Egyptian-Israeli negotiating team to reach a peace agreement or treaty, dealing with territory and the other issues. The same would be done between Syria and Israel on the Golan Heights. Then we would let the occupied territories

of the West Bank be dealt with in a Jordanian-Israeli group, with Palestinians in the Jordanian delegation. This group would deal with the status of the West Bank territories, including the possible arrangements for autonomy, a Jordanian relationship, or some division of the area. If Syria and Egypt were to insist on the right of approving any agreement reached between Jordan and Israel, that would be up to you.

There would remain the problem of the Palestinian refugees. Our hope is that if Israel and you can agree to accept negotiations on that issue, there would be a multinational group, including Palestinians and the PLO from various Arab countries. They would negotiate as a team to represent the refugees, to deal with the questions of compensation and return. This would not be part of the peace treaty negotiations, but would be separate and simultaneous. We don't object to having this done in Geneva, or in Cairo for that matter, but it would be an additional problem.

The Soviets, of course, are co-chairmen at Geneva, and we will have to work out with them anything that we agree to with you. I cannot accommodate the wishes of all the parties and I cannot assure the success of these negotiations, but it is my belief that this is the best approach.[27]

This was the president of the United States speaking, not some staff lawyer or State Department negotiator. The president was committing an extraordinary amount of time and detailed study to this cumbersome and unworkable process, but appeared no closer to resolving the issues than he had been upon taking office. His frustration was increasingly evident in his many meetings on the subject. Who would find a way to cut through all these Gordian knots?

According to Quandt, "Given the difficulty of working all this out smoothly without agreement among the Arabs themselves, Carter was tempted to go over the heads of the regional parties, who seemed hopelessly mired down in procedural arguments, and work out a joint invitation to Geneva with the cochairman, the Soviet Union."[28] After three weeks of negotiating over the wording, the Americans decided to try that. Vance and his Soviet counterpart, Andrei Gromyko, issued the invitation on October 1, in the form of a joint statement.

"The United States and the Soviet Union believe," the crucial paragraph said, "that the only right and effective way for achieving a fundamental solution to all aspects of the Middle East problem in its entirety is negotiations within the framework of the Geneva Peace Conference, specially convened for these purposes, with participation in its work of the representatives of all the parties involved in the conflict, including those of the Palestinian people, and legal and contractual formalization of the decisions reached at the conference." The statement said the conference should be held "not later than December 1977," but noted that "there still exist several questions of a procedural and organizational nature which remain to be agreed upon by the participants to [sic] the conference."[29] To the dismay of Israel and its supporters in Congress, the text called for "insuring the legitimate rights of the Palestinian people," and made no mention of Resolution 242's language on security. Moreover, it appeared on its face to restore Moscow's position as an equal power in the negotiations.

The statement did not say how those "questions of a procedural and organizational nature" were to be resolved now when they had eluded resolution up to this point, leaving Sadat in the same position as before: he wanted peace but no mechanism existed for bringing it about. Not only were the inter-Arab issues unresolved but Israel rejected the joint communiqué out of hand. In a confrontational meeting with President Carter on October 4, Dayan said it was "totally unacceptable."

Carter could not understand that. He argued to Dayan that the communiqué was tilted Israel's way on several key points. "It would be helpful to know what you cannot accept," he said testily. "In the past, the Soviets have always, along with the Arabs, referred to the national rights of the Palestinians [as opposed to 'legitimate rights,' the wording that was used]. We did not allow that [wording]. The Soviets have always claimed that the PLO were the only representatives of the Palestinians, and we refused to let the PLO be mentioned. The Soviets and the Arabs have always said that Israel should withdraw to the 1967 borders, and that is not included. The Soviets have always claimed that Israel should only get non-belligerency as part of the settlement, but in the statement we issued it calls for contractual agreements or peace treaties to be concluded. The statement also calls for normal diplomatic relations."

Carter and Vance told Dayan that the Israelis were not required to accept the statement and were free to say whatever they wanted about it. They could say they would go to Geneva specifically on the basis of Resolutions 242 and 338 if it made them feel better. The important thing was to get to Geneva.

"We do want to go to Geneva," Dayan assured the president, "and we have a positive attitude. We are not here to react to the U.S.-Soviet statement. I can use this: I don't agree with all or some of the provisions, and I am not going [to Geneva] on the basis of that statement, but on the basis of resolutions 242 and 338 and other agreements. I have to go back to Israel some day. It must be clear that we did not accept the statement."

"I would like to ask you," Carter said, "that when you make your public statements to be as constructive as possible. That would put the Arabs on the defensive. They don't accept it all either."

"I don't think the Arabs are so sensitive," Dayan retorted. "I will say what I think."[30]

In Dayan's version of what he called this "gloves-off talk," he said he told Carter that Israel's aim

> was to reach an agreed arrangement with the Palestinians on a pattern of co-existence, but we had certain vital interests in the West Bank and Gaza District which we could not give up. We would never return to a situation which left the populated part of the State of Israel squeezed into an eight-mile-wide coastal strip without an early-warning system in the West Bank and a military presence along the River Jordan. As a man, I said to the President, I did not think I was a coward; but as a Jew I feared for my people. We had suffered too many catastrophes in our history to ignore the possibility of their recurrence in the future. We could not afford

to be lulled by the comforting but illusory thought that "it can't happen to us." Moreover, the security aspect was not our only consideration. We regarded the West Bank—Judea and Samaria—as part of our homeland. We were not strangers there, and we could not give up our right to settle and acquire land in those areas.[31]

This extraordinary conversation went on for some time, Carter becoming increasingly agitated as he accused the Israelis of introducing new conditions and obstacles and warned Dayan against a "confrontation" with the United States. He did not want that, he said, again urging Dayan to adopt a positive tone in whatever he would say publicly.

To the Arabs, Carter reported that the Israelis had yielded on a few key points, such as allowing PLO-affiliated Palestinians to go to Geneva so long as they did not advertise the connection, and said it was time for the Arabs also to set aside their differences and get to the negotiating table. He proposed working terms for the planned conference and on October 21, he sent a handwritten letter to Sadat pleading with him to accept them. "When we met in Washington," the letter said, "I was deeply impressed and grateful for your promise to me that, at a crucial moment, I could count on your support when obstacles arose in our common search for peace in the Middle East. We have reached such a moment, and I need your help." He said Vance had suggested answers to all the procedural questions, and "the time has now come to move forward. . . . This is a personal appeal for your support." The letter was signed, "Your friend, Jimmy Carter."[32]

The cumulative effect of all this was to leave Sadat even more frustrated. Here was a situation in which the president of the United States was willing to confront and squeeze Israel and was asking him, an Egyptian, for help, the superpowers appeared to be in agreement, the PLO had offered a compromise on the representation issue by accepting a Palestinian-American professor to speak for them, and Israel had acquiesced—and there was still no reason to think that Geneva was imminent, or could succeed if convened. It was time for another daring stroke.

This Year, in Jerusalem

In the power struggle of 1971 in which Sadat had triumphed over Nasser's allies, and in the preparations for the October War, Sadat had controlled the agenda and could make decisions on his own initiative. Now he was in a different position; he had no control over what Israel and Syria would do. Under pressure, Sadat had a habit of unnerving professional diplomats and confounding his allies by making proposals and offering ideas seemingly out of the blue, making things up as he went along. Now, at the beginning of November 1977, he did it again. In a letter to Carter, he proposed to convene an international summit conference in "the Arab sector of Jerusalem" to devise "a just and lasting peace in the region." The participants would be "the leaders of the United States, the Union of Soviet Socialist Republics, the People's Republic of China, France, the United Kingdom, Israel, the Arab Republic of Egypt, the Syrian Arab Republic, the Hashemite Kingdom of Jordan, Lebanon, Mr. Yassir Arafat, and the United Nations Secretary-General."

The "terms of reference" for this event would include "the termination of the Israeli occupation of all Arab territories occupied since 1967." Sadat told Carter that he would make this proposal publicly in a speech to the People's Assembly he was scheduled to deliver six days later, on November 9.[33]

The whole idea was preposterous. The other Arabs would never agree to go to East Jerusalem while it was under Israeli control. China had nothing to do with any of this. Israel was not going to sit down with Arafat, and it certainly would not accept "terms of reference" that would require it to withdraw to the 1967 lines.

Carter's response was unequivocal: forget it. "After serious reflection," the president wrote, "I must tell you that this public announcement may seriously complicate, rather than facilitate, the search for peace in the Middle East. Without careful and private agreement being reached that the leaders of Israel, Syria, the Soviet Union, and other nations would attend, their public rejection might be embarrassing both to them and to those who would be willing to participate . . . my own limited experience and study of history indicate that a summit conference is often a better forum for confirming agreements previously arrived at through quiet diplomacy than for reaching new agreements, and especially when the views of participants are as divergent as they are with respect to the final terms of a Middle East peace settlement."[34]

Sadat had the good sense to accept Carter's advice, and he never made this proposal publicly. That left him scheduled to address the parliament in a few days with little progress to report on the peace negotiation front, so he made up another new initiative.

In a very long address to parliament on November 9, Sadat said that everyone was pushing for peace except the Israelis. Israel, he said, "dreads Geneva," and was avoiding it by raising endless procedural questions and issues of semantics. "Before you and before the Arab nation, I repeat that procedural issues are of little concern to me," he told the parliament. "I am ready to go to Geneva. You must have heard me say that I would go to the end of the world to spare an injury to one of our men, much more the death of one. Israel must be greatly surprised to hear me say that I am even ready to go to the Knesset and discuss with them."[35]

The members of parliament applauded, but it was hard to take seriously the idea that a president of Egypt would go to Jerusalem to propose peace to the Israeli parliament. In an analysis the next day, U.S. ambassador Hermann Eilts said, "Sadat's offer to go to the Knesset is a first for an Arab leader and should be seen as his way of dramatizing lengths to which he prepared to go to achieve peace, not as serious possibility."[36] He was wrong.

Sadat told Walter Cronkite of CBS News a few days later that he was "just waiting for the proper invitation" from Begin. The only condition, he said, was that he have an opportunity to address the Knesset and "put out the full picture and detail of the situation from our point of view." He said he was prepared to make the journey within a week.

Begin, interviewed separately, said this was "very good news," and promised to deliver an invitation through American diplomatic channels the next day.[37]

He did. Sadat accepted. When the news broke, I was in Tunisia at a gathering of the Palestinian National Council, an umbrella organization of all the Palestinian factions. The reaction of the delegates could best be described as stunned silence. Sadat then went to Damascus to explain his decision to Assad, the only Arab leader he consulted before making his groundbreaking trip. The cautious, calculating Syrian leader, Sadat's temperamental opposite, refused to endorse the idea. Assad never did anything on impulse and did not see what was to be gained by handing the Israelis de facto recognition for which they would pay no price.

Sadat was out on a very fragile limb by himself. Vance, fearful of the consequences for Sadat, and for peace, if other Arabs also disdained Sadat's gamble, sent a strongly worded message to Crown Prince Fahd bin Abdul Aziz of Saudi Arabia, pleading with the kingdom to support the Egyptian leader.

"The president and I firmly believe," Vance wrote, "that history will judge this latest initiative by President Sadat as a major contribution to breaking through the psychological barriers that have made peace elusive for much too long. We have been impressed with its courage, imagination and decisiveness. . . . One of the major underlying reasons for the often inflexible positions the Israelis have taken has been their deep conviction that the ultimate Arab objective remained the dismantling of Israel as a sovereign Jewish state. Nothing could have been better designed to break through that suspicion than Sadat's offer to go to Israel." The response of the other Arabs, Vance said, would be a test of whether they were sincere in their professed desire to make peace.[38]

On this point, Sadat and the Americans were doomed to disappointment. The other Arabs failed this test of statesmanship. They could have endorsed Sadat's courage and vision, knowing that if Israel did not respond generously it would be the Israelis who took the blame in world opinion; instead, they turned against Sadat and fell back on the slogans and posturing that had brought them nothing in all the time since the October War. They had no new or realistic ideas about how to deal with Israel, but they could not bring themselves to support what Sadat was doing.

Sadat said he had told no one, not even his closest advisers, what he would say in his speech to the Egyptian parliament, and no one was sure how the people of Egypt would react to his radical idea. They might feel as Assad did that by going to Jerusalem Sadat would give away his trump card—recognition and acceptance—with no guarantee of any return. In one ominous sign, Foreign Minister Fahmy resigned. Ambassador Eilts reported that most Egyptians, while astonished, seemed supportive, but "officials who follow negotiating process are shocked, and deeply apprehensive" about what might happen if Sadat "comes back empty-handed." These officials, Eilts said, feared that the "impact will be greater in domestic Arab political context [than that of an] American president visiting Hanoi at the height of fighting in Vietnam and domestic turbulence."[39]

Egypt's foreign policy professionals, like the leaders of other Arab countries, were trapped in unproductive conventional thinking. Sadat was not. On the evening of November 19, he took off on a journey that no one had foreseen ten days before. Fearing a popular backlash, he departed after dark from a remote airstrip. The time and place of embarkation were not announced in advance. But when he landed at Ben-Gurion Airport outside Tel Aviv at 8:30 p.m., the bright lights were on and everyone who was anyone in Israeli politics was there to welcome him, along with a guard of honor and a military band to play both national anthems. This astonishing event was televised around the world.

In an instant, a taboo was shattered; the Middle East would never be the same as it was before Sadat's plane landed. It was the Middle East equivalent of President Nixon's trip to China. Stunned, emotional Israelis wept and cheered as the leader of the country that had always been their most dangerous enemy was welcomed to their capital with full military honors.

Sadat's trip was essentially a public relations gesture, one of the most audacious ever undertaken. It was a breathtaking development that riveted the world; journalists from Brazil to Japan, including many with skimpy knowledge of the Middle East, poured into Jerusalem for saturation coverage. Their reporting about Sadat was adulatory; he was a hero again, perhaps not in the Arab world, but all across Asia, Europe, and the Americas.

In the ceremonial parts of the visit, Sadat gave the Israelis everything they could have wanted. Just by arriving in view of the television cameras, he effectively accepted Israel as a legitimate state. He stood at attention for the Israeli anthem, laid a wreath at a memorial to Israeli soldiers who had died fighting the Arabs, and prayed at the Mosque of al-Aqsa on the Temple Mount, a holy site of Islam to which Israel had controlled access since 1967. He even paid the obligatory visit to Yad Vashem, Israel's Holocaust memorial. But on the substance of the issues, which he addressed in his speech to the Knesset, he gave nothing away.

Speaking in Arabic, he acknowledged to the members of the Knesset that "most of those who contacted me following the declaration of this decision [to go to Jerusalem] expressed their objection because of the feeling of utter suspicion and absolute lack of confidence between the Arab states and the Palestine people on the one hand and Israel on the other that still surges in us all.

"Many months in which peace could have been brought about have been wasted over differences and fruitless discussion on the procedure of convening the Geneva conference. All have shared suspicion and absolute lack of confidence."

Nevertheless, Sadat said, he believed that it was his "obligation of responsibility before God and before the people that I should go to the far corners of the world, even to Jerusalem," to talk to members of the Knesset and "acquaint them with the facts."

Among the "facts," Sadat said, were that he had been declaring since 1971 that he wanted peace; that "no one can build his happiness at the expense of the misery of others"; that "the call for a permanent and just peace based on respect for United Nations resolutions has now become the call of the entire world"; and that "the Arab nation, in its drive for permanent peace based on justice, does not proceed from a position of weakness. On the contrary, it has the power and stability for a sincere will for peace."

Sadat said he had not come to Jerusalem in search of a separate peace between Egypt and Israel, nor to seek a limited agreement ending the "state of belligerency" without full, normal relations. He wanted "full peace, based on justice."

What would that entail?

"Ladies and gentlemen, to tell you the truth, peace cannot be worth its name unless it is based on justice and not on the occupation of the land of others," Sadat said. "It would not be right for you to demand for yourselves what you deny to others. With all frankness and in the spirit that has prompted me to come to you today, I tell you that you have to give up once and for all the dreams of conquest and give up the belief that force is the best method for dealing with the Arabs. You should clearly understand the lesson of confrontation between you and us. Expansion does not pay. To speak frankly, our land does not lend itself to bargaining, it is not even open to argument. To us the national soil is equal to the holy valley where God Almighty spoke to Moses, peace be upon him. We cannot attempt to take away or accept to seek one inch of it nor can we accept the principle of debating or bargaining over it." Jerusalem, he said, was above annexation by Israel or anyone else: it should be "a free and open city for all believers."

If for Israel the definition of peace was to live alongside its Arab neighbors in safety and security, with whatever international guarantees it might want, "I say yes." The days when Arabs referred to the Jewish state as "the so-called Israel" and refused to talk to its representatives should come to an end, he said.

As a finale, Sadat addressed "the people of Israel. I pledge myself with true and sincere words to every man, woman, and child in Israel. I tell them, from the Egyptian people who bless this sacred mission of peace, I convey to you the message of peace of the Egyptian people, who do not harbor fanaticism and whose sons, Moslems, Christians, and Jews, live together in a state of cordiality, love and tolerance." He urged all those who had lost fathers, brothers, or sons in war to "fill the air and space with recitals of peace" and encourage their leaders to make the decisions necessary to achieve it.[40]

Sadat spoke eloquently and with obvious sincerity, but beyond the rhetoric the message was blunt: land for peace. You cannot have both.

Sadat need not have worried about how the people of Egypt would respond to this headline-making move. Cairo was as quiet as the inside of the Great Pyramid while he was in Jerusalem, and he returned home the next day to a massive, rapturous welcome. Hundreds of thousands of Egyptians lined the route of his motorcade from Cairo's airport through the teeming city, to his residence across the Nile in Giza. They cheered, whistled, ululated, and shouted "Sadat! Sadat! The man of peace!" True, some of those Egyptians were "rent-a-crowd" bused in from the countryside by the government, but to those of us who witnessed the procession as he waved from an open car, in the dark of night, there was no doubt that he had touched the aspirations of his countrymen, who wanted what he wanted—an end to a fruitless, debilitating struggle, and a new era of development and prosperity. They were exhilarated, and so was he. What would come of it was up to Israel.

5 The Separate Peace

Sadat was pleased with the reception he got in Israel and he relished the international adulation, but he was soon disabused of the illusion that his grand gesture would move Prime Minister Begin to flexibility on the issues. Begin set him straight before they left the Knesset chamber, with a speech in response to Sadat's that yielded nothing on matters of substance.

The Israeli leader began with his customary history lecture, about the historic travails of the Jews and Israel's struggle to defend itself against the unrelenting hostility of its Arab neighbors. "With the help of God," he said, "we overcame the forces of aggression and assured the survival of our nation, not only for this generation but for all those to come." At Yad Vashem, he said to Sadat, "With your own eyes you saw what the fate of our people was when this Homeland was taken from it" in biblical times. That Jewish homeland, he said, would not be taken again. "No one came to our rescue," he said, "not from the East and not from the West. And therefore we, this entire generation, the generation of Holocaust and Resurrection, swore an oath of allegiance: never again will our wives and our children—whom it is our duty to defend if need be, even at the cost of our lives—be put in the devastating range of enemy fire."

He said Israel fervently desired peace, and urged the Arabs, "Let us not be daunted by memories of the past, even if they are bitter to us all." But he also said that Israel was determined to maintain its right to "Eretz Israel," as the Likud Alliance had pledged to do in its successful election campaign six months earlier.

"Today Jerusalem is bedecked with two flags, the Egyptian and the Israeli," Begin said. "Together, Mr. President, we have seen our little children waving both flags. Let us sign a peace treaty and establish such a situation forever, both in Jerusalem and Cairo. I hope the day will come when Egyptian children will wave Israeli and Egyptian flags together, just as the Israeli children are waving both of those flags together in Jerusalem, when you, Mr. President, will be represented by a loyal ambassador in Jerusalem, and we, by an ambassador in Cairo. . . . We propose economic cooperation for the development of our countries," he said, to abolish "poverty, hunger, and homelessness."[1]

He would have given that speech no matter what Sadat had said, because it reflected Israel's position: it would welcome peace with all its neighbors, but in the meantime, it sought a treaty with Egypt that would establish bilateral diplomatic and commercial relations while leaving the West Bank, the Golan, and East Jerusalem in Israeli hands. Begin did not even mention the Palestinians.

"It was clear that he was unable to rise to the occasion," the Israeli historian Avi Shlaim wrote, and Sadat "failed to grasp Begin's real aims and aspirations." The Israeli leader was willing to make peace with Egypt but "had no intention of including in the price any territory outside the Sinai Peninsula."[2]

The Likud platform, on the basis of which Begin had been elected, meant what it said. It was not a campaign slogan to be forgotten after the election; it was a statement of deeply held belief, and it could not be reconciled with Sadat's equally sincere belief that Israel could gain peace only by giving up the territories Likud had pledged to retain.

The Americans had anticipated such a response from Begin and had tried to head it off. The day before Sadat was to arrive in Israel, Secretary of State Vance instructed U.S. ambassador Samuel Lewis to tell Begin that "Sadat has staked his place in history and his immediate political fortunes on the proposition that an honorable peace can be obtained. . . . It hardly needs saying that if he fails to get it he will be in the most serious trouble." Vance warned that if Sadat were backed into a separate peace, political rivals at home and critics in other Arab capitals would use it against him "to serious effect."[3]

A few days after the Knesset session, when everyone except Sadat himself could see that Begin had stonewalled him, Vance told President Carter, "It is clear that Sadat himself has not thought through precisely all of the implications and that he is overly optimistic about the ease and speed with which his negotiations with the Israelis can proceed. He will almost certainly at some point come to us for help in moving the Israelis on specific issues."[4]

For a brief period after Sadat's return from Jerusalem, the Egyptians, Israelis, and Americans went through the motions of embarking on a new path to peace negotiations. Geneva was now irrelevant. Sadat invited the United States, the United Nations, Israel, the Palestine Liberation Organization, and a few other Arab leaders to a peace conference in Cairo, but only the Israelis, the United Nations, and the Americans agreed to attend.

He announced in American television interviews, on the Sunday after his return from Jerusalem, that he had already issued invitations to his proposed conference and it would be held, whether all those invited came or not.[5] He said he would invite television cameras into the meeting room to show the empty chairs for the missing Arab delegations, in the belief that this would reveal to the world their pointless intransigence. The Americans talked him out of it; what such a display would really show, the Americans said, was that Sadat had no support from his fellow Arabs and was on his own.

The Israelis arrived in Cairo bearing negotiating documents that said nothing about Israeli settlements, borders, or other practical matters. The Egyptians countered with a list of principles for peace that began with full Israeli withdrawal to the 1967 lines, as if they believed Begin and his Likud allies had changed their minds about this virtually overnight. Nothing could come of this posturing, and nothing did.

"The Cairo Conference proved a total failure," Israeli foreign minister Moshe Dayan wrote afterward. "The dialogue between Egypt and

Israel was sterile. . . . Both sides knew they were only going through the motions of conferring, and the game they were playing was like a dialogue between two deaf people who could not yet lip-read."⁶ Sadat could not believe that Begin would adhere to all the positions he had staked out before the Jerusalem event, as if nothing had happened. "Apparently," he complained to Carter, the Israelis "are still thinking and behaving with the old mentality and complexes. The pre-initiative spirit persists, even though the Israeli people left no doubt that their yearning for peace is the paramount factor in their life. They received my message with enthusiasm and hope. To me, their response was gratifying. Nonetheless the Israeli delegation remained seized by the worn-out concepts and the old suspicion. In a nut shell, I want them to wake up, look beyond mere words and rise to the level of the great events we are creating."⁷

Sadat's tone reflected unhappy reality: he had little to show for his grand initiative and, predictably, found himself under fire. He broke diplomatic relations with five of the hardest-line Arab states—Iraq, Syria, Libya, South Yemen, and Algeria—after they accused him of selling out the Arab cause. Then he turned his ire on another critic, the Soviet Union, which Egypt said was fanning the flames of Arab rejection. Sadat ordered the Soviet Union and four of its Warsaw Pact allies to close their consular and cultural offices in Alexandria, Port Said, and Aswan.

The effect of these moves was to increase Sadat's dependence on Begin to deliver some positive developments; his vituperative attacks on other Arab leaders cut off his fallback position, namely a return to a united Arab front and partnership with Moscow should Begin fail to respond. Pressure mounted on Carter and Vance to lean on Begin, as Vance had predicted. The situation now was that Sadat was eager, even desperate for peace, but had no further leverage over the Israelis. He had not persuaded the other Arabs to support him, at least not openly. Prime Minister Begin was unyielding on the withdrawal issue, and he was unmoved by Sadat's pleas that he respond generously to the spirit of the Jerusalem initiative.

"Did you not tell me," he wrote to Sadat, "that we should put our cards openly on the table, to speak with each other in complete candor? Did we not understand after our respective speeches from the rostrum of the Knesset that we have differences of opinion?"[8]

Carter and Vance did not want Sadat's initiative, and all their efforts over the previous year, to end in total failure or in a separate peace. Carter believed the Israelis were primarily responsible for the impasse, but he was constrained in the amount of pressure he could be seen to put on Begin because he could not afford to alienate Israel's many supporters in the U.S. Senate, which was then considering whether to ratify a treaty returning the Panama Canal to Panamanian sovereignty, one of Carter's most cherished goals.

Pressure Mounts on Sadat

To the handful of American journalists who were giving these developments their full attention and had good access to Sadat's policy advisers and to diplomats at the U.S. embassy, it was apparent by the time of the abortive Cairo Conference that Sadat's resistance to the idea of an agreement negotiated only with Israel was eroding; the triple pressures of Israel's immovability, the refusal of other Arab states to participate, and his own need to collect some return on his gamble, were forcing his hand. Neither Sadat nor anyone on his staff was prepared to say such a thing in public, and Sadat would continue to reject the idea of a straight bilateral deal that contained nothing for the Palestinians in any form; he hoped for an agreement under which Israel would at least agree in principle to "land for peace," with details on fronts other than Sinai to be negotiated by other Arabs. If, for example, he could persuade the Israelis to acknowledge that they were obliged in principle to surrender the Golan Heights, then it would be up to Syria's Assad, not Sadat, to negotiate the terms. But in the absence of any such commitment by Israel, Sadat's options were narrowing.

A few weeks after Sadat went to Jerusalem, State Department intelligence analysts calculated that "Sadat is continuing to receive strong support at home," but warned that "should Sadat feel compelled to abandon the quest for a comprehensive settlement and seek instead a separate deal with Israel, the public mood could change abruptly."

If Sadat could extract "concessions from Israel that are meaningful in a pan-Arab context" and the other Arabs rejected the agreement anyway, the analysts said, he could make the case that he had achieved what they could not and they were foolish to disdain it. In the absence of such meaningful movement by Israel, Sadat could face trouble at home, especially from the armed forces, which "would be torn between the prospects of recovering the Sinai without war for which they are ill-prepared, and being held up to the charge of abandoning the wider Arab struggle."[9]

In a way this assessment and others like it only stated the obvious: Sadat had given Israel quite a bit, and if he failed to bring back an acceptable outcome it could be politically fatal. His army might turn against him, his financial backers in Saudi Arabia might abandon him. But those were not Israel's primary concerns.

Begin went to Washington in mid-December 1977 to offer his version of what a peace deal would look like. Israel would indeed withdraw to the 1967 lines in Sinai, to which it had no biblical or historic claim, but would keep some troops in a buffer zone for three to five years. Diplomatic relations would be established with Egypt when the withdrawal was complete. For the Palestinians of the West Bank, Israel would grant administrative autonomy under an elected council—the right to manage their own affairs—and would suspend its own claim of sovereignty for five years. This was to be self-rule for the Arabs who lived there, but not control of the land. Israel would retain a "security border" in the Jordan Valley.

When President Carter asked him about implementing Resolution 242, Begin restated his argument that "Resolution 242 does not oblige Israel to total withdrawal." To Israel, he said, the important part of 242 was that it called for "secure boundaries," and there was no way to create those along the 1967 borders. "If we withdraw to the 1967 lines, there will be permanent bloodshed," he said.[10]

In Vance's estimation, this proposal "fell far short of what we believed necessary for an interim solution," because it would leave Israel in control of Arab immigration and it provided no negotiating role for Syria and Jordan. The one positive note was that Begin at least acknowledged the existence of a "Palestinian problem" and offered a basis for negotiations about it.[11]

The Cairo Conference debacle began a period of several months in which there was no fundamental movement on the issues. The only difference between this period and the frustrating year before the Jerusalem trip was that now Egypt and Israel were talking directly to each other, rather than exclusively through the Americans. This bilateral dialogue began when Begin made his first visit to Egypt, in December 1977, to meet with Sadat at Ismailia, on the Suez Canal. The meeting took place on Christmas Day; the schedule disrupted the family lives of Western diplomats and journalists but that was of little concern to the Jews of the Israeli delegation or to Sadat and his fellow Muslims.

The Ismailia meeting was remarkable for the circumstances that surrounded it—an Israeli prime minister landing in Egypt in an El Al jetliner, along with a large entourage of Israeli journalists seeing the land of their longtime enemy for the first time and receiving a generous welcome. Several of these journalists made their first visits to Cairo after the session in Ismailia. The manager of the Mena House Hotel, near the Pyramids, even sought out Jews in Cairo's American community and press corps to find out what the Israeli guests would eat. The symbolism was unmistakable, but in terms of negotiating progress, Ismailia achieved little. Sadat and Begin could not even agree on wording for a joint communiqué and issued separate statements. The only firm point of agreement was that negotiations would continue in the form of two committees: military, headed by the defense ministers, to meet in Cairo to discuss security matters such as troop levels; and political, headed by the foreign ministers, to meet in Jerusalem to discuss the Palestinian question. The two leaders were unable to agree on whether the objective was "self-rule" or "self-determination" for the Palestinians, so they omitted mention of the concept. Begin did agree to accept the pre-1967 line as a permanent border with Egypt only, but asked that Israeli settlements in Sinai be permitted to remain. Sadat refused. The Israeli military team at the meeting asked that

Israel be allowed to keep two airfields in Sinai; Sadat responded that they should be "plowed up."[12]

Begin and Sadat tried to put the best face on it at a joint news conference. Begin, who had achieved the previously unthinkable just by landing in Egypt and being received as a peace negotiator, said he had "arrived as hopeful prime minister and I am leaving as a happy man." Sadat said there was "no going back" to the days of war. But he also said that peace must be based on full Israeli withdrawal from the occupied territories, to which Begin responded, as always, "Resolution 242 doesn't commit Israel to total withdrawal and therefore this is a matter for negotiation, to establish those secure and recognized boundaries which are mentioned in the second paragraph."[13]

The Short Life of the Political Committee

The two committees were duly established, but they began their work in a new atmosphere of anger and recrimination, mostly from the Egyptians, over the impasse. Harsh rhetoric flowed from both sides, but the Egyptians went overboard. The press, which always reflected the government's views, even insulted Begin personally, with references to "Shylock."

Sadat's position now, as he reported it to U.S. ambassador Hermann F. Eilts, was that he had in effect given the Israelis what they wanted in the context of the "nature of peace," which was all he had to give. Now it was up to the Israelis to make some concessions. Sadat did not regard the offer of withdrawal from Sinai as a concession, since the Israelis were on Egyptian territory illegally. He said he hoped that his actions had given President Carter "full maneuverability" to urge the Israelis to be responsive."[14]

That handed the ball back to Carter, who decided to run with it. But he was caught, and would remain caught, in the twilight zone between Sadat's quest for a settlement that would provide for the Palestinians and Begin's determination not to agree to one. That would not change, through many months of proposals and counterproposals, and angry charges and countercharges. The president viewed Begin as stubborn and inflexible, and believed the Israelis had responded grudgingly rather than generously to all that Sadat had done, but he could not just turn his back on the Israeli leader; to do that would accomplish nothing except alienate Israel's many supporters in the United States.

At the beginning of January 1978, Carter went to the Middle East. (That was the trip that began in Iran with the infamous New Year's Eve celebration at which Carter toasted the Shah as "an island of stability" in the region.) In Saudi Arabia, King Khaled told the president that he had put aside his initial irritation at Sadat's failure to inform him in advance of the Jerusalem trip, and now the kingdom "was doing its best to remain in support of Sadat."[15] Reassured on that point, the president then flew to Aswan, Egypt, to see Sadat. He pointedly omitted a visit to Israel during this tour.

In a public statement after he talked to Sadat, Carter proclaimed, "Your bold initiative in seeking peace has aroused the admiration of the entire world." The quest for peace "must succeed," he said, and to do so the negotiations would have to be based on fundamental principles: Israeli withdrawal from "territories occupied in 1967," "secure and recognized borders for all parties," as called for in Resolution 242, and "a resolution of the Palestinian problem in all its aspects. The problem [he meant the solution] must recognize the legitimate rights of the Palestinian people and enable the Palestinians to participate in the determination of their own future."[16] This was not different in substance from anything the Americans had said previously, but in the context of January 1978 it put the United States on the Egyptian side of the negotiations, in opposition to Israel.

On the same day that Carter issued his Aswan statement, the Israelis began work on four new settlements in Sinai. This news infuriated Sadat and made Carter especially angry because he thought Dayan had promised him that would not happen. When he returned to Washington, the president wrote Begin a blunt letter laying out his view on this subject, reminding him that the U.S. position on settlements had been consistent since 1967:

As you know, the position of the United States has been consistent on the issue of Israeli settlements in territory occupied in the

1967 war. We publicly articulated our position as early as September 26, 1967. On numerous occasions since that time, United States representatives have expressed disapproval of, and opposition to, the establishment of Israeli settlements in the occupied territories on the grounds that these actions contravene the Fourth Geneva Convention on the Protection of Civilians in Time of War, to which Israel is a signatory, and also that these actions are prejudicial to the achievement of a Middle East peace settlement. As concerns this latter point, we have mentioned that settlements in themselves convey at the very least the impression of permanence of Israeli occupation which clearly is not conducive to creating the appropriate atmosphere for productive peace negotiations. It must be recognized that, if considered as permanent and under Israeli military protection, the settlements per se are inconsistent with Security Council Resolution 242 which is the only framework for negotiations and which clearly envisages Israeli military withdrawals in exchange for peace.[17]

Over the next few weeks, in the early part of 1978, the atmosphere of the entire peace negotiating process deteriorated and the impasse deepened. Begin accepted some proposals about wording and timing, but clung to his fundamental positions: Israel was not required to withdraw from all the occupied territories and would not do so, no settlements would be dismantled, Jerusalem was not negotiable, and no arrangement for the Palestinians could lead to the formation of an independent state. The Israeli obsession with words and details was frustrating to Sadat and Carter, but for the Israelis it was a matter of substance, not just a tactical annoyance. Begin and his team insisted on nailing down every syllable out of fear that Egypt would find some excuse in future to abrogate the treaty or, worse, that the Palestinian autonomy provisions would lead to an independent state. The Israelis believed any such entity would inevitably be pro-Soviet and hostile to Israel. Assessing the state of play in a memo to Brzezinski, Bill Quandt wrote, "I see no sign that Begin is ready to accept the principle of withdrawal, to say nothing of the principle of self-determination. He might agree to the vague language of the President's Aswan statement, but that would not represent any real change in policy and would not be enough to bring King Hussein [of Jordan] into the negotiations. At best it could serve as a very thin fig leaf behind which Sadat might try to conclude a separate deal with Israel."[18]

The words "fig leaf" would be heard again and again in the months to come, because Quandt's assessment was correct. The military committee that had been established in Ismailia made good progress on technical matters involving Israeli redeployment from Sinai, but the political committee quickly ran aground on the shoals of Palestine.

At its first session, Vance, representing the United States, offered what he called "a fair and balanced draft" of a proposed "declaration of principles" that would form the basis for a settlement. It was based mostly on the language of Resolution 242 and on the statement Carter had issued at Aswan two weeks earlier. It called for "full implementation of the principles of UN Security Council Resolutions 242 and 338 in all their parts," "withdrawal of Israeli armed forces from territories occupied in the 1967 conflict and secure and recognized borders for all parties," and "a just resolution of the issues relating to the West Bank and Gaza which recognizes the legitimate rights of the Palestinian people and enables them to participate in the determination of their own future." The Egyptians and Israelis introduced their own drafts. Israel offered "[w]ithdrawal of Israeli armed forces from territories occupied in the 1967 conflict," but not, of course, "all territories," and offered the Palestinians of the West Bank and Gaza "administrative autonomy—self rule." As could have been expected, the Egyptian version stressed "the inadmissibility of acquisition of territory by war" and called for "self-determination" for the Palestinians. These differences in wording were not just semantics. The Egyptian version would have required Israel to withdraw from all the occupied territories and would have opened the door for the Palestinians to declare an independent state. For Israel, both propositions were out of the question.

On January 18, Sadat yielded once again to his instinct for the impetuous. He terminated the political discussions and ordered the Egyptian delegation home from Jerusalem. Sadat said the military talks could continue, because the Israeli delegation was headed by Defense Minister Ezer Weizman, the only Israeli he actually liked, but the political talks were over. Carter, shocked, telephoned Sadat to ask him to reconsider, but Sadat said his decision had already been announced. "The Israelis need a lesson," he said. "They cannot deal the way they have been dealing with us."[19]

The next day, the Israeli Foreign Ministry issued a statement that blamed the Egyptians for the breakdown of the talks:

> The abrupt Egyptian announcement proves once more that the Egyptian Government was under the illusion that Israel would surrender to demands that at no time were acceptable to Israel. The Egyptian delegation demanded of the Israeli delegation the withdrawal of Israeli forces from Sinai, the Golan, Judea, Samaria and Gaza. The Egyptian Foreign Minister, on his arrival in Israel, did not hesitate to demand that Israel transfer the Old City of Jerusalem to foreign rule, and further demanded the establishment of a Palestinian state in the territory of Eretz Yisrael in Judea, Samaria, and in Gaza. Such a Palestinian state would have extinguished any prospect of peace, and would have created a danger to the very existence of the Jewish state. There has never been, and there will never be, a government in Israel that would agree to such conditions.[20]

In taking the position that the military committee, which was concerned primarily with redeployments in Sinai, could continue, but the political committee, which dealt primarily with the Palestinian question, could not, Sadat inadvertently strengthened what was becoming an inexorable turn toward a separate bilateral Israeli-Egyptian agreement; it implied the possibility of an agreement on Sinai, the one territory Begin was prepared to yield, while seeming to foreclose a comprehensive settlement.

In fairness to Begin, he found it just as difficult to deal with Sadat as Sadat did with him. Sadat was distressed by Begin's unyielding positions on the issues; what bothered Begin was Sadat's erratic decisionmaking and inattention to detail. Begin told Vance that he was becoming impatient with what he saw as Sadat's penchant for agreeing to something in their one-on-one conversations, only to reverse himself when he told his foreign policy professionals what he had done. "Sadat is not a rational man," he complained.[21]

Some members of the American team agreed with him. Quandt complained to Brzezinski that "Sadat takes initiatives without informing us in advance; he holds back on what he is saying to Weizman; he lets his officials turn out worthless legalistic documents in the guise of serious negotiating proposals; and yet he seems to be disappointed with our reluctance to become a full partner. We do not have a satisfactory political understanding with Sadat as we enter a crucial phase of the negotiations. The reason, in my view, is that he has little idea of how to proceed and counts on us to bail him out. His impatience with details is becoming a real problem, as is his reluctance to engage in sustained negotiations."[22]

This harsh assessment of Sadat's weaknesses as a negotiator would prove to be accurate. He was impatient and impetuous; Begin was neither.

In February Sadat traveled to the United States to assess the situation with Carter, Brzezinski, and Vice President Walter Mondale. Carter said he recognized that Sadat and other Arabs were disappointed that so little had come of the Jerusalem initiative. Then he gave the floor to Mondale for an appeal to Sadat's vanity.

"I think you know that there have been few things in my political career that have made more of an impression than your historic trip to Jerusalem," Mondale said. "You swept aside barriers in a simple human stroke. You risked your career and your life to change a framework of 30 years, and the reaction here was indescribable. More people watched your speech to the Knesset than almost anything in American history. In 48 hours, in the minds of Americans you became one of the world's leading apostles of peace and [leading] statesmen. I believe that it is very important for the evolution of Israeli policy that you continue to be seen in that light. The Israelis should be asked what they are doing to reciprocate. You should not let the Israeli government off the hook by saying that what you did was a one-time thing. Begin should not get you in a position where he can say that he has had no response to his moves."

Carter picked up the theme: "I won't mislead you," he told Sadat, "but without you and your support in American public opinion, I can't force Israel to change. With your support, I can put pressure on Israel to change."

Carter, who was to meet next with Begin, asked Sadat point blank whether, if King Hussein of Jordan refused to join the negotiations, he would accept a bilateral peace treaty with Israel. In response, Sadat offered his fallback position: he could live with an agreement in which Israel accepted the principle of withdrawal from the captured territories but would not actually be required to pull troops and settlers out until the leaders of Jordan and Syria sat down with the Israelis to negotiate the details. Israel would have peace with its most powerful neighbor, Egypt would regain all its lost land, and what the other Arabs did would be up to them.[23]

That sounded reasonable, but it was unrealistic. Begin had not accepted and would not accept the "principle" that Israel was required to withdraw from all the occupied territories. He would never accept a "principle" that would violate his personal beliefs and, in his view, expose his people to grave danger. Thus the stalemate continued, while the Americans considered what to do now that Sadat had pulled the plug on the political committee. The Israelis, Vance observed wryly, "are certainly not inclined to be more flexible on issues after this move."[24]

In the second week of March, PLO chairman Yasser Arafat went to Moscow to meet Soviet leader Leonid Brezhnev and Foreign Minister Andrei Gromyko. The Palestinian leader had been striking a conciliatory pose in messages to President Carter, and the Kremlin wanted to stiffen his resolve.

Brezhnev and Gromyko reported on the conversations to their Politburo colleagues: "We put particular emphasis on the importance of facing Sadat's capitulationist course with increasing counter-measures within the Arab world." Expressing approval of the creation of a resistance front by hard-line Arab states, they said, "We also noted that the Arabs' and their friends' rebuff of American-Israeli intrigues and Sadat's capitulationist course was already yielding some fruit," because Sadat could no longer discount the strength of the "anti-imperialist forces."

The Soviets warned Arafat that "some elements in the Arab world have not yet rid themselves of the illusion that the Americans can induce Israel to make meaningful concessions to the Arabs. However, those who think this way are making a clear political miscalculation. Making concessions to the aggressor in hopes of cajoling him into negotiations cannot bring about the assurance of your own national interests."

Arafat, they said, "affirmed that the PLO intends to continue to steadfastly oppose the capitulationism of Sadat, the separate deals between Egypt and Israel, imperialist scheming, and Arab reactionaries in the Middle East."[25]

Terrorists Strike in Israel

The day after Arafat left Moscow, eleven guerrillas from his Fatah movement entered Israel by boat from Lebanon, seized a bus and its passengers, and engaged in a shootout with Israeli security forces. It was one of the bloodiest episodes in the long history of terrorist attacks: thirty-eight Israelis died, including thirteen children. If there had ever been any inclination within the Begin government to yield ground on the issues of territorial withdrawal and secure borders, this ghastly incident snuffed it out. Israeli troops promptly marched into southern Lebanon in "Operation Litani," a drive to take out strongholds established there by Palestinian fighters.

By April, Vance recalled, "we had concluded that the gap between Israel and the Arabs on this problem [of withdrawal] was so great that no final settlement could be negotiated as part of the current peace effort," but at the same time "we could not allow the stalemate to continue because of the risks it posed to Sadat and to our interests in the Middle East."[26] Nevertheless, it did continue.

The Israelis and Egyptians sent proposals and counterproposals back and forth, through Washington, with no outcome. Sadat adopted a new tactic in his public remarks, blaming Begin personally for his obstinacy and pointedly praising other senior Israelis, such as Weizman, who were supposedly more flexible. The Americans warned him that this rhetorical ploy was counterproductive because it would lead Israelis to rally around their prime minister and alienate Israel's friends in Congress, but Sadat had reached a point where protocol was almost irrelevant. When the Israelis turned down his request that they unilaterally return the Sinai town of El Arish to Egypt as a goodwill gesture and Begin sneered that "nobody can get anything for nothing," it reinforced Sadat's belief that Begin and his government had completely misunderstood what his peace initiative meant: he was not offering "nothing," he was offering the peace Israel always said it wanted.[27]

Vance told Carter, "[I]t is becoming increasingly apparent that Sadat has ruled out [the] possibility of arriving at agreement with Begin." That may have been the case, but Sadat plodded ahead because he and Carter saw no alternative to doing so.[28]

In July, Vance met with Dayan and Egyptian foreign minister Mohammed Ibrahim Kamel at Leeds Castle in Britain. This gathering received extensive coverage in the international news media, but it produced no results because the Israelis and the Egyptians largely clung to the positions they had already stated over and over. The Israelis said they did not want to rule the Palestinians of Judea and Samaria—the Arabs there should govern themselves—but Israel would retain control of the land, and Jews would have a right to settle there, with Israeli security forces to protect them. Absolutely not, the Egyptians replied. That arrangement would be a sham that would leave the Palestinians stateless because Jordan would not participate in it. The only positive news from these meetings was that Vance persuaded the Israeli and Egyptian delegations to dine together for the first time.

Sadat then sent Carter a long letter in which he said there was no point in any further meetings because "the parties would only repeat their positions." Adopting a "more in sorrow than in anger" tone, he said he had concluded that "Mr. Begin wants to treat the peace process as a commercial transaction and solve it by barter. This is a distortion of the spirit of my initiative, and will lead us nowhere. We ask for no concessions, the land is ours and we cannot concede it."[29]

It was a moment of decision for President Carter. He had invested countless hours, and a great deal of political capital, in the effort to forge a peace agreement and he had nothing to show for it. Moreover, Sadat had begun to make the argument that the Sinai II agreement was due to expire in October, raising the possibility of a new military conflict.[30] The president's sense of urgency was also growing because by this time it was clear that a genuine revolution was unfolding in Iran and that the position of the Shah, a critical regional ally, was eroding. With nothing else left in his tool kit, Carter rolled the dice: he invited Sadat and Begin to join him in September at Camp David, the presidential retreat in the Maryland hills, for a final effort to break through the impasse.

The Great Gamble: Camp David

This initiative was daring to the point of recklessness. The president of the United States invited two strong-willed men who disliked and mistrusted each other to sit with him for an open-ended attempt to reach a solution that had eluded the most skillful negotiators for the better part of a year because their positions were irreconcilable.

At a White House news conference on August 17, the first reporter the president called on asked the obvious questions: Why are you doing this, and what happens if it fails?

"It is a very high risk thing for me politically," the president said, "because now I think if we are unsuccessful at Camp David, I will certainly have to share part of the blame for that failure."

> But I don't see that I could do anything differently, because I'm afraid that if the leaders do not meet and do not permit their subordinates to meet in a continuing series of tough negotiations that the situation in the Middle East might be much more serious in the future even than it is now. So, I decided on my own, and

later got the concurrence of my top advisers, including Secretary of State Vance and the Vice President and others, to invite both those men to meet with me at Camp David.

We do not have any assurance of success. I do not anticipate being completely successful there and having a peace treaty signed in that brief period of time. But if we can get them to sit down and discuss honestly and sincerely their desires for peace, to explore the compatibilities among them, to identify very clearly the differences, try to resolve those differences, then I think we can set a framework for peace in the future. It may result only in a redetermination or recommitment to continue subsequent negotiations. We might make more progress than that. But we will go there as a full partner in the discussions, depending primarily, however, on the two national leaders themselves to work out the differences between them.

I pray and I hope the whole Nation, the whole world, will pray that we do not fail, because failure could result in a new conflict in the Middle East which could severely damage the security of our own country.

Carter said he believed he knew Begin and Sadat quite well and was "absolutely convinced" that both wanted peace.

It was extraordinary for a president to convene a summit conference with no understanding in advance of what might be accomplished or whether anything might be accomplished, so another reporter asked Carter if he had extracted anything new from Sadat or Begin that would signal the possibility of an agreement. No, he said. Both leaders showed "good faith" by agreeing to come, "but I do not have any commitment from them to change their previously expressed positions as a prerequisite or prelude to coming to Camp David."[31]

Naval Support Facility Thurmont, better known as Camp David, is a secure two-hundred-acre compound operated by the U.S. Navy in the woods of Catoctin Mountain Park, about sixty-five miles northwest of Washington near the little town of Thurmont, Maryland. Every president since Franklin D. Roosevelt has used it as a recreational getaway or as a place for private conversation with foreign leaders, sequestered from inquisitive journalists. Carter, Begin, Sadat, and a handful of their senior advisers gathered there on September 5, 1978, and would emerge only once for thirteen days.

Carter was not the only one for whom Camp David was politically risky. Sadat was in a very delicate position. If the conference succeeded in producing an agreement, which it could do only on terms Israel would accept, Sadat would further alienate his fellow Arabs and increase Egypt's isolation. If it failed, he would have given Israel legitimacy and recognition while gaining nothing in return. At the U.S. embassy in Cairo, Ambassador Eilts's professional diplomats, who liked Sadat, viewed the event with apprehension because they understood his vulnerability.

One of them, Edward L. Peck, said that Carter "wanted peace and love and brotherhood and understanding and friendship. Anwar Sadat wasn't really sure what he wanted except something different from what he'd had. The only person in that triumvirate who knew precisely what he wanted and had known for a long, long time was Menachem Begin."

Another, Arthur Lowrie, said that by the time of Camp David, "the feeling in the embassy political section was that we, at the behest of the Israelis, had asked so many concessions of Sadat, most of which he had given, that his position was already becoming almost untenable. . . . By that time, of course, Sadat had nowhere to go."[32]

Thus there was a critical imbalance among the participants from the first minute of the conference: Sadat and Carter needed an agreement, but Begin did not. And because he did not need an agreement, the Israeli leader was not prepared to yield on his fundamental positions in order to achieve one.

Brzezinski sensed that problem in advance. In a memo to Carter, he noted that "Sadat cannot afford a failure and he knows it; both Sadat and Begin think that you cannot afford failure; but Begin probably believes that a failure at Camp David will hurt you and Sadat, but not him. He may even want to see Sadat discredited and you weakened, thus leaving him with the tolerable status quo instead of pressures to change his life-long beliefs concerning 'Judea and Samaria.'"[33]

As described by participants, Camp David was a marathon of negotiating brinkmanship, bouts of anger and moments of humor, haggling over words and phrases, threats and retreats, stubbornness and flexibility, multiple drafts and endless revisions. Carter discovered on the very first day that the personalities and negotiating styles of the other two would be difficult to mesh: when Carter proposed that the three issue "a call for the world to join us in prayer for the success of our efforts," Sadat agreed immediately while Begin "liked the idea, but first he wanted to see the text. This characteristic response was a prelude to our relationship at Camp David," Carter recalled.[34]

Uncharacteristically for all of them, after the appeal for prayer they issued no public statements during the entire time. They said nothing to the press even when they left the compound for the only time, on the sixth day, Sunday, to visit the nearby Gettysburg battlefield.

Sadat's Awkward Position

For Sadat, the determination to avoid any deal that could be construed as a separate, bilateral peace with Israel put him in the awkward position of negotiating on behalf of the Palestinians, but he had no mandate from them. Ambassador Eilts saw in stark terms the difficulty this would present.

"I frankly am at a total loss as to how Sadat can conclude a full peace treaty or something less on the West Bank by himself," he wrote in a memo to Secretary Vance. "It would be nice if he could, as he sometimes says he will, but he cannot do so and hope to make it stick. Nothing that he negotiates in the West Bank gives any form of legitimacy to the interim regime [that would be created there]. As I have previously stated, it will be building on quicksand and will not endure."[35] His assessment was all too accurate. Within weeks, Carter himself concluded that "Sadat should not have been asked to negotiate for the West Bank."[36]

On the first full day of discussions at Camp David, Sadat told Carter that he was "convinced that Begin really wanted to keep the West Bank," just as Brzezinski had said he did, and as the Likud platform had promised. Much of the often heated discussion over the next eleven days consisted of an unsuccessful search for a formula that would bridge Begin's position and Sadat's, which was that all territories seized in 1967 had to be given back and that Palestinian refugees must be allowed to go home. Carter was furious when, after nearly a week of discussion, Begin said a final document should contain no reference to Resolution 242 because the 1967 war had been "defensive" while 242 applied only to territory acquired through aggression. "What you say convinces me that Sadat was right," the president snapped. "What you want is land!"[37]

Sadat's stated positions were just as absolute and inflexible as Begin's; the difference was that Begin had a well-developed strategy for reaching a well-defined bottom line, while Sadat had neither. By Carter's account, Sadat knew where the Israelis wanted to come out—"They want the West Bank, and are willing to give back the Sinai to me in exchange for the West Bank"—but the Egyptian had neither the leverage nor the negotiating creativity to block them from getting there. If the Americans asked Sadat to modify his positions to accommodate the Israelis, his inclination was to do so because he trusted Carter.

Ambassador Eilts recalled afterward that "Vance several times said to me, 'You know, I'm surprised that Sadat's agreeing with all of this. But if he agrees I must assume he knows what he's doing.'"[38]

As Carter described the negotiations after the conference, "During the last two weeks, the members of all three delegations have spent endless hours, day and night, talking, negotiating, grappling with problems that have divided their people for 30 years. Whenever there was a danger that human energy would fail, or patience would be exhausted or good will would run out—and there were many such moments—these two leaders and the able advisers in all delegations found the resources within them to keep the chances for peace alive."[39] In his memoir, Carter said he believed at the start that as Sadat and Begin got to know each other better, they would find greater rapport but in fact, "for the last ten days of negotiation leading up to our final agreement the two men never spoke to one another, although their cottages were only about a few hundred yards apart."[40]

Begin said the participants "used to go to bed at Camp David between 3 and 4 o'clock in the morning, arise, as we are used to since our boyhood, between 5 and 6, and continue working. The President showed interest in every section, every paragraph, every sentence, every word, every letter of the framework agreements. We had some difficult moments—as usually there are some crises in negotiations, as usually somebody gives a hint that perhaps he would like to pick up and go home. It's all usual. But ultimately, ladies and gentlemen, the President of the United States won the day."[41]

By Vance's account, the differences over the fate of the Palestinians in the West Bank and Gaza were so profound that they nearly torpedoed the entire effort. The Egyptians saw the proposed period of administrative autonomy as a prelude to self-rule and Israeli withdrawal, the Israelis as limited self-government in which Israel retained actual control. Begin clung to his position that Resolution 242 did not require withdrawal from all the occupied territories and sought to maintain the settlements Israel had established in Sinai. Vance said that Sadat "chafed over what he regarded as Begin's haggling over minutiae," but to Begin these "minutiae" were critical to Israel's security and to the future of Zionism.[42] Sadat insisted that peace with Israel be formally linked to resolution of the Palestinian question; Begin, and to some extent Carter, sought the opposite—a self-contained peace treaty between Israel and Egypt, with the Palestinian issue to be resolved by some other process, at some point in the future.

The first participant who gave "a hint that perhaps he would like to pick up and go home," as Begin put it, was Sadat. Carter himself had concluded on the eleventh day that there was no point in further discussions and was thinking about damage control when this news became public, but the one who actually announced that he was leaving was Sadat. He told Vance he was going home because of Begin's insistence on keeping Israeli settlements in Sinai and his inflexibility on the Palestinian issue. When Vance told Carter, the president was "shocked" and called Sadat to say he would come immediately to talk to him.[43] They met privately for an hour. Carter told Sadat that "he would be publicly repudiating some of his own commitments, damaging his reputation as the world's foremost peacemaker, and admitting the fruitlessness of his celebrated visit to Jerusalem. His worst enemies in the Arab world would be proven right in their claims that he had made a foolish mistake." Sadat stayed.[44]

Even on the last day, after Begin had yielded on the Sinai settlements—which he had always been prepared to do—and language had been crafted that might paper over the differences on Palestine, the entire effort nearly blew apart over an issue that had not even been part of the discussions: the status of Jerusalem. There had been extensive conversations about the holy city and access to its shrines, but no agreement because Begin and his delegation said the city's future was nonnegotiable: Israel had annexed East Jerusalem immediately after the 1967 war, and the city would never again be divided. Israeli sovereignty was not subject to bargaining. That could not be reconciled with the American or Egyptian view, which was that the annexation was invalid and the status of East Jerusalem was to be resolved through negotiation. So the conferees decided to finesse it—each of the three parties would attach to the agreement a separate "side letter" stating its position.

That ought to have been a straightforward procedure because each of the three positions was well known and unchanged, but the issue was so sensitive that reiteration could inflame the atmosphere and threaten to undo the fragile agreements that had been achieved on other points. Dayan, Vance, and Quandt provided dramatic accounts of that final Sunday, as the exhausted negotiators were staggering toward the finish line.

As expected, the Israeli letter said that East Jerusalem was and would remain the undivided capital of Israel and that there was nothing to be negotiated. The Egyptian letter stated the opposite: Resolution 242 applied to East Jerusalem as well as to the other territories, the annexation was invalid, and "Arab Jerusalem should be under Arab sovereignty." The American letter stated simply that the position of the United States on Jerusalem remained unchanged from what had been declared at the United Nations by Ambassador Arthur Goldberg in 1967 and by Ambassador Charles Yost in 1969: the United States "does not accept or recognize" Israel's annexation of East Jerusalem, and the "final and permanent status" of the city remained to be negotiated.[45]

This American statement was old wine in old bottles, but it infuriated Begin and Dayan. Now it was Begin's turn to threaten to walk out. He said Israel would not sign any document that contained any reference whatever to Jerusalem. Dayan said that if the Israelis had known Jerusalem would come up, they would not have come to Camp David in the first place. The Americans, they said, could not tell them that the Western Wall, Hebrew University, Hadassah Hospital, and other Jewish institutions in East Jerusalem rightly belonged to Jordan. Why did Jordan, which had seized the city by force in 1948, have a higher claim than Israel, which had seized it by force in 1967? Carter, equally angry, demanded to know if Israel was trying to dictate what the United States could say about its own position on a matter of international policy.

At that point it would have been a normal human reaction for the participants to give up and walk away in frustration, but that it is not how statesmen and professional diplomats respond in such a situation. They do not give in to outbursts of temper. They return, warily and wearily, to the bargaining table, because the consequences of failure would be politically unacceptable and strategically dangerous. So Vance and Israeli attorney general Aharon Barak, Begin's legal adviser, went back to work.

The resolution proved to be surprisingly simple. The United States restated its longstanding position; it referred to the statements by Goldberg and Yost but did not quote them. That somehow appeased the Israelis, who accepted the American and Egyptian letters because, as Dayan put it, "they were not of an operational nature."[46]

Thus the Camp David "Framework for Peace in the Middle East" survived. The agreements it contained had the virtue of making war even less likely than before, and of resolving most issues affecting only Israel and Egypt, but they were also deeply flawed because they failed to resolve the fundamental and irreconcilable positions between Israel and the Arabs over the future of the West Bank, Gaza, and East Jerusalem and over the political status of the Palestinians. Those issues were left for future negotiations. Nearly forty years later, they remain unresolved, a constant source of tension and intermittent violence.

Flawed Agreement, Flawed Outcome

The Camp David framework was not a peace treaty. It was a set of agreements that would make it possible for Egypt and Israel to reach a treaty. But by the nature of those agreements it was now inevitable that the treaty between Israel and Egypt would be exactly the bilateral peace that Sadat had said he would never accept. Begin had exploited all of Sadat's diplomatic and strategic weaknesses at Camp David to arrive at arrangements that reflected all of Begin's bottom-line demands. In theory, the establishment of peace between Egypt and Israel was linked to a resolution of the Palestinian question; in reality, the language of Camp David on that subject was so full of loopholes, so full of aspirational language that was not self-fulfilling or enforceable, that there was no pressure on Israel to deliver.

In the Camp David Accords, Israel and Egypt agreed to negotiate a full-service peace treaty that would reflect the "land for peace" foundation first laid out in Resolution 242. The Sinai would be restored to Egyptian sovereignty all the way back to the 1967 line and Israel's armed forces would withdraw. Israel's military airfields in Sinai would be converted to civilian use. A highway across the southern tip of Israel would connect Egypt with Jordan. The Suez Canal, the Gulf of Tiran, and the Strait of Aqaba would be open to ships of all nations. Egypt would extend to Israel "full recognition, including diplomatic, economic, and cultural relations" and an end to the economic boycott of Israel. Those essential elements of a peace agreement between Egypt and Israel met Sadat's most fundamental requirement, restoration of all territory lost in 1967, as well as Israel's, full peace with its most powerful neighbor.

The Camp David framework asserted that Israel and Egypt were committed to the achievement of a comprehensive regional settlement that would reflect the "principles" of Resolution 242 "in all its parts." But when it came to specifics, the very first paragraph revealed that this was a sham, or to use what had quickly become a common term, a "fig leaf," designed to disguise the bilateral nature of the agreement:

"Egypt, Israel, Jordan and the representatives of the Palestinian people," it said, "should participate in negotiations on the resolution of the Palestinian problem in all its aspects." There was no mandate, nor could there have been because Jordan and "representatives of the Palestinian people" were not parties to the agreement. Egypt and Israel could not order them to the negotiating table.

That flaw permeated the entire document. The Palestinians were to gain self-governing autonomy, it said, and "Egypt, Israel, and Jordan will agree on the modalities for establishing the elected self-governing authority in the West Bank and Gaza." No document signed at Camp David could compel future negotiators to agree, especially when one of the designated negotiating parties, in this case Jordan, wanted nothing to do with the process. The use of the term "West Bank," as opposed to "Eretz Israel," was a rhetorical concession by Begin that involved no commitment as to outcome. Similarly, the framework declared that "a strong local police force will be constituted by the self-governing authority. It will be composed of inhabitants of the West Bank and Gaza." It was inherently contradictory to order the supposedly self-governing authority to establish a certain kind of police organization, and who was to decide if any force that was established was sufficiently "strong"? In any case Israel and Egypt could not order Arab residents of the territories to participate in such a force if they rejected the entire idea as a cover for continued Israeli rule.

As the side letters to this agreement revealed, some issues that would have been essential to a comprehensive peace were set aside entirely, including sovereignty over Jerusalem and the status of Israeli settlements, even those in Sinai. Begin promised to ask the Knesset to approve elimination of the Sinai settlements but could not guarantee the outcome.

These flaws were readily apparent to Egypt's professional diplomats. Foreign Minister Mohammed Ibrahim Kamel resigned, just as his predecessor, Ismail Fahmy, had resigned over Sadat's trip to Jerusalem. Others complained privately that Sadat had accepted the framework over their objections, but in public they acquiesced. For Sadat, there was no turning back. The treaty—and with it, recovery of all Egyptian land—still lay ahead, and he was still expecting "linkage," a direct tie between implementation of an Egyptian-Israeli accord and a sufficient package of Israeli concessions to the Palestinians to make it acceptable to them and to other Arabs. He trusted Carter to deliver this "linkage." As Vance put it, "A major step forward had been taken, but in a sense we had only just begun."[47]

If anything, the negotiating atmosphere deteriorated after Camp David. On the most difficult issue, the political status of the Palestinians, Begin now adopted the same bargaining strategy he had used in the past when referring to Resolution 242: If it was not in the Camp David texts, Israel was not obliged to do it. And since the Camp David Accords had left this issue unresolved, with only a vague promise of an ill-defined Palestinian autonomy, Israel was in a strong position to maintain its military presence in the West Bank and to continue adding to its settlements there. At this point the Israelis raised two new issues: retention of, or a guaranteed replacement for, the oil they had been extracting from the Sinai fields, and insertion of a separate clause in the proposed treaty specifying that it would take precedence over Egypt's defense commitments to other Arab states.

Carter was running out of patience. He was tired of the haggling, and he had other pressing matters to deal with: the Iranian revolution brought about the downfall of the Shah in January 1979, and the United States was in the final months of difficult negotiations with the Soviet Union on the nuclear arms reduction treaty known as SALT II.

Sadat, outmaneuvered at Camp David, had put himself in a bind. The other Arabs were threatening economic and political reprisals against Egypt if he signed a peace treaty based on the Camp David agreement. Sadat needed to establish much firmer linkage to the Palestinian issue to persuade them that he was not agreeing to a separate peace, but Begin was just as determined to avoid more specific linkage as Sadat was desperate to achieve it.

Sadat, with optimism real or feigned, told the people of Egypt after Camp David that the accords contained "definite provisions for the solution of the Palestine question, in all its aspects" and that Begin was facing "a terrible dilemma" in trying to reconcile those provisions with his commitment to "Eretz Israel."[48] But in reality the Camp David agreements were toothless. Brzezinski warned Carter that "the Israelis are now launching a concerted effort to imply that any form of linkage is a deviation from Camp David. This is not the case, and it is important for us to establish this fact."[49] Eventually the president's national security adviser came to believe that Begin never took the Palestinian autonomy agreement seriously at all.[50]

The Israeli leader had his own political problems—he was being criticized at home for having given away too much at Camp David. He responded by insisting that nothing in the accords went beyond limited Palestinian autonomy under continued Israeli military control. Those statements, in turn, reinforced pressure on Sadat to deliver something more.

Within a few days after leaving Camp David, Carter concluded that Begin did not intend to fulfill even the limited commitments he had made on the subject of the Palestinians. His diary entry from September 19 noted that Begin "is behaving in a completely irresponsible way." The Israeli leader was making public statements in which "he continued to disavow the basic principles of the accords relating to Israel's withdrawal of its armed forces and military government from the West Bank, negotiations on an equal basis with the Palestinians and other Arabs, and the granting of full autonomy to the residents of the occupied areas." Carter realized what had been apparent to others since Likud published its campaign platform the previous spring: "Begin wanted to keep two things: the peace with Egypt—and the West Bank."[51]

Begin had an advantage, because the imprecise wording and lack of enforcement mechanism in the Camp David texts left him abundant room to maneuver, as he had intended. Arguments about what the accords really meant and what the participants were required to do dragged on through months of what Vance called "tedious hairsplitting," complicated by a public dispute between the Israelis and the Americans over the length of a moratorium on settlements to which Begin had agreed in one of the Camp David side letters.[52] The Israeli parliament voted to approve the Camp David agreements and to remove Jewish settlers from Sinai, a development that Americans viewed as positive but was in accord with Begin's overall strategy: to give back Sinai as the price of peace with Egypt, while keeping the West Bank.

When Vice President Hosni Mubarak went to see Carter in Washington near the end of 1978, the president appealed to the Egyptians to understand Begin's position. "The Israelis have already made great concessions," he said.

It is hard for you and President Sadat to know how difficult these decisions are for Prime Minister Begin. He gave more in Sinai than the Labor Party would have given. They wanted to keep a corridor to Sharm el-Sheik, and they wanted to keep the settlements. They would not recognize the Palestinians' right to self-government. Begin has made tremendous concessions, and President Sadat has also made generous concessions, but there is a tendency in Egypt not to see how far Begin has come. In the Camp David agreements, linkage is clearly spelled out. The linkage is already there. After hours, after weeks, we have Israeli agreement on linkage. This is done both in the treaty and in other documents. Nothing could be clearer than the commitment to begin negotiations within one month of the ratification of the treaty on the West Bank and Gaza. This is tangible and clear. We have gotten that commitment from the Israelis. This will take place before anything else has happened in terms of implementing the Egyptian-Israeli treaty. This is a very clear linkage. We cannot make more of a commitment in the treaty than was made at Camp David, and at Camp David there was already a complete linkage guaranteed and approved by Begin and Sadat.

Mubarak was not convinced. "No one now believes that Israel will give full autonomy," he said.[53]

Carter, who had spent New Year's Eve of 1977 celebrating at a lavish dinner and party hosted by the Shah of Iran, spent New Year's Eve 1978 huddled with Vance at Camp David, contemplating what to do about the disintegration of the Shah's regime and the new impasse in the Middle East negotiations. Not only had the other Arabs refused to join the Camp David process, they were openly denouncing it as a sellout of the Palestinians and threatening reprisals against Sadat if he signed a treaty based on the Camp David framework. Sadat, bested in the Camp David negotiations, had seriously miscalculated the reactions of other Arab leaders and put himself in a position somewhere between discomfort and desperation.

Carter and Vance were tired of the whole process—tired of Begin's maneuvers, of Sadat's twists and turns, of the refusal of Jordan, Saudi Arabia, and the Palestinians to take part in negotiations that would be in their own interest. But they could not just walk away; the president had invested too much time, effort, and political capital to abandon the quest, and he believed U.S. interests in the Middle East required him to keep trying. And so they beat on, boats against the current.

In February 1979, Vance met at Camp David with Dayan and Egyptian prime minister Mustafa Khalil, a dapper, sophisticated politician whom Sadat had assigned to negotiate details of a treaty. This gathering proved to be "short, cold, and sterile," as Dayan put it. The participants made no progress either on the major outstanding issue, the future of the Palestinians, or on short-term items of lesser import, such as the priority of a peace treaty over Egypt's mutual defense agreements with other Arab countries and Israel's oil supply from the Sinai wells.

Before the fall of the Shah in early 1979, Iran had been a major supplier of oil to Israel. With that source now cut off, Israel wanted a clause in the peace treaty guaranteeing its right to buy oil from Egypt; Vance responded that Egypt could not be forced to sell oil to any particular customer. The issue was finally resolved by a U.S. guarantee to assure Israel's supply of oil for fifteen years, but only after the Israeli cabinet first rejected it as a de facto continuation of the Arab economic boycott.

A Last Roll of the Dice

After the failure of Vance's discussions with Khalil and Dayan, Carter—with no other plausible move to make—rolled the dice one more time. He decided to go to Egypt and Israel for a final effort, knowing that failure, coupled with the fall of the Shah, could cripple his prospects for reelection the following year.

According to Carter's memoirs, when he and his wife arrived in Cairo on March 8, 1979, they "felt a glow of welcome, warmth, and friendship which remained throughout the visit." When he told Sadat he was "concerned about his isolation in the Arab world," which had deepened since Camp David, Sadat replied, "My friend, you take care of the Israelis and I will take care of the Arabs." The two presidents reached agreement on the remaining issues within an hour.[54]

The remainder of Carter's stay in Egypt was a kind of premature victory lap, including a visit to the Great Pyramids and a slow ride to Alexandria, with Sadat at his side, aboard an open-sided train. Carter told American reporters aboard the train that some details still remained to be worked out, but Sadat said there were no more issues on the Egyptian side. "Let me tell you this," he said. "We must get rid of the distrust, because, unfortunately, there are still some shades of distrust until this moment, and it is not from the Egyptian side. We have dropped all complexes and everything through my visit to Jerusalem. It is a word here, a word, but I don't see any difficulty in reaching an agreement upon the main principal issues."[55]

Carter then went to Israel, believing that a final agreement on treaty language was now in hand. He got a rude awakening as soon as he had a conversation with Begin.

"Begin then told me for the first time," Carter wrote afterward, "that he would not sign or initial any agreement; that I would have to conclude my talks with him, let him submit the proposals to the cabinet, let the Knesset have an extended debate, going into all the issues concerning the definition of autonomy, East Jerusalem, and then only after all that would he sign the documents. I couldn't believe it." Begin, he now felt, did not really want a peace treaty—"he was obsessed with keeping all the occupied territory except the Sinai."[56]

By that time it should not have been a surprise to Carter that Begin wanted to keep all the lands seized in 1967 except the Sinai in exchange for peace with Egypt. Begin was betting, as he had at Camp David, that Sadat would eventually accept that bargain because he had no other option. Carter was furious at the Israeli leader because his own prestige and political future were on the line. He wanted a document signed while he was in the Middle East; he did not want to go back to the United States and wait for the outcome of some interminable debate in the Israeli parliament, with no assurance about the outcome.

For Sadat, this was on one level a moment of satisfaction: he had driven a very large wedge between the American president and Israel. He, Sadat, was the peacemaker, the statesman; Begin was the land-grabbing obstructionist. But on another level, Sadat had his back to the wall. He had given all he could reasonably give without abandoning the Palestinians and further alienating the other Arabs, but it was still not enough. He had given Carter his authorization to negotiate whatever points remained in dispute, and Carter was finding Begin stubborn and immovable, so Sadat would have to give still more.

After Carter's dismaying meeting with Begin, whose positions were far more rigid than those of Weizman and even Dayan, the Israeli cabinet met to review the situation. At one point, according to Dayan, the cabinet agreed to "the Egyptian request to change a word ('derogate' to 'contravene') in the 'interpretive note' to Article 6 (5)" because, Carter told Begin, the Egyptians found the word "derogate" difficult to accept. We have tried to find a synonym that would be acceptable to you."[57] (No wonder Carter complained that "[f]or the last 18 months I, the President of the most powerful nation on earth, have acted the postman."[58]) The Israelis agreed to withdraw from the town of el-Arish, administrative capital of the Sinai, earlier than previously planned and acceded to Egypt's wish to phase in diplomatic relations as the Sinai handover progressed in stages, but two issues remained. The Israelis would not agree to the stationing of Egyptian liaison officers in Gaza, and they insisted on the right to buy oil directly from Egypt, without an American intermediary.

"The Camp David accords," Dayan noted, "had made no mention of Egyptian liaison officers in Gaza, and we would not have them there." As for oil, it was less a matter of fuel supply than of politics: direct Israeli access to oil from Egypt would pierce the longstanding Arab economic boycott of Israel.

Carter was scheduled to go home the next day and did not see any point in staying longer. He planned to stop briefly at the Cairo airport to break the bad news to Sadat. Facing this disastrous outcome, Dayan, Vance, and other officials labored through the night to craft language that would bridge the differences.

On oil, there would be a clause stipulating that Israel had the right to buy Egyptian oil, but not requiring Egypt to sell it. If Egypt did not, the United States would guarantee to cover Israel's needs for fifteen years, no minor matter given the supply shortages in the United States and the skyrocketing price of oil in global markets. With peace, Egyptians would be able to move freely into the territory of Gaza, but there would be no mention of liaison officers.

After a last breakfast with Begin, at which the prime minister agreed to relax some restrictions on the movement of Palestinians so that families could be reunited, Carter returned to Cairo with new requests: accept the amendments offered by the Israeli cabinet, drop references in the proposed text to Egyptian access to Gaza, offer a pipeline from the Sinai oil wells to Israel, and invite Israeli president Navon to visit Egypt. Sadat agreed to all of them and the deal was finally done. The treaty was to be signed in Washington on March 26, 1979.

The Reality of a Separate Peace

Jimmy Carter hailed Sadat as "the world's foremost peacemaker."[59] Sadat and Begin shared the Nobel Peace Prize in 1978, after Camp David. But the treaty they signed left gaps in the regional order that plague the Middle East, and the United States, even now. It was indeed the separate peace that Begin sought and Sadat always insisted he would not accept.

"I was still convinced," Carter wrote, "that an effort to carry out all the provisions of the Camp David accords in good faith would lead to the realization of the legitimate goals of Israel, its neighbors, and the Palestinians. But this was not to be."

That was because the treaty itself said nothing about the future of the West Bank or the political status of the Arabs who lived there, except for an "agreed minute" specifying that the text "shall not be construed as contravening the provisions of the framework for peace in the Middle East agreed at Camp David." In a side letter, Sadat and Begin promised Carter that within a month of ratification of the treaty, the two countries would begin negotiations on "the modalities for establishing the elected self-governing authority (administrative council), define its powers and responsibilities, and agreed-upon other related issues." They set a goal of completing these negotiations within a year. Jordan was to be invited to participate, but of course could not be compelled to do so.[60]

This language reflected all the loopholes that were in the Camp David documents: there was no enforcement mechanism, and no punishment for failure to carry out the provisions for Palestinian autonomy. Israel retained military control of the West Bank. The treaty did nothing and promised nothing for all the Palestinian refugees who lived in camps in Jordan, Syria, and Lebanon—as they still do, a generation later. It left the status of Arab residents of East Jerusalem even murkier than that of the West Bankers, because Israel took the position that they lived within Israel and thus were not to be part of the autonomy process. If Israel chose not to be forthcoming on these matters, Egypt could do nothing but protest; it had given up its leverage.

In the end, the autonomy talks went nowhere, partly because Begin had no intention of loosening Israeli control over the West Bank, partly because Israeli settlements there continued, partly because Jordan refused to participate, and partly because continued intransigence and attempted terrorist attacks by the Palestinians hardened Israeli opinion.

The Carter Presidential Library has posted on its website a sort of "lessons learned" paper about Camp David and its aftermath that offers this observation: "Sovereign states cannot be made to enforce treaties and negotiated settlements. They must *want* to abide by the agreement."[61] Menachem Begin's Israel did not want.

Robert S. Dillon, who became deputy chief of mission at the U.S. embassy in Cairo while the fitful posttreaty autonomy talks were being conducted, said he soon concluded that the lesson Israel had learned from all the negotiations since the war "was not that Sadat was a great man but that if you hit the Arabs long and hard enough they would eventually cave in. The ideas that they put forward in enormous detail, and which they kept pushing in the autonomy talks, were really not addressing 'autonomy' in the normal definition of the word. There was no autonomy for land, no autonomy for water resources. There was autonomy for people. In essence this really meant the privilege for the Palestinians of being second- or third-class citizens in lands controlled by other people. They could pick up the garbage, which they were already doing, but nothing beyond that."[62]

Ambassador Eilts used even stronger language: "Nobody was quite sure what autonomy meant. For Egypt it meant self-determination, or leading to self-determination. To Israel, it meant a kind of bondage status." Begin, he said flatly, "really had not intended to carry through on the Palestinian side of the bargain" and "reneged on his commitments about settlements in occupied territories. It was clear that he had agreed that there were not to be any further settlements but he continued to push them."[63]

Eilts and other American negotiators, and the Egyptians, no doubt believed that Begin "reneged on his commitments about settlements," but in fact no provision of the Camp David Framework agreement, the peace treaty, or any of the associated annexes, protocols, or side letters said specifically that Israel would halt the expansion of Jewish settlement on the West Bank. The documents contain language about "territorial integrity" and about implementation of "Resolution 242 in all its parts," but Begin out-negotiated Sadat and Carter on this subject. The language of the texts left him free to interpret the agreements differently.

Throughout 1980, the process of defining and implementing autonomy for the Palestinians died a lingering, painful death. Carter, Sadat, and Begin repeatedly pledged to keep going, but the diplomatic record is replete with statements and messages reflecting anger, frustration, and even despair. President Carter's advisers warned him that the Soviet invasion of Afghanistan at the end of 1979 had raised the stakes in the autonomy talks, because the United States needed to show the Arabs that it could deliver on its promises while Moscow offered only armed force. That may have been accurate, but it did not help the Americans find a way to break the impasse.

The autonomy negotiators set a May 26 target date for completion of the talks, but it was apparent by spring that the deadline could not be met. In March, the stalemate prompted Sadat to offer yet another of his half-baked ideas: he would go to Washington and address the U.S. Congress. He would explain the situation, make public the letters he had exchanged with Begin to demonstrate the Israeli's "intransigence," and invite the American lawmakers to write a sample treaty based on what might be executed between the United States and any friendly nation. Sadat told Ambassador Eilts that he would sign that treaty "without reading it."[64] This proposition was unwelcome in Washington because it would amount to a proclamation that the Camp David process had failed, so nothing came of it.

In April, Sadat wrote to Begin saying that if the talks did not begin to show progress, the United Nations might take up the matter once again to establish "new terms of reference," outside the Camp David framework, on the future of the Palestinians. If that were to happen, Sadat said, it would "give credence to the allegations that the peace accords we signed constitute a separate peace arrangement. We reject this categorically. As I told you in our first meeting in Camp David, I would never accept a separate or partial agreement. I need not emphasize this any further."[65] The target date passed without tangible progress. Israeli settlements on the West Bank continued to expand.

On July 30, the Knesset passed by a vote of 69–15 a bill to make Jerusalem the legal, permanent capital of Israel. It changed nothing on the ground, but it sent a clear message, which Carter understood.

He said it "almost puts the final nail in the coffin of the Camp David negotiations between Israel and Egypt."[66]

In the years that followed the treaty, the limbo-like status of Gaza bred despair and resentment that led to the rise of the radical resistance group Hamas and to periodic outbreaks of armed conflict with Israel. Limitations on the number of troops Egypt could station in Sinai created a security vacuum to be filled by smugglers, illegal migrants, and terrorists. Jerusalem is still seen by everyone except the Israelis as an open issue. And Israeli settlers continue to move to the West Bank. Resolution of the West Bank question has eluded every American president since Carter, even though a deal briefly seemed achievable after the Oslo agreements of 1993, when Israel finally agreed to negotiate directly with the PLO. Oslo produced an unforgettable image comparable to Sadat's appearance before the Knesset: Yasser Arafat and Yitzhak Rabin shaking hands at the White House before a beaming President Bill Clinton, but that moment of good will was only an ironic memory when the second Palestinian *intifada*, or uprising, broke out in 2000. In 2014, after months of intense but fruitless negotiations aimed at a permanent settlement based on a "two-state solution," with an independent Palestine alongside Israel, President Barack Obama's secretary of state, John F. Kerry, abandoned the quest.

The peace treaty between Egypt and Israel, on the other hand, has withstood the turbulence and conflict that have scarred the Middle East for all the years since it was signed, because maintaining it has been in the interests of both countries. Sadat often argued that his deal with Israel, however flawed, had one overriding virtue: Egypt was the only Arab country, and he was the only Arab leader, to regain any of the lands lost in 1967. That was true at the time, but it only reinforced the argument of his critics that Sadat had accepted a separate peace that benefited only Egypt and Israel. And the treaty had the perverse effect—just as Sadat's many critics had predicted—of nullifying the greatest restraint on Israeli policies. Israel, still facing the enmity of all Arab countries except Egypt, could do what it felt was necessary without fear of Egyptian response.

On June 7, 1981, Israeli warplanes destroyed a nuclear reactor that

Iraq was building with French help at Osirak, near Baghdad. The Iraqis never fired a shot, the raid lasted two minutes, and all the Israeli planes returned home safely. Iraq at that time was in compliance with nuclear safeguards established in the Nuclear Nonproliferation Treaty, and Israel's action prompted strong criticism around the world. At the United Nations, the United States voted for a harshly worded UN resolution saying that the Security Council "strongly condemns" Israel's action.[67] Sadat was furious, but aside from calling off a planned visit to Egypt by Shimon Peres, then the leader of Israel's opposition Labor Party, he did nothing about it. Israel was scheduled to complete its withdrawal from Egyptian territory the following year, and Sadat did not want to give Israel any reason to interrupt that process. His inaction was understandable, but it outraged critics at home and throughout the Arab world; they could see that Israel was holding back on Palestinian self-government and charged that Sadat had given Israel a free hand to use its military power.[68]

Peres and Labor then lost an election they had been expected to win as Israelis rallied around Begin and Likud. The new cabinet was devoid of relative moderates on the subject of Palestine, such as Dayan and Weizman. It now consisted almost entirely of hard-liners such as Yitzhak Shamir, Ariel Sharon, and Yosef Burg, a leader of the National Religious Party, whom Begin selected to lead the Israeli team in the negotiations on Palestinian autonomy. Given that Burg's party believed that Judea and Samaria belonged to Israel by divine right, this was a prescription for failure in the talks. U.S. ambassador Lewis reported to Vance that "[t]he fundamental idiocy of the way the Israeli negotiating team and structure has been put together will put an enormous boulder in the road no matter how we try to ignore it."[69]

The autonomy negotiations sputtered on for many months afterward, but never resolved the fundamental questions: What powers would the Palestinian self-governing group have, what would be the status of Jerusalem, and to what extent was implementation of the Egypt-Israel bilateral treaty linked to these other issues? Begin had told Carter that "there shouldn't be any doubt in your mind or with President Sadat that we want to implement the autonomy."[70] But before autonomy could be implemented it had to be defined, and it never was. In the minds of the Israelis, the more power the self-governing body was to have, the more it would resemble an independent state, which almost by definition would be hostile to Israel and armed by the Soviet Union.

Six months after Begin's reelection, his government proclaimed the annexation of the Golan Heights, brushing off Carter's warning that it would be "a serious mistake" because it "would in effect signal to the rest of the world an abandonment by Israel of a commitment to UN Resolution 242.[71] By that time Sadat had been dead two months, succeeded by his plodding, unimaginative vice president, Hosni Mubarak, who was the stylistic opposite of Sadat but equally determined to adhere to the peace treaty. Even in 1982, when Israel staged a full-scale invasion of Lebanon, marched all the way to Beirut, and drove out the Palestine Liberation Organization, Mubarak resisted calls to abrogate the treaty. He was no friend of Israel—in all his years as president he went there only once, for the funeral of Yitzhak Rabin—but Egypt lacked the military and economic resources to return to the battlefield.

And so even now, after all that had happened in Egypt since Mubarak was overthrown in 2011, including a year in which Egypt was run by the Muslim Brotherhood, the peace treaty remains in force while Israel retains control of the West Bank, and Gaza remains an open sore, as demonstrated vividly by the war between Israel and Hamas in 2014. That was the separate peace into which Sadat was maneuvered by Menachem Begin and, in the end, by Jimmy Carter. For all his courage and vision, Sadat was undone by his naïveté about the Israelis. He believed that the October War would induce Israel to embrace full peace with its Arab neighbors, on terms the Arabs could accept. And then he believed that his trip to Jerusalem would produce that outcome. The truth was that nothing that he did or could have done would have produced that outcome, for the same reasons that nothing that has happened since has done so.

Moshe Dayan provided an appropriate epitaph for the daring quest Sadat began with his visit to Jerusalem: "While his initiative, and his presence in Israel's capital, will long be remembered, his speech will not. Future historians will examine the text, compare it with what subsequently happened, and quickly discern those parts that were realized and those that remained mere words on paper, soon forgotten."[72] He did not say who was to blame for that unhappy reality.

6 The End of Arab Nationalism

In *The October Working Paper,* the ambitious political and personal manifesto that he published in 1974, not long after the October War, Anwar Sadat extended generous tribute to the fellow Arabs whose support had made the triumph possible.

"Arab national feeling," he wrote, was "foremost among the elements of victory [and] our success in fighting Israel on two fronts. I seize this opportunity to salute once again my brother, President Hafez El Assad, who had the courage to participate with me in taking the decision to fight. I also salute the brave Syrian armed forces and the heroic Syrian people."

He was equally effusive about the oil states that had participated in the embargo. "The rallying of the Arab countries around the frontline countries and the moral and material support they extended in addition to employing the oil weapon in the battle doubtless contributed in achieving victory. The Arab kings and heads of state and their people supported us, and thanking them for their efforts is a duty. Perhaps one of the most important results of the October War is that Arab nationalism has transcended the confines of being a mere slogan to become a palpable, well-defined action. The October War has raised the prestige of all Arabs."[1]

Sadat's comments reflected the spirit of the Egyptian constitution of 1971, the first year of Sadat's presidency, which declared that the people were "convinced that Arab unity is a call of history and of the future, and a demand of destiny; and that unity can materialise only under the protection of an Arab nation capable of warding off any threat, under whatever pretexts." But his encomiums were wishful thinking at best, cynical manipulation of the facts at worst. Sadat must have known that Assad was deeply aggrieved over what he believed was the Egyptian leader's duplicity about his war aims. He knew Libya's Muammar Qaddafi opposed even his basic cease-fire agreement with Israel. Beyond that, the unilateral peace initiative upon which Sadat would soon embark, combined with the fratricide of the civil war that erupted in Lebanon in April 1975, would shatter whatever good feelings existed within the Arab world as a whole after the October War. With each landmark on the road to peace—the Sinai II agreement, the Jerusalem trip, Camp David, and finally the treaty—Sadat further separated himself and Egypt from their Arab brothers. By taking Egypt out of the struggle against Israel, Sadat put an end to the great aspiration that had inspired Arabs for generations: to function as a collective brotherhood of national spirit that would transcend mere geographic boundaries.

Sadat really had no choice. Had he and Egypt remained captives of pan-Arab rhetoric, he would never have lifted from Egypt the unsupportable burden of the conflict with Israel. Sadat understood that it was necessary to separate Egyptian policy from the sterile posturing that passed for Arab diplomacy in the years between the wars. It might have been politically gratifying to refuse to acknowledge the existence of Israel or to negotiate with it, as the Arabs collectively had done at the 1967 Khartoum summit, but doing so would not produce any positive results.

The hard truth was that the other Arabs were not ready to make peace with Israel on any terms Israel would ever accept, and therefore Sadat had no option but to go it alone. At the beginning of this journey, he truly believed that if Egypt regained its land through negotiations, the other Arabs would follow. Was he not their hero, the Hero of the Crossing? Yes, he had been, but that was then. With his trip to Jerusalem, the Arabs' esteem vaporized.

Secretary Vance heard this message bluntly from King Hussein of Jordan when they met in Amman shortly after Camp David. The king said he was "flattered and touched" to have been included in the agreement, but he did not intend to participate in negotiating the future of the Palestinians because the Camp David Accords failed to answer the most fundamental question: "How can Palestinians determine their own future or organize the way to self-government under even a partial Israeli occupation?" Hussein told Vance that Camp David "spells out a separate Egyptian/Israeli agreement which is unconnected or binding with the other aspects of the Arab/Israeli problem. This will lead to the isolation of Egypt and the paralyzing of the peace process. We feel this very strongly, particularly since a separate peace has been a primary Israeli objective throughout."[2]

The king then gave an interview to the *New York Times* in which he said, "The Arab world is a family, [and] it is not a situation where Egypt is the shepherd and the rest are a herd that can be moved in any direction without question."[3]

Hussein could have been speaking for Morocco or Saudi Arabia or any of the other so-called moderate Arab states, to say nothing of the hard-liners who rejected the entire idea of negotiating with Israel.

After Sadat's death, Jordan eventually came around to his position, as did the Palestine Liberation Organization when it entered into the doomed Oslo I agreement of 1993. No other Arab states have followed Egypt and Jordan on the path to peace because the price they want, in advance, is the price Israel will never pay: full withdrawal to the 1967 lines of demarcation. At the instigation of Saudi Arabia, the entire Arab League formalized that offer in 2002: peace in exchange for all the land, including East Jerusalem. That was a giant step forward from the "Three No's" of 1967, but Israel was not going to accept that offer then and has never done so.[4]

At the time of his peace initiative, Sadat failed to understand that rejection of Israel was the only glue other than language holding together an "Arab nation" that encompassed monarchies and pseudo-republics, religious regimes and secular governments; the Arab states were rivals as much as they were brothers. Sadat did what he had to do, but most of his fellow Arabs never forgave him.

Toward the end of his presidency he made half-hearted attempts at reconciliation, but only after his death was Egypt restored to Arab good graces. Under Sadat's successor, Hosni Mubarak, Egypt remained uncomfortably at peace with Israel and out of the conflict; the other Arabs accepted it back into their fold only when it was no longer run by the man they regarded as a sellout and a traitor.

One Language, One People?

Who is an Arab? The standard answer is that an Arab is anyone whose native or first language is Arabic, whether that person is born in Mauritania or Iraq. Arabic binds the peoples of many cultures, in North Africa, in the Arabian Peninsula, and in the Levant—more so even than Islam, for many of those Arabic speakers are Christians. The League of Arab States, formed in Egypt in 1945, describes itself as a group of "independent Arab states," but its charter offers no definition of the term Arab. Djibouti and Somalia, in the Horn of Africa, are members, as is Comoros, a tiny island nation in the Indian Ocean.

The league has twenty-two members, including Palestine. Their citizens differ in skin color, dress, and colonial histories; most were occupied for centuries by the Ottoman Turks, and later by the French, the British, or the Italians. What they share is a fierce desire not to be occupied again by any foreign power and a sense that their culture, once overpowered by outsiders, is worthy of respect.

In the first half of the twentieth century, that collective desire came to be expressed in a political movement, or more accurately a political philosophy, known as Arab nationalism, defined by the scholar Albert Hourani as the belief that "those who speak Arabic form a 'nation,' and that this nation should be independent and united." For most of the people in the regions where it is spoken, Arabic is a natural binder because it was the language of the Prophet Muhammad and of the Koran. As a political force, however, the primacy of the language was a late arrival. Through most of the twentieth century, the language of business and commerce was French in North Africa and Christian parts of Lebanon, and English in the Gulf.[5] It was a strong statement when independent Algeria, free of French domination, switched the language of education from French to Arabic.

Egyptians spoke Arabic, but until the 1952 revolution Egypt remained on the margins of the Arab unity movement; it was distinct because of its unique pre-Arab cultural history and its links to Africa, upstream on the Nile. That sense of separateness changed when Nasser enshrined Arab unity as a central tenet of his political philosophy.

Mahmoud Masadi, a prominent Tunisian educator, wrote that the main "elements" of Arab nationalism are "the unity of our language, which is Arabic; the unity of our literature, which is Arab; [and] the unity of our culture and civilization," despite the incorporation of ideas from other cultures. "The elements in question are partly spiritual and partly historical and inherited; some are rooted in the past, others are features of the modern world." Regardless of politics, Masadi wrote, Arabs share a "psychic factor," which he defined as "the shared will to live together as a community."[6]

This belief in a collective Arab nation, or *watan*, a fraternity of the spirit that transcends boundaries of state or even religion, has proved irreconcilable with the modern organization of government known as the nation-state, but it remains an emotional aspiration of the Arab people collectively. It has been nurtured by schoolbooks that celebrate the glories of medieval Arab civilization, the early achievements of Arab science, and the victories of the "Arab Revolt," as the uprising against the Ottomans during World War I is known.

Perhaps the most eloquent statement of Arab national aspirations was delivered by the young Prince Faisal of Arabia, later king of Saudi Arabia, at the Versailles Peace Conference after the Great War. With T. E. Lawrence, "Lawrence of Arabia," translating, Faisal told the delegates, "The aim of the Arab nationalist movement is to unite the Arabs eventually into one nation. We believe that our ideal of Arab unity in Asia is justified beyond the need of argument." The prince's father, Abdul Aziz al-Saud, would create the modern Saudi Arabia a few years later by capturing Mecca and Jeddah by force of arms and uniting the Arabian Peninsula under his control. That is, this apostle of Arab unity would achieve power by sending his Arab warriors to defeat another Arab leader's Arab warriors. Faisal, however, said

Abdul Aziz was "convinced of the ultimate triumph of the ideal of unity, if no attempt is made now to thwart it or hinder it by dividing the area as spoils of war among the Great Powers." The Arabs, he said, "expect the Powers to think of them as one potential people, jealous of their language and liberty, and they ask that no step be taken inconsistent with the prospect of an eventual union of these areas under one sovereign."[7]

Faisal's apprehension about a division of the former Ottoman lands as "spoils of war" was well founded, for he and everyone else at Versailles knew by then that Britain and France, having lured the Arabs into supporting them against the Ottomans during the war, had secretly agreed to do just what he had feared: establish European colonial rule in place of the Ottomans. In the Sykes-Picot Agreement of 1916 Britain, France, and Czarist Russia, their ally in the war, had arranged to divide among themselves the lands to be stripped from the Turks, rather than grant them independence. The agreement was revealed after the Bolshevik Revolution when the new Russian government withdrew from the war, repudiated the agreement, and made it public. The new post-Ottoman map of the Arab lands known as the Levant was drawn not by the Arabs but by Britain, France, and the League of Nations at the San Remo Conference of 1920. Under different forms of mandates, direct rule, and nominal independence, France gained control of Syria and Lebanon; Britain took over Iraq, Transjordan as it was then known, and the territory of Palestine. Britain also retained de facto control of a nominally independent Egypt. This great-power treachery, combined with Britain's Balfour Declaration of 1917 promising to support the creation of a "national home for the Jewish people" in Palestine, led to an acceleration of Zionist migration into Palestine and further stoked collective Arab opposition to rule by outsiders. On that principle the Arabs were in agreement, but otherwise Arab unity was a myth. As the historian Martin Kramer deftly put it, "they did not wish to be ruled by foreigners from over the sea. But neither did they desire to be ruled by strangers from across the desert, even if those strangers spoke Arabic."[8]

"Arab" as a political concept is a relatively recent development: the

Kingdom of Saudi Arabia became the first to include it in the name of a country when it was founded in 1932. Only years later did it emerge as common in national names, as in today's United Arab Emirates and Arab Republic of Egypt. Nevertheless, Arabs embrace the *watan* as if it were factual, at least in their rhetoric and in the narratives of their own societies. It is a political fraud but a sentimental reality. Those who truly believe in it, such as the late King Abdullah of Saudi Arabia, are destined to be frustrated by their inability to achieve it.

Arab nationalism was the basic principle of the Arab Baath, or Renaissance, Party, which was founded in Syria in 1947. Rival wings of the Baath controlled Iraq under Saddam Hussein and Syria under the Assads, father and son. To the Iraqi Baathists, individual Arab countries were essentially provinces of a single nation, which would eventually be united under one government. (It was consistent with this view to invade and take over neighboring Kuwait, as Iraq did in 1990.) Iraq put the *watan* philosophy into practice by allowing visa-free entry to any citizen of an Arab League country, but at the same time an irreconcilable split developed between the Iraqi and Syrian wings, demonstrating the difficulty of achieving "Arab unity" on a transnational scale. The Arab League, supposedly the collective voice of the Arabs to the rest of the world, made this clear in its founding document, its 1945 charter, which stipulates that it is "composed of independent Arab states," and that its purpose is "to achieve cooperation between them and safeguard their independence and sovereignty"— not to supplant them as a political entity.

Arab unity is like world peace—always an aspiration, never achieved. An old joke tells of a young man sitting outside Arab League headquarters in Cairo holding a trumpet. A passing friend asks what he is doing.

"This is my new job," the young man says. "I wait for Arab unity, then blow the trumpet to report it to the world when it is achieved. I get paid 40 pounds a month."

"That's a miserable salary," his friend says.

"Maybe so, but it's a lifetime job."

The professed desire of the Arab people to be *al-watan al-arabi*, the

Arab nation, is incompatible with the modern nation-state. (The same is true of the transnational "caliphate" proclaimed by Islamist insurgents in Iraq and Syria in 2014.) Virtually all Arabs agree that they are against imperialism and Zionism, but they cannot agree on what they are for. Even in the time of Gamal Abdel Nasser, when he was widely admired for standing up to the West and promoting Arab nationalism, Egypt and Saudi Arabia were fighting a proxy war in Yemen. Nasser went so far as to engineer a merger of Egypt and Syria into a "United Arab Republic." It lasted three years before Syria withdrew. It fell apart because, as a French scholar, Olivier Carré, noted, the Syrians had been motivated to join it not out of any desire for unity with Egypt but out of fear of Iraq. When the Iraqi monarchy was overthrown in a coup in July 1958, Syria no longer needed Egyptian protection. With the ouster of the Iraqi monarchy, "Syria no longer had to fear Hashemite encirclement," Carré wrote, referring to the Hashemite dynasties created by the British in Iraq and Transjordan after World War I.[9]

In today's world, with Arab fighting Arab in Iraq, Syria, Yemen, and Libya, the ideal of Arab solidarity seems laughable, but it was not always so, at least not in the popular imagination.

There was a brief period of Arab unity in the time of the Prophet Muhammad and for the first decades after his death in 632, but schisms, power struggles, and tribal rivalries soon disrupted the new community of Muslim believers that he created. As Islam expanded, non-Arab peoples, including those of Egypt and Morocco, were grafted on to, and inevitably eroded, the unified Arab community. In the modern world, if the term Arab is taken to mean anyone whose first language is Arabic, the Arabs are nearly as diverse as they are alike. Within the independent Arab countries of today, most people are Muslims but many are Christians. (Before the creation of Israel, there were also large Jewish communities in Morocco, Egypt, and Iraq, but most of those Jews fled or were driven out.) Some Arabic speakers are darkskinned Africans; some are olive-skinned people of the Mediterranean. Other than Egypt, Yemen, and Saudi Arabia, most of the countries the Arabs inhabit exist within boundaries drawn by conquerors and colonizers, not by the people themselves.

"The Arabs have been living in a period of decadence for several centuries, not just since their colonization by the West," wrote Michel Aflaq, the Syrian Christian who developed the ideal of Arab unity into a political platform through the creation of the Arab Baath Party. "The conditions which have developed in our countries of the last several hundred years have very deeply perturbed and disfigured the structure of the nation and have caused a disjunction between the idea of an Arab nation and the reality, so that our nation is no longer able to react in a healthy way to the demands of life."[10] As a Christian, Aflaq sought to maximize the appeal of Arabism as a political unifier, because the likely alternative was Islamism.

Nasser and other Arab leaders, including the Baathist rulers of Iraq and Syria and, later, Libya's Qaddafi, preached Arab unity and solidarity, but they failed to achieve it. The disaster of the 1967 war exposed the emptiness of Arab nationalism as a political force. Before it was restored briefly by the October War, the ideal of Arab unity had vaporized in defeat by Israel, in the collapse of Egypt's short-lived union with Syria, and in inter-Arab bloodletting such as Black September and the war in Yemen. But in their rhetoric, Arab leaders still revered this mummy. A few weeks after the 1967 conflict, at a summit conference in Khartoum, Sudan, the Arab leaders adopted a policy known as the "Three No's": no peace with Israel, no recognition of Israel, no negotiations with Israel. This sort of rhetorical posturing rendered their diplomacy as impotent as their armies. At the time, no Arab leader had any idea how to regain the lands lost to Israel, but neither did any Arab leader have the vision or the courage to acknowledge that the façade of collective action was not the answer.

The end of colonialism had given the Arabs independence for the first time in centuries, but not the educational or economic resources to manage it. Lacking genuine political institutions, they were vulnerable to manipulation by outside powers and home-grown demagogues. The unifying forces of language, religion, and hostility to Israel were overpowered by rivalries—between monarchies and republics, between countries aligned with Moscow and those aligned with the West, between religious and secular regimes, and between those that had oil money and those that did not.

No Arab leader sought to manipulate these differences more flagrantly than Anwar Sadat. He preached Arab solidarity and unity when it suited his purposes, turned from it when it did not. Early in his presidency, for example, he announced plans for a union with Libya, but he did it as a ploy to outmaneuver leftover Nasserists blocking his consolidation of power.[11] A few years later he went to war briefly with Libya in a dispute over oil wells near the border. As I wrote at the time, "The Sadat who sent his bombers to smash Libyan airfields is not the Sadat of the 1973 Middle East war but the more recent Sadat who has been willing to use his armed forces to influence events in Africa. It is the Sadat who sent Egyptian pilots to Zaire and concluded a defense pact that commits him to fight alongside Sudan in the event of war with Libya or with the Marxist government of Somalia"—that is, the Sadat who used Egypt's geographical location on the African continent to promote the country's African heritage, its Nile Basin heritage, and to show the other Arabs that Egypt lived in a wider world than they.[12]

Sadat broke with Syria in the aftermath of the 1973 war, but neither he nor Syria's Assad accepted the breach as final. Despite their mistrust of each other, they tried again in December 1976, announcing that they would set up a "unified political command" to guide them toward eventual union.[13] That arrangement would not survive Sadat's trip to Jerusalem the following year.

Sadat clamped down on Palestinians who lived in Egypt when they became restive, and he turned away from Arabism itself when other Arab countries rejected his peace initiative—denying all the while that he had turned his back on the principle of Arab solidarity. Just before he went to Jerusalem, he proclaimed before parliament that "in all our actions, we provide the Arab nation with the most powerful and effective weapon, that of genuine Arab solidarity. . . . No one could be more intent on Arab solidarity than we are, nor can anyone believe in the need for coordinating the Arab stand more than we do or strive in this regard."[14] A few days later, when he arrived in Israel, angry demonstrators took to the streets from Algiers to Baghdad, burning Egyptian flags and denouncing him as a traitor to the Arab cause.

Two weeks after that, five hard-line Arab countries and representatives of the Palestine Liberation Organization, meeting in Libya, agreed to form a united "resistance front" to oppose Sadat. His response was to break diplomatic relations with Libya, Syria, Algeria, and South Yemen. So vituperative was Sadat's language that President Carter instructed Secretary of State Cyrus Vance to deliver a warning: "It is important for Sadat to understand that movement towards peace in the Middle East will require the involvement of other Arab parties, and notably moderate Palestinians, the Jordanians, and the Saudis. He should therefore refrain from actions or rhetoric that have the effect of dividing the Arabs and focusing international attention on Arab extremism rather than on the need for Israeli moderation. Sadat risks engaging in self-defeating policies if his initiatives detract from the need for serious negotiations beyond the purely Israeli-Egyptian relationship."[15] Sadat paid little heed to these prescient words from Washington. On the contrary, his language grew more intemperate as Arab resistance hardened.

Even after his fellow Arabs expelled him from their ranks as punishment for his peace initiative, even as he insisted that they were the isolated ones, not Egypt, because Egypt stood above them all, he continued to proclaim that he cherished and defended the true Arab Nation. In the end his rhetorical posturing could not save him. The Egyptian people were deeply unsettled by their country's alienation from their Arab brothers, a malaise that contributed to the evaporation of popular support for him toward the end of his rule.

The great hero of Arab nationalism was Nasser, who got rid of the British and led Egypt into a position of honor as a leader of the so-called Non-Aligned Movement. He fought a proxy war against Saudi Arabia in Yemen, and he failed in an attempt to build the *watan* across national boundaries when his union of Egypt and Syria broke apart, but he stood as the embodiment of postcolonial aspirations. Anwar Sadat went down a different road, and in the Arab soul that road led to a dead end.

Sadat was not the only person responsible for the exposure of Arab nationalism as a fake. The Egypt-Syria union broke apart before he became president. "Black September," the brief war in which Jordan crushed the armed forces of the Palestinians as Syria refused to intervene, also occurred while Nasser was still in office, as did the first civil war in Yemen. The outbreak of the civil war in Lebanon in 1975 exposed deep existing fissures in a divided society. Sadat was not the Arab ruler who invaded and claimed to annex a neighboring Arab country; that was Iraq's Saddam Hussein, taking over Kuwait years after Sadat's death. Syria, the Palestine Liberation Organization, Iraq, Libya, and Saudi Arabia all involved themselves in that conflict in one way or another, playing out their rivalries in support of warring factions. But as fractious as they were, these Arabs remained united in their views about Israel. It was Sadat who crossed a spiritual red line; he sacrificed the ideal of Arab unity on the altar of peace with Israel. The Western world honored him for it; the people of Egypt and their fellow Arabs did not. One of the main reasons that Islamic activism is prevalent today across so much of the region is that Arab nationalism, which crossed religious lines, was snatched away as a competing aspiration. The failure of Arab nationalism, like the failure of all other "isms" that the Arabs have tried in their search for an organizing principle for their societies, convinced many that the rule of Islam was the only remaining option.

A Brief Era of Harmony

The winter of 1973–74 marked a brief, triumphal peak for the Arabs as a group. The era of humiliation—of subjugation by outsiders, of crushing defeat by Israel—was behind them. Arab armies, fighting together, had vindicated themselves on the battlefield. Arab oil producers had prevailed over the foreign corporations that had controlled their greatest asset. The Arabs worked effectively together to promote anti-Israeli measures in the United Nations General Assembly, including a resolution condemning Zionism as a form of racism.

Yet even while the October War was in progress, disagreements developed about it. Lebanon's Christian president, Suleiman Franjieh, allowed Palestinian guerrillas into southern Lebanon, from where they could attack Israel, only because he feared they would attack the Lebanese army if he did not, the CIA reported at the time. King Hussein of Jordan knew that "Jordan would face certain defeat and the destruction of his armed forces" if it entered the war, the agency reported, but he faced intense pressure from Jordan's large Palestinian population. Libya's Muammar Gaddafi was said to be "extremely angry about the Syrian-Egyptian offensive" because he had not been told about it in advance and because he thought it was aimed only at "diplomatic" gains, not at the destruction of Israel, and there was nothing in it for him.[16] In Iraq, which took part in the war, Egypt was "very popular for 10 days," but the Iraqis were "shocked" when Sadat accepted the first cease-fire plan, and they urged Syria not to go along, according to a cable to the State Department from Arthur Lowrie, then based in Baghdad.[17]

It did not take long for the exhilaration of the war to dissipate and inter-Arab disputes to reappear. The Arabs would prove themselves utterly incapable of managing their success, turning on themselves in conflicts across the region, from Oman to the Western Sahara. As the Lebanese-American scholar Fouad Ajami observed, failure had united the Arabs, but success unhinged them. "In the aftermath of the June [1967] defeat, the dominant order sought to put together an answer of its own to the defeat, as it had to if it were to survive," he wrote. "Grim as its task was (for it knew that a military victory against Israel was not in the cards) it operated from givens shared by the overwhelming majority of the masses. The defeat was culturally, psychologically, and politically unacceptable, and it had to be dealt with." They shed those unifying grievances with the October War, but then "the world brought about by October 1973 blew away the cobwebs of Arab society. Buffeted by mighty winds and propelled by temptations and possibilities unknown before, its cultural container ruptured. It strutted on the world stage for a brief moment, then the breakdown came. There were great victories on distant stages and paralyzing wounds at home."[18]

The inherent instability of Lebanon's sectarian divisions blew up into civil war in the spring of 1975, pitting Arab against Arab, Muslim against Christian, Lebanese Arabs against Palestinian Arabs, Syrians against Lebanese, in a conflict that would last for fifteen years and still threatens to break out anew. And then Sadat went his own way on the road to peace with Israel, leaving the Palestinians stranded and all Arabia divided against itself. Even the Palestinians, who had no country but wanted one, turned against each other. The Arabs collectively had recognized Yasser Arafat's Palestine Liberation Organization as the official voice of the Palestinians, but there were multiple factions within the Palestinian national movement, some more willing than others to compromise with Israel, and Sadat's moves shredded their façade of unity. Given Arafat's malign reputation among Americans and Israel's refusal to negotiate with the PLO, this fracturing of the Palestinian movement might have seemed like a positive development, but most of the other Palestinian groups took a harder line than the PLO.

"Sadat's peace initiatives have thrown the Palestinian movement into chaos," the State Department's intelligence bureau reported shortly after Sadat's trip to Jerusalem. Sadat "shattered" the consensus that had been built around Arafat, the bureau reported, "thereby threatening not only Arafat's leadership but the very legitimacy of the PLO. Arafat is being challenged from within the PLO, by rejectionists, and by other Palestinians who are supported by various Arab states." In the West Bank and Gaza Strip, this report said, many Palestinians were willing to let Sadat's initiative play out and judge by the results, but "outside the Occupied Territories Arafat is facing a serious challenge from the rejectionists led by George Habash's PFLP [Popular Front for the Liberation of Palestine]. The relatively moderate PLO leadership under Arafat, those who are willing to state that they will negotiate a settlement which recognizes Israel's right to exist, are being criticized for being too closely associated with Sadat."[19] The description of the PLO as "relatively moderate" differed from the official U.S. and Israeli position, which was that the PLO was a terrorist organization, and would have created an uproar if it had become public at the time; but the fact was that the PLO leaders, unlike the rejectionists, would have accepted an agreement with Israel if it included creation of an independent Palestinian state. That is still the official Palestinian position today and is consistent with the Arab League initiative of 2002.

After the peace treaty was finally signed in 1979, the near-unanimity of Arab opinion against it forged a brief new period of solidarity among the Arab states other than Egypt, but it soon broke apart. It was overpowered by regional and tribal rivalries, by differences over Lebanon, and by the unbridgeable ideological gaps between the radical rejectionists and the moderates, between the pro-Western and anti-Western regimes, and between the religious and the secular. The intellectuals of the early twentieth century who dreamed of Arab unity could not have imagined that 1991 would see Egyptians and Syrians fighting side by side, in an American-led coalition, to drive the army of Arab Iraq out of occupied Arab Kuwait, nor could they have fathomed the Arab versus Arab conflicts of 2014.

The News from Baghdad

On a sunny early spring day in 1979, several journalists from the United States and Europe gathered in a garden outside a meeting hall in Baghdad, awaiting news from inside. Foreign ministers and ministers of economy from nineteen Arab countries were meeting, trying to agree on how to punish Anwar Sadat for signing a peace treaty with Israel.

The ministers had been at it for days. The conventional wisdom among the journalists was that the delegates would be unable to come to agreement because of deep political and ideological differences between their countries. Syria and Iraq, ruled by rival wings of the Baath Party, were barely on speaking terms; Syria was on record as favoring peace with Israel, provided the terms were acceptable, whereas Iraq rejected any such acceptance of what it called "the Zionist entity." Saudi Arabia, an ally of the United States, wanted nothing to do with the regimes of such radicals as Libya's Qaddafi. The monarchies, generally pro-Western, were pitted against the pseudorepublics such as Iraq and Algeria, generally aligned with the Soviet

Union. These feuding despots, we assumed, could never take unified, effective action.

Our conventional wisdom was wrong. The delegates put aside their differences and agreed to impose a total economic boycott on Egypt, recall their ambassadors, and break diplomatic relations within a month. This outcome went far beyond what Egypt was expecting. Sadat and President Carter had been counting on Saudi Arabia, whose economic support was essential to Egypt, to hold out for some milder response. Washington had appealed to Saudi Arabia and Jordan to give Sadat's plan for negotiations on Palestine a chance and to use their influence to entice some Palestinians into the proposed autonomy talks. In the immediate aftermath of Camp David, Crown Prince Fahd, de facto ruler of Saudi Arabia, had promised the United States that the kingdom would give "strong support" to Sadat and encourage Jordan to do the same.[20] Neither kingdom was able to hold out against the pressure of the radicals and of Arab public opinion.[21]

This outcome at Baghdad should not have been so surprising as it appeared at the time. Delegates at an Arab summit conference the previous November had warned Sadat not to sign a treaty with Israel and threatened to boycott Egypt if he did so. Moreover, the CIA had forecast the Baghdad event with remarkable accuracy. An intelligence memorandum dated March 15, 1979, said,

> Arab renunciation of President Sadat and the Egyptian-Israeli treaty is building toward a crescendo. We expect the effort by Iraq, Syria, and Libya to stampede the more moderate Arabs into unqualified condemnation of the treaty to be largely successful. The culmination of the effort will be a new conference in Baghdad—possibly timed to open the day a treaty is signed—and a vote to impose sanctions against Egypt. We detect some initial ambivalence on the part of Saudi Arabia and Jordan toward "punishing" Sadat. It will be difficult to keep them that way until the early, largely hostile Arab reaction has run its course. The sentiment, moreover, is tentative and the full weight of anti-Sadat pressure has not yet been applied. That will occur at Baghdad, where there will be few

significant countervailing pressures. We doubt that the moderates have the self-confidence to stand against the hardliners given their own reservations about the treaty. The day of reckoning that the Saudis have long feared appears to be at hand.[22]

Nevertheless, as had happened with the October War itself, and with the oil embargo, the firm belief that something would not happen—in this case, the belief that the Saudis would not take part in such drastic measures—led to astonishment when the kingdom did so.

Ambassador Hermann Eilts said that the Egyptians and Americans alike had made the mistake of assuming that the Saudis would come around. "Somehow," Eilts said, "Carter had gotten the impression that [Saudi Crown Prince] Fahd, in that typical notional way in which he tends to speak, would go along with whatever Carter had worked out. And it came as a shock to Carter that the Saudis didn't agree. It also came as a shock to Sadat." At Camp David, according to Eilts, when Sadat said the Saudis would not accept some provision of the agreement, Carter had reassured him: "Don't worry about the Saudis, Mr. President. I'll take care of the Saudis." Eilts, who had been ambassador to Saudi Arabia before he was posted to Egypt, observed that "this view that Saudi Arabia was a client state of the U.S. was one that Sadat had had for a long time," partly because Washington expressed the same assumption.[23]

Bill Quandt, who had been a member of the American team at Camp David, came to a more cynical conclusion: Sadat was "deliberately seeking to polarize the Arab world in the belief that Saudi Arabia would have to side with him against the pro-Soviet radicals." In a memo to Zbigniew Brzezinski, Quandt said, "The Saudis will be most reluctant to weaken their support for Sadat if the alternative in the Arab world consists only of radical Arabs with strong Soviet backing."[24] Sadat and the American negotiators, including Carter, failed to perceive that even under the mild-mannered King Khaled and his generally pro-American brother, Prince Fahd, Saudi Arabia had a well-developed sense of its position as a leader of the Arab and

Muslim worlds and could not separate itself entirely from popular sentiment, from the "Arab street."

In one sense this was the last hurrah of Arab solidarity: countries with long histories of rivalry and mistrust rose above their differences to promote a common goal. Their universal dismay over what they saw as Sadat's betrayal of the Arab cause united them as nothing else could. Opposition to the treaty even brought about a short-lived reconciliation between Iraq and Syria, which had been at sword's point for years; had they not reconciled, no common ground could have been reached by the ministers at Baghdad.

In another sense, however, the Baghdad outcome represented the irreversible end to the ideal of the Arab nation. What was the *watan* without Egypt? And what would Egypt be without the economic support of Saudi Arabia and the other Gulf monarchies, who kept Egypt afloat then as they do today? Some of the Arab countries would reconcile with Egypt after Sadat's death, but the Arabs as a people could have no more illusions about their unity of spirit.

The Baghdad boycott had been brewing since Egypt signed the Sinai II disengagement agreement after the October War, committing itself not to go to war again. Syria was already angry at the time because President Assad thought Sadat had deceived him during the conflict.

"Egypt betrayed Syria and all she had done in the 1973 war," Assad's senior political adviser, Adib Daoudi, told me. "Also it accepted the second Sinai disengagement agreement, which contained nothing for the Palestinians. We had plenty of opportunity to make a second disengagement agreement for the Golan, as Egypt did in Sinai, but we didn't do it because of the Palestinian position."[25]

As long as Sadat's stated intent was to reconvene the Geneva Conference and achieve a comprehensive settlement through negotiations in which Syria and the Palestinians would participate, he was able to persuade moderate Arab states such as Tunisia and Jordan to give him the benefit of the doubt. Even these moderates were shocked by Sadat's trip to Jerusalem, and they were put off by his angry rejection of their objections.

"In response to Arab criticism," a CIA analyst reported, "Sadat usually thinks that his erstwhile allies are taking the easy way out at Egypt's expense and fails to see that they are attempting at least in part to curb Egypt's independent actions and to salvage at least the appearance of having options of their own. It is possible that Sadat is simply trying to force Syria, the Soviets, and even Arab moderates such as Jordan and Saudi Arabia to make the hard choices he has made and commit themselves to a concerted peace effort. His actions are more likely, however, to deepen suspicions that Egypt has been planning all along to negotiate a separate settlement with Israel."[26]

In the five months between Camp David and the signing of the peace treaty, those suspicions deepened and attitudes hardened. Almost immediately the Arab League, based in Cairo since 1945, decided to hold its future meetings in other capitals. The announcement was made by the secretary-general, Mahmoud Riad, an Egyptian himself, who said that the league would meet elsewhere until Sadat "returns to the Arab camp." He said it "would not be logical to keep the League headquarters in Egypt, where there will be an Israeli embassy."[27]

Assad, Sadat's wartime ally, became a leader in organizing Arab opposition to Sadat's initiative. The Syrian leader put together a "Steadfastness and Liberation Front" of committed hard-liners: Syria, Libya, Algeria, South Yemen and the Palestine Liberation Organization. (Iraq was just as strong in its opposition but initially refused to join this group because it was organized by Syria.) Addressing this group's first gathering, Assad said Sadat had "defected to the enemy" by giving up "not only Jerusalem but the whole Arab cause." He said Sadat had "forgotten all his speeches and promises," the ones in which he pledged not to make a separate peace with Israel.[28]

In fact, the more Sadat proclaimed his determination not to accept any peace deal that failed to resolve the Palestinian question, the more other Arabs suspected that he would do just that. Most of them thought the Camp David accords showed they had been right. Had Sadat been less impetuous and less arrogant—had he, for example, consulted or even notified the Saudis and the Algerians before going to Jerusalem and explained what he was up to, instead of announcing it on CBS Television—he might have gained at least sullen tolerance of his tactics. Instead he plunged ahead over their objections and insulted them when they spoke out against him. He made a point of separating himself from other Arabs and of embracing Western leaders such as "my friend Giscard," President Valéry Giscard d'Estaing of France.

After Camp David, the war of words escalated, and Sadat held little back. The Baghdad meeting and the Arab boycott were the logical culminations of deteriorating relations between Egypt and the Arabs, a deterioration that Sadat fueled with rhetorical attacks on his critics. He called them "dwarfs" and "ignoramuses."[29] He said they were "ostriches with their heads in the sand" about the reality of Israel.[30] He said that "their adolescent, materialistic, and hysterical behavior jeopardizes Arab causes."[31] He said his solo diplomacy was necessitated by "the cheap auctioneering and unbecoming actions of our Arab brothers."[32] Egypt, he said, was the "throbbing heart, sword, and shield of the Arab Nation," and would not be pushed around by "nouveaux riches."[33] He called Assad a "bully" who was guilty of "hooliganism" in Lebanon.[34] If the Arab League moved out of Egypt, good riddance, he said in an interview with a Kuwaiti newspaper: "If the Arab League expresses Arab reality as illustrated in Baghdad, Egypt does not want any part of it."[35]

In the same interview, he said that "Egypt is not like any other country: it holds respect for values, because of its heritage and its deep roots," and cannot be bought off by oil money. He stressed the point in his memoir: "The Egyptian people differ from many other peoples, even within the Arab world. We are no longer motivated by 'complexes'—whether defeatist 'inferiority' ones or those born out of suspicion and hate."[36]

"The Arabs Are Zero"

In one speech Sadat said of his Arab critics, "Their main decision was to starve the Egyptian people, those dwarfs who have been fed, protected and educated by Egypt and are still being educated by Egypt," a reference to all the teachers Egypt had provided to Arab countries that had no educated class of their own. "You heard me say that Egypt was not only sending professors and teachers to one of these dwarfs' emirates but also schoolbooks, pencils and chalk. . . . Without Egypt, the Arabs are zero. Egypt is the heart and mind of the Arab world and for the next generations to come they will never catch up with Egypt, and it is not oil that builds Egypt, no. The fortune of Egypt is not like Saudi Arabia and the others, it is here a complete economy of agriculture, industry, assets, all this. And the biggest asset in Egypt is the human being, the Egyptian man, who is a doctor, engineer, laborer, teachers, with 13 universities here and with all the pride and heritage of seven thousand years."[37]

Those comments reflect an attitude common among Egyptians at the time. Unlike the postcolonial Arab countries that came into existence only in the twentieth century, Egypt has been a unitary state for thousands of years and has a rich overlay of cultural history dating to the time of the Pharaohs. Egypt had railroads and factories when the other Arabs were herdsmen. And as Sadat frequently reminded the Saudis and other Gulf Arabs, Egyptians shed blood in the Sinai in the cause of liberation while they were collecting oil money and vacationing in Europe. In Sadat's time Egyptians were contemptuous and resentful of oil-rich Arabs who came to Cairo in the summer to purchase young wives and to gamble at casinos where betting required dollars, which few Egyptians had. Egyptian doctors routinely griped that they, specialists trained in Britain and Germany, had forty-year-old equipment and antiquated hospitals, while the Saudis, who then did not even have any native-born physicians, were buying state-of-the art equipment from the United States and Japan and installing it in gleaming new hospitals staffed by foreigners.

"Sadat had been an Arab nationalist, believed in Arabism of the Nasser variety for a period of time," Ambassador Eilts recalled. "By the time he became president, however, he seemed to have developed to a point where he was more Egyptian rather than Arab. . . . That did not mean that he discarded or discounted other Arab concerns, including Palestinian concerns, but Sadat was an Egyptian first and foremost. In typical Egyptian fashion he saw Egypt as a civilization of 5,000 years. He was a devout Muslim, yet he recalled that Egypt was building pyramids while the Arabs elsewhere were having difficulty putting up tents. And he showed that typical attitude of condescension toward other Arabs which so many Egyptians tend to do."

According to Eilts, who worked more closely with Sadat than any other American, it was this primacy of Egypt and Sadat's focus on recovering Egypt's lost land, on regaining the Sinai first, that enabled the Israelis to outmaneuver him in the peace negotiations.

Even after Camp David, Eilts said, "Sadat, as an Egyptian, could not believe that other Arabs would be prepared to alienate themselves from Egypt. They needed Egypt. I remember, after Camp David and the peace treaty, when Egypt was expelled from the Arab League and the Islamic Conference, saying once to Sadat, 'Mr. President, I'm very disturbed about Egypt's isolation in the Arab world.' And Sadat replied with total conviction, 'Hermann, Egypt isn't isolated in the Arab world, the Arabs are isolated from Egypt.'"[38]

A few weeks after Sadat went to Jerusalem, State Department intelligence analysts observed, "As a result of this bold stroke, Sadat sees himself as having thrust Egypt back into its 'proper' leadership role, created new hope for regaining the Sinai and presented himself as the seeker of peace on behalf of all Arabs." If Syria and the Palestinians declined to participate in peace negotiations, the analysts said, "Sadat could probably justify to the Egyptian people, including the military leadership, an attempt to strike a separate deal. In the absence of Israeli concessions, it becomes very difficult to predict the reaction to a bilateral agreement; elements of the armed forces would be torn between the prospects of recovering the Sinai without [another] war, for which they are ill-prepared, and being held up to the charge of abandoning the wider struggle."

In that struggle, the analysts calculated, "the role of Saudi Arabia becomes crucial." If Israel showed itself genuinely ready to pull out of at least some occupied lands and make other concessions, and if Syria and the Palestinians declined to seized the opportunity, that would make it easier for Saudi Arabia to endorse or at least tolerate Sadat's initiative.[39]

Unfortunately, the assassination of King Faisal of Saudi Arabia two years earlier now contributed to Sadat's alienation from other Arab rulers. Faisal had been universally respected. Sadat frequently sought his aid and counsel. Faisal was no advocate of peace with Israel; he equated Jews with communism and communism with Jews, and despised both. Yet he also recognized that Israel would continue to be a fact of life at least as long as it had the support of the United States, and he would have acquiesced to a peace agreement, if it returned Israel to its pre-1967 borders. Were he still alive at the time of Camp David, he would certainly have had Sadat's ear as the Egyptian navigated his way to peace, and he might well have persuaded Sadat to adopt a more conciliatory approach to Arabs who did not agree with what he was doing. Faisal's successor, King Khaled, was an avuncular and kindly person but a weak king whose influence among the other Arabs could not match that of Faisal and who was unable to resist their pressure at the Baghdad meeting. Crown Prince Fahd, who was running the kingdom's day-to-day affairs, could not approach Faisal's stature among other Arabs.

In a speech shortly after the Baghdad boycott was announced, Sadat said he would not engage in a public argument with Saudi Arabia out of respect for Faisal, who he said had been a generous friend and whose successor was not of the same caliber.[40] This gratuitous insult to King Khaled reflected Sadat's disappointment at Saudi participation in the boycott—he had devoted much time and effort since Camp David to seeking at least tacit Saudi consent—as well as his growing penchant for rhetorical intemperance that infuriated people he would have done better to placate.

When Eilts suggested that he might want to tone down his rhetoric and try a new approach to Jordan and Saudi Arabia, Sadat replied, "Let Hussein and the Saudis stew in their own juice awhile." He said that "more than 90 percent of the Arab world" supported him. To Brzezinski, Sadat described Saudi Arabia as a "scarecrow" and "a U.S. protectorate," and complained that the United States showed the kingdom too much deference.[41]

Despite Sadat's superior attitude and his insistence that it was the other Arabs who were isolated, not Egypt, the resolutions taken at Baghdad had real negative consequences. Besides cutting diplomatic relations and moving the Arab League to Tunis, the other Arabs cut off economic aid. Saudi Arabia pulled back funds it had allocated for an Egyptian purchase of American fighter jets. The Saudis and other Gulf states killed off the Arab Organization for Military Industrialization, a weapons-building venture the Egyptians were developing with Arab money.

Some of the economic blow was cushioned by a flow of aid from the United States and other Western countries, but the rupture between Egypt and the other Arabs was about more than economics. In the aftermath of Baghdad, the flags of Arab nations were lowered on their embassies all across Cairo as they severed ties with Egypt, while the flag of Israel was going up in accordance with the peace treaty. It was deeply unnerving for the Egyptian masses to be excommunicated by their Arab brothers. Much of what Sadat was saying about the other Arabs was true, but the relentless intemperance of his language violated the Egyptian people's sense of commonality with their fellow Arabs; they became increasingly uncomfortable and restive as Sadat engaged in his long-running rhetorical flogging of all Arabs who did not agree with him. It was fair to criticize the policies of Syria's Assad, but it was not fair for Sadat to refer to him in speeches as "the Alawite," a below-the-belt reference to Assad's membership in the quasi-Muslim minority sect that dominated the country. He aimed another cheap shot at King Hussein of Jordan, whom he dismissed as "schizophrenic like his father," King Talal, who had suffered from mental illness.[42]

The Egyptian people had welcomed the prospect of peace with Israel because they thought their lives would improve, but they did not anticipate that the price would include a rupture of their ties to the rest of the Arabs, which they had long been taught to value. Being Arab mattered. Hundreds of thousands of Egyptians lived and worked in the Arab oil countries. Uncounted numbers had made the Muslim pilgrimage to Mecca. The most eminent writers and scholars of the Arab world in modern times were Egyptians. Arabs from across the region had come to Egypt for education. The people's separation from these deep bonds left a feeling of alienation, stoked by the growing ranks of Sadat's political opponents, that would soon contribute to his downfall. Sadat seemed to have forgotten his own words in *The October Working Paper*: "Our people believe deeply in their affiliation to the Arab nation."[43]

Sadat's closest advisers and confidants were well aware of, and uncomfortable with, the growing rift between Egypt and the other Arabs as Sadat stridently went his own way. At a crucial point in the negotiations that led to the treaty, Prime Minister Mustafa Khalil pleaded with the Israelis to understand the potential consequences and to be more forthcoming about the Palestinian question. He argued, according to Moshe Dayan, "that the United States and Israel should be urging Egypt to make alliances with the moderate Arab countries . . . only Egypt could rush to their help against the wave of radicalism and Khomeinism that was sweeping the area—but not if Egypt were to be isolated and considered a stranger. Since Sadat's visit to Jerusalem, and the denunciation of Egypt as a traitor, Egyptian technicians working in the oil states were being replaced by Koreans and Pakistanis. This was a danger to the stability of [the Gulf] regimes, to Egypt, and to the West—particularly the United States."[44] Only by extracting substantial concessions from Israel on the Palestinian question could Egypt forestall those developments, Khalil argued, to little avail.

Egypt's intellectuals, academics, and leftist politicians led the way in articulating the sentiment that the peace treaty brought too little gain for what Egypt gave up. Sadat argued correctly that with the treaty Egypt became the only Arab country to regain its lost land and that by signing the treaty, Israel had, for the first and only time, set a firm, permanent border with an Arab neighbor, a brake on expansion. The corollary, however, was that Israel could now act as it wished to its north and east without fear of response from its west. The critics' view that the treaty left Israel free to throw its weight around was reinforced when Israel bombed the nuclear reactor under construction in Iraq in 1981 and faced no Arab retaliation. Sadat was already dead by the time of Israel's massive invasion of Lebanon in 1982, but the resentment he had incited with the treaty, among many Egyptians as well other Arabs, was inflamed anew by Egypt's inability to do anything about it. Adherence to the treaty precluded even token military action. Without Egypt, the other Arabs were as impotent as they were angry.

To some extent they took out their frustrations on each other, as in the contest between Morocco and Algeria over the Western Sahara territory. When Iraq foolishly invaded non-Arab Iran in 1980, Syria backed Iran because President Assad's Syrian wing of the Baath Party—a party founded on the principle of Arab unity—had again broken with Saddam Hussein's Iraqi wing; the brief reconciliation in response to Sadat was forgotten. That was the dawn of the alliance between Syria and non-Arab Iran, which continued for more than thirty years, through the Arab Spring rebellion against Assad's son and successor, Bashar, whom Iran supported in his struggle to remain in power while his fellow Arabs in Saudi Arabia and other countries backed the rebels trying to overthrow him. When Iraq invaded Kuwait in 1990, most of the other Arabs condemned it, but Jordan, Yemen, and the PLO supported Saddam Hussein.

"Egypt's opting out" of the struggle against Israel, Mohamed Heikal wrote, "had a centrifugal effect on all the other Arab countries, diverting their attention from what had long been the dream of unity—however imperfectly understood or pursued, yet a noble and stimulating dream—into barren territorial rivalries, religious conflicts, and social strife. The Arab world had become well and truly Balkanized."[45]

He wrote that in 1982, but he could have written it with equal resonance in 2014, a year in which Arabs from Libya to Yemen were turning their guns against themselves while Israel was blasting the Palestinians of Gaza with bombs and artillery fire and Egypt, bound by its treaty, could do nothing to stop the carnage. Sadat did not put an end to Arab solidarity, because it never really existed. He exposed it as an empty and futile pretense.

7 The Rise of the Islamists

When Walter McClelland arrived in the historic Mediterranean port city of Alexandria in 1978 to take up his duties as United States Consul General, he was surprised to find that the job came with a high level of security protection for himself and his colleagues. "I had a personal bodyguard with me at all times," he recalled. Egypt was free of street crime—nobody was going to stick a gun in McClelland's ribs and demand his wallet. The reason for the security was that, as McClelland put it, "Muslim extremists threatened all kinds of trouble."[1]

Alexandria in 1978 was not what it had been before Nasser's time. Nasser got rid of the Greeks, Italians, Cypriots, Lebanese, Jews, and of course Britons who had made it a great cosmopolitan metropolis. The Alexandria of Lawrence Durrell's *Quartet* was long gone; the city was shabby, disorganized, and provincial, but only recently had it become dangerous. If McClelland had arrived in Egypt six years earlier, or at any time in the 1960s, when Nasser was president, he would not have perceived any threat from "Muslim extremists," because there was none, at least none that could be discerned in daily life. The "extremists" were in prison and their organizations had been crushed, or driven deep under ground. But in Egypt, as in many Muslim countries, the contest between believers who accept the religious status quo and those who would overthrow it, by force if necessary, is never settled. What McClelland observed was a new turn in this seemingly endless cycle, instigated not by clandestine conspirators but by the president of the republic himself, Anwar Sadat.

When Sadat became president, he was an accidental leader thrust into power by Nasser's early death. To bolster his personal constituency and neutralize the influence of the political left, he unleashed the forces of Islamism—that is, of individuals and groups who believe and demand that all functions of the state and society be regulated entirely by religious doctrine and Islamic law, to the exclusion of any secular or foreign input. Sadat, believing that he could manage or co-opt the power of political Islam, released its practitioners from prison and allowed—even encouraged—their organizations to regroup. Then as now, the largest and best organized of these groups was the Muslim Brotherhood (Ikhwan al-Muslimin), founded in Egypt in 1928.

Some advocates of Islamizing state and society argue that it can be done while individual liberty and democratic processes are protected, but history says otherwise. Many if not most of those who could be grouped under the heading "Islamist" are not extremists or advocates of violence. But even those who profess nonviolence, as the Brotherhood did in the 1970s, endorse lines of thought and political objectives that are incompatible with freedom of thought, social liberalization, and multicultural tolerance. Their differences with the extremists involve tactics, not objectives. Sadat's political ploy in encouraging them was a misjudgment that haunts his country and the Muslim world even today, reflected in the power struggle between the Egyptian armed forces and the Muslim Brotherhood that led to the military coup of 2013.

Sadat was a pious Muslim, but his motivation was political rather than religious. In the summer of 1972, Sadat wrote in his memoirs, he learned that "the Soviet Union was preparing to infiltrate and incite students in an uprising when the Egyptian universities reopened in October, in accordance with a plan drawn up by the Arab Communist parties (though issued, naturally, by Moscow) for Soviet agents within our universities."[2] Whether or not Moscow was actually engaged in such a plot, there was no doubt that the political discourse on campuses was dominated by leftist groups and individuals who were still loyal to Nasser and grateful to the Soviet Union. Thus there was a certain logic to Sadat's encouragement of religious elements as a counterweight. The university students of the 1970s whom Sadat encouraged to embrace religious activism are today the graying adults who promote an Islamist agenda.

Sadat was not responsible for the sectarian violence that has plagued the world of Islam from Algeria to Afghanistan for the past three decades but he did make fateful decisions and implement policies, including peace with Israel, that facilitated the spread of extremist ideas.

Sadat's visible religiosity was not, or was not entirely, a pose for public consumption. As Kirk J. Beattie put it in his study of Sadat's presidency, "One cannot overestimate the importance of Sadat's religious training during his childhood. His initial, formal instruction was acquired at the village *kuttah*, or Koranic teaching school. It provided the basis for religious beliefs that would mark many of Sadat's values for the rest of his life."[3] Nevertheless, his decision to release activists of the Muslim Brotherhood from the prisons to which his predecessor had confined them and to encourage religious activism on university campuses and in professional syndicates was political rather than religious in nature, aimed at shoring up his weak power base.

When he became president, Sadat was surrounded by leftist rivals firmly aligned with Moscow. The armed forces were trained and equipped by the Soviet Union. Soviet diplomats and journalists were everywhere in Cairo and Alexandria. Cairo newspapers reprinted articles from *Pravda* and *Izvestia*. All major industries had been nationalized, and state planning dominated the economy. Leftist groups dominated university campuses and the trade unions. The prevailing official ideology was Arab nationalism. Nasser had essentially excluded Islam from Egyptian politics and public life after a wing of the Brotherhood tried to assassinate him in 1954.

In a brilliant book about the rise of political Islam in Egypt, Geneive Abdo observed that Nasser in effect nationalized the faith just as he nationalized the economy, ensuring that the state took firm control of the *ulema*, or religious elders, and of religious institutions such as al-Azhar University. The ruler controlled the apparatus of faith, to the distress of those who preferred the opposite. The Egyptian public mostly accepted these policies because Nasser was their great national hero, at least until the defeat of 1967, and the government did not interfere with their personal devotions. But at the same time, there developed new clandestine cadres of religious activists who wished to restore control of the mosques to the believers.[4]

About 10 percent of Egypt's people are Christians, but otherwise Islam is the foundation of society. Especially in the countryside and small towns, Islam is present and visible everywhere. It is often said that Islam is not just a religion, practiced at church or synagogue at fixed times, but a way of life, practiced everywhere at all times. When the uniformed guard outside a Cairo bank lays a square of cardboard on the grimy sidewalk and drops to his knees in prayer, he is entirely unselfconscious about it, and passersby hardly notice. Nobody thinks it an oddity worthy of being photographed.

Sadat, who labeled himself "the believer president," often boasted about his rural origins and his religious faith. Before the 1952 revolution, he had been the conspirators' liaison with the Brotherhood. On his forehead he displayed the *zabeeb*, or raisin, the dark spot that some men develop over years of pressing the head to the ground for prayer. (Some of his detractors joked that the *zabeeb* was makeup, applied only for public appearances. Others said it was created by Nasser, who in meetings of the leadership would slap Sadat on the forehead and say, "You, shut up.") As president, Sadat calculated that he could harness the deep religious sentiment of the people into a political force that he could wield against the leftist ideas, secular politics, and pro-Moscow sentiment of the officials and institutions he inherited from Nasser. He was wrong. He and his advisers failed to see, or to acknowledge, new forces that had overtaken the traditional sources of religious activism.

In his autobiography, Sadat recalled meeting Hassan al-Banna, the Brotherhood's founder and Supreme Guide, in 1940, and inviting him to address his army unit. "His choice of subjects was excellent, his understanding and interpretation of religion profound, and his delivery impressive. He was indeed qualified, from all points of view, to be a religious leader. Besides, he was a true Egyptian: good-humored, decent, tolerant," Sadat concluded.

Before that encounter, Sadat thought that the Brotherhood "was merely a religious society aimed at reviving the values of Islam and working for moral advancement; but now that I heard Sheikh al-Banna, I began to think differently." He understood that al-Banna and the well-organized Brotherhood had a political as well as a moral agenda.[5] And he soon discovered that the Brotherhood was recruiting members among the officer corps. And yet as president he believed the Brotherhood could be an asset to him, rather than a liability.

Sadat failed to recognize the larger historic context in which the Brotherhood and like-minded groups in other Muslim countries had developed. He preached the separation of politics and religion, but Islam makes no such distinction—in fact the religion teaches that all human activity is governed by the rules of the faith—and therefore it was natural that those who professed full allegiance to Islam would also develop political agendas. In the Arab world of the mid-twentieth century, those agendas involved restoring Islam's pride and power after long years of economic and cultural domination by the West, and ridding society of laws and institutions adopted from the West, such as secular criminal codes and modern banking practices.

The details of the religious activists' agendas differ, as do their tactics; only a minuscule minority advocate the murderous absolutism of the Islamic State, the all-or-nothing group that seized parts of Iraq and Syria in 2014. Violence aside, however, Islamist groups in general all agree on three fundamental objectives: implementation of sharia, or Islamic law; dealing out the punishments prescribed in the Koran for transgressors and criminals; and the exclusion of non-Muslims from public life. Many members of Islamist groups are not deeply knowledgeable about theology but are committed to a political agenda formulated around Islamic ideals.

Almost by definition, that agenda would not include making peace with Israel, which in the Islamist view was a non-Muslim entity forced into the heartland of Islam by colonial powers, by infidels who exhibited the same disregard for Islam as the crusaders of medieval times. The U.S. Central Intelligence Agency warned in 1947 that creation of an independent Israel would be detrimental to U.S. interests; one of the reasons the agency cited was that the existence of a separate Jewish state would become a casus belli for violence-prone Islamist groups hostile to Western encroachment.

"The Arabs are capable of a religious fanaticism which when coupled with political aspirations is an extremely powerful force," the agency's analysis said. The Muslim Brotherhood "regards Westernization as a dangerous threat to Islam and would oppose any political encroachment of Zionism on Palestine with religious fanaticism."[6] And that was before the Brotherhood spawned the radical offshoot groups that surfaced in Egypt in the 1970s.

"These groups," the religious scholar Charles J. Adams wrote perceptively, "present Islam as an alternative to the modern Muslim experiments in liberalism, democracy, republicanism, socialism, economic planning, military dictatorship, and so on, all of which they consider to have foreign origins and to be discredited by their lack of an Islamic basis and their failure to alleviate the fundamental problems of the Muslim societies. Their wrath is directed, not at modernization as such, but at the things which have accompanied it and the people who have led it: the increasing dependence upon alien values, continuing military impotence (resulting in part from the strength of U.S.-supported Israel) and economic subjugation to foreign powers, the always-growing secularization of society and its institutions, and exploitativeness and ineffectiveness of allegedly corrupt and inefficient leadership."[7]

Some of these groups are willing, even eager, to resort to violence to advance their cause. Among these in Sadat's Egypt were conspiratorial, secretive, and compromise-averse offshoots of the Muslim Brotherhood.

"The authorities refused to recognize that new forces were at work among the students and beneath the surface everywhere," Egypt's most prominent journalist, Mohamed Heikal, wrote after Sadat had been assassinated. "They continued to assume that as far as religion was concerned the people they had to deal with were either simply the unorganized mass of Moslem believers or known organizations like the Moslem Brotherhood. Yet they had been warned that much more was involved, if only they had been willing to read the warning properly."[8] The regime and its compliant supporters, Heikal wrote, "were creating a monster, and one day, sooner probably than they expected, it was going to turn and rend them."[9] Violence-prone extremist groups within the armed forces were organizing clandestine cells, and the Brotherhood itself now included more radical elements than Sadat perceived.

"One thing that President Sadat never realized," the Egyptian-American sociologist Saad Eddin Ibrahim observed years later, "is that the Muslim Brothers whom he knew were different from the Muslim Brothers he released from jail in 1971. What he did in 1971 was to negotiate with the elders of the Muslim Brothers, people of his age cohort. What he did not realize was that the Muslim Brothers had gone through a very deep split in the late 1960s, in prison."[10]

"Sadat's policies of co-optation failed for a variety of reasons," another shrewd analyst wrote. He "profoundly miscalculated the appeal and resilience of the Islamist groups. In so doing, he willfully ignored the splintering of the Islamist groups during the late 1960s and 1970s, mistakenly perceiving a unified, well-organized Islamist opposition fronted by the Brotherhood. . . . Equally destabilizing was failure of the Sadatist agenda to advance a consistent and well-institutionalized program of Islamization," which Sadat did not do because he was always ambivalent and equivocal about the role of religion in Egyptian life.[11]

Those analysts wrote with the benefit of hindsight, but the phenomenon they described was evident even at the time. Writing in 1980, Nazih N. M. Ayubi reported, "By most accounts many of the Islamist groups that exist in Egypt today are more militant than the Brothers and may represent a less orthodox orientation similar to what the new left represents within socialist circles."[12]

Rival factions had developed within the Islamist movement, Ibrahim and other scholars said. Radical groups formed, willing to use violence to promote an extremist agenda. Throughout the second half of the 1970s, Sadat—despite his piety and his promotion of overt religiosity—pursued policies that fueled the deepest resentments of the religious activists, even those who were not themselves espousing violence. He failed to perceive that growing numbers of people were antagonized by the readily perceptible gap between what he said and the way he conducted his presidency, and that the most radical among them were impatient as well as angry.

In simplest terms, the differences between the clandestine radicals and the traditional Islamists reflected differences in Muslim thinking that have reoccurred many times in the religion's long history: the radical factions believed that the entire state system was un-Islamic and corrupt and therefore should be destroyed and rebuilt. The others believed in reforming the state through preaching, charity, education, and good example.

"It was this second camp with which Sadat negotiated," Ibrahim said. "But many of the younger ones who were released at the same time were followers of [Sayed] Qutb," the Egyptian religious thinker whose radical ideas were later embraced by violence-prone extremists, including al-Qaeda.

Some members of the Brotherhood emerged from prison alienated from the state and seeking revenge for what had happened to them, according to Michael Yousef, who wrote one of the early analyses of the trend toward extremism. They believed, as Qutb had, that all of society was living in *jahaliyah*, the state of pagan ignorance that predated Islam, and thus by definition had to be dismantled. Society could not be reformed; instead, "a completely new Islamic society must be established." It was necessary for the believers to separate themselves entirely from society and then "after its collapse, return to build it anew."[13] Those who held this view were the *takfiris*, from an Arabic word that is difficult to express in English but often translated as "separation" or "migration."

Qutb was executed, on Nasser's orders, in 1966, but he remained and remains an ideological beacon for radical Islam. Seeds that he planted sprouted in the dark greenhouses of radical activists. Within three years of Sadat's first release of religious activists and members of the Muslim Brotherhood, breakaway extremist groups began violent attacks against the government and against prominent figures of the conventional religious establishment. Their tactics and their choice of targets would be familiar today in Iraq or Afghanistan. The first episode of violence was a spectacular attempt in 1974 to take over the Military Technical Academy, outside Cairo. By 1976, the Central Intelligence Agency was detecting signs of more trouble ahead.

In a prescient report to headquarters on "Sadat's Domestic Position," the CIA station in Cairo said that "the abortive putsch at the Cairo military cadet academy in 1974 . . . was led by a putative Islamic zealot who mobilized middle-class youth. The Moslem Brotherhood seems recently to have grown in influence, especially in the military and in government agencies. Supported by money (and arms as well) from Libya, its long-term aim is to exploit the shortcomings of Sadat's regime. The Brotherhood has traditionally derived most of its strength from families of merchants and shopkeepers and from the peasantry, but it also includes many intellectuals. Xenophobic in outlook, its aim has long been to combine a fundamentalist Islamic political system with modern social reforms."

Sadat, the CIA report said, was playing a dangerous game: "Sadat's regime has sought to capitalize on the reservoir of Islamic sentiment in Egypt by encouraging Muslim leaders to carry out propaganda attacks on Egyptian leftists and seek to counter leftist influence among students. The government-orchestrated call for a return to Islamic values is a two-edged sword, however, since a 'back to the mosque' movement risks arousing public denunciation of the secular aspects of Sadat's social, political, and economic 'open door' policies."[14] That assessment was prophetic.

The following year, 1977, readers of Egyptian newspapers found on the front pages a photograph of a wild-eyed figure who looked a lot like Charles Manson, the California mass murderer. Egyptians are vociferous people but usually good-humored and generous; the man in this photo, with glaring eyes, unkempt beard and unmistakable sneer, hardly looked Egyptian at all, which was why the state-controlled papers used the picture. The government wanted to discredit the man pictured, a radical religious extremist named Shukri Ahmed Mustafa.

The reason the government wanted to discredit Mustafa, despite its own encouragement of religious activism, was that he and his group crossed the line separating tolerable activities such as preaching, writing, teaching, and community organizing, from intolerable actions and violence that challenged the regime. That is the same wall that was breached in Saudi Arabia in 2003, when the local branch of al-Qaeda began to attack foreign residents and oil installations, in Pakistan and Afghanistan with the rise of the Taliban, in Somalia with the militias of al-Shebab, in Iraq with the Islamic State, and in many other Muslim countries. This struggle long predated Sadat, but Egypt's size, influence, and position in Islamic history made it the critical arena.

At the age of twenty-eight, Shukri Ahmed Mustafa was no doubt a criminal, but his crimes were not motivated by money or ambition. He resorted to violence in an effort to bring down an Egyptian state that he and his followers regarded as anti-Islamic and to replace it with a new caliphate. That is, they envisioned a return to what they believed was a purely Islamic society, untainted by foreign or infidel influence, as it supposedly existed under the early caliphs, or successors to the Prophet Muhammad. Their target was not just Sadat but the entire political and social structure of Egypt, which Mustafa said was tainted by hedonism, materialism, and alien—meaning Western—ideas.

Mustafa headed a band of desperadoes known as Takfir w'al Hijra (Separation and Migration, or Anathema and Exile), reflecting their belief that they had to separate themselves altogether from society and the state as it existed and build a new Egypt on Islamic principles. Theirs was a radical program, at that time far outside the main stream of political Islam, but the world of Islam today offers many examples of how such ideas have spread, such as the Boko Haram group in Nigeria and of course the Islamic State in Iraq and Syria.

Sadat "let the genie out of the bottle," said Alfred Leroy "Roy" Atherton, who succeeded Hermann F. Eilts as U.S. ambassador to Egypt in 1979. "There were spin-offs of the Brotherhood, militant spin-offs, clandestine spin-offs, who definitely looked to violent political action as a way of trying to change the regime. Their objective was to achieve what Islamic fundamentalists basically had as their goal—to get the country back to the Koran, to make the Koran the law of the land, Islamic law and Islamic tradition, governing education, governing all aspects of society and all policies of the government."[15]

The subterranean currents of extremism and violence that have always existed within Islam were largely dormant in Egypt before Sadat opened the dam. His decision to turn loose the Muslim Brotherhood can now be seen as one of the major developments that produced the violence-plagued Muslim world of today, though hardly the only one. Sadat's policies were not responsible for the religious revolution that took over Iran in 1979; for the 1980s anti-Soviet war in Afghanistan, which the United States and Saudi Arabia allowed the leader of Pakistan to transform from a political conflict into a religious one; or for the dispatch of more than five hundred thousand foreign, mostly American, troops to Saudi Arabia for Operation Desert Storm, a campaign that enabled extremist ideologues, including Osama bin Laden, to claim that the infidel West was waging war on Islam. The U.S. invasion of Iraq in 2003, another example of the West's "war on Islam," reinforced religious, anti-Western sentiment that had been brewing among Muslims for decades. On an intellectual level, however, the developments in Egypt during Sadat's time were critical. He was an enabler of the radicals.

In Egypt in the 1970s, Takfir w'al Hijra organized itself underground and was unknown to the public before it surfaced with the kidnapping and murder of an innocuous former minister of religious affairs. Egyptians were shocked, and Mustafa was hanged a year later, but by that time other violence-prone extremist groups were growing. They were the people whom Walter McClelland found to be threatening "all kinds of trouble" in Alexandria.

McClelland perceived that while Sadat could control the senior imams and scholars in government ministries and al-Azhar University, who were employees of the state, his peace initiative and gaudy personal style had alienated the pious rank and file. "Sadat tried to bring the religious establishment along with him," McClelland recalled, "but what the [imams] preached in the mosque on Friday often was highly

critical of what Sadat was doing. Not only did they oppose an opening to Israel, but they were very anti-Western and anti-Christian. Their
influence was everywhere, in the university, labor unions, clubs, etc."[16]

Operation Badr

A collective sense of defeat and disillusionment had settled over Egypt
after the catastrophic war of 1967. Many ordinary people, not members of any organization clandestine or otherwise, sought solace in an
embrace of Islam as their guiding ideology, understanding that Arab
nationalism and Nasser's socialism had failed them. Sadat encouraged such sentiment by assigning to the restorative war of 1973 the
code name Operation Badr, which as all Muslims knew was the site
of a crucial victory in the Prophet Muhammad's struggle against the
pagans of Mecca.

Mohamed Heikal—Egypt's most prominent writer at the time of
the war and a confidant of Sadat's until their falling out—reported
that shortly after the crossing, the army distributed to all members of
the military a pamphlet asserting that the triumph had been inspired
by a vision of "the Prophet Muhammad dressed in white, taking with
him the Sheikh of al-Azhar, pointing his hand and saying, 'Come
with me to Sinai.'" Heikal said he found this sort of religious propaganda "inappropriate," partly because it diminished the valor of
the troops who did the fighting. "There were signs of growing religious fanaticism as war fever mounted, so that eventually the President [Sadat] felt obliged to announce publicly that the commander
of the first infantry brigade to cross the canal was a Copt," that is, a
Christian, not a Muslim.[17]

Heikal was a bit unfair, in that Sadat frequently made public gestures intended to show that the Copts were equal, patriotic citizens.
His minister of state for foreign affairs, Boutros Boutros-Ghali, later
secretary-general of the United Nations, was a member of a prominent Christian family. Boutros-Ghali made no secret of the fact that
his wife was Jewish.

Nevertheless, it was true that Sadat elevated the role of Islam in
public and political life; the symbolism of Operation Badr was part

of this effort. After the war, with the citizenry inspired anew by the faith, the Muslim Brotherhood liberated to recruit and organize, and religious groups encouraged by Sadat's government seizing political control of campus organizations and professional syndicates, it was not surprising that a wave of religious sentiment swept over Egypt. Sadat had encouraged it, but he could not control it. In fact, he inflamed it by accepting a peace agreement that left infidels in control of Jerusalem's al-Aqsa Mosque and by flaunting a luxurious and self-indulgent personal lifestyle that alienated many of his people.

Even foreign residents of Egypt at the time such as myself, a non-Muslim with a limited command of Arabic, could see that this development had reached a point where people in the West needed to be aware of its significance. It was part of a phenomenon that was transforming the Muslim world from Algeria to Afghanistan and had strategic implications that reached far beyond Egyptian campuses. I wrote an article that appeared on the front page of the *Washington Post* on January 21, 1979—five days after the religious revolution in Iran forced the Shah to leave the country—describing "the resurgence of Islamic orthodoxy and puritanism that is one of the strongest trends in Egyptian society today. . . . Repelled by materialism and corruption, and frustrated by the lack of political and economic opportunity, many of the 40 million Egyptians are seeking spiritual solace or an outlet for their energies in a campaign of Islamic fundamentalism. It goes beyond the deep and abiding piety of the average Egyptian farmer or workman into social and occasionally political activism."

After the exhilaration of the 1973 war, a combination of persistent poverty, flagrant corruption, Western cultural encroachment, and the failure of any other ideology to deliver a better life created a fertile environment for an "Islam is the answer" sentiment among the people just at the time Sadat was encouraging Islamist groups to organize.

"Sadat's policies played a decisive role in the broadening of an Islamic opposition," as the American scholar Raymond A. Hinnebusch wrote. "His relaxation of police controls and the encouragement he initially gave to Islamic revival as a way of winning mass legitimacy and defeating the threat from the left, gave Islamic groups the oppor-

tunity to proselytize and organize without fear of government moles-
tation," he wrote.[18] As a result, by the late 1970s, "the mobilization
capacity of the Islamic movement, while perhaps still falling short of
its peak in the thirties, produced one of the most formidable political forces in Egypt."[19]

Most of these devout people did not espouse the violence of Takfir
w'al Hijra but they sympathized with many of its views, just as millions of Muslims today deplore the violence of al-Qaeda but endorse
its stated goals. By design and by accident, policies implemented by
Sadat fostered this growing religious sentiment among the people.
His Labor Ministry, for example, organized the migration of hundreds of thousands of Egyptian laborers to Saudi Arabia and other
Gulf states, where they absorbed conservative religious and cultural
attitudes that they later brought back with them. As Abdo and others have noted, a massive expansion of public universities in the 1970s
outstripped the ability of the schools to provide adequate faculty,
classrooms, or housing for the students; their discontent was fed by
the campus religious groups Sadat encouraged for political reasons.[20]
The religious groups won popular favor by providing textbooks for
poor students and transportation that spared women the indignities
of the ramshackle public bus system.

Moreover, not long after the Iranian revolution had inspired a wave
of religious ambition across the Muslim world and become a political if not doctrinal model for Muslim malcontents everywhere, Sadat
threw fuel on that fire by giving refuge to the exiled and reviled Shah.

The triumph of the Iranian revolution early in 1979 marked the
start of a year in which events all across the Muslim world inspired a
surge of religious zeal. Participants in these dramas differed in geography, history, and language, but were united by a common goal: establishment of Islam as the foundation of law, society, and government.
The military ruler of Pakistan, Zia ul-Haq, executed his worldly predecessor, Zulfikar Ali Bhutto, and declared Pakistan an Islamic state.
Zia acted out of political expediency rather than religious conviction, but he fostered an atmosphere in which religious fervor grew.
In Afghanistan, the population was in open rebellion against a com-

munist puppet government—an insurgency that prompted the Soviet invasion in December and the intervention in the war that followed of Arab religious radicals led by Osama bin Laden. Sadat signed a peace treaty with the Zionists that left Jews in control of Jerusalem's al-Aqsa Mosque. The rulers of Saudi Arabia, terrified by an armed takeover of the Great Mosque in Mecca by religious fanatics, committed billions of dollars of their swelling oil wealth to spread their xenophobic, absolutist form of Islam around the world. And the Saudis, with American encouragement, spent additional billions to support the Afghan mujahedeen and the so-called Afghan Arabs in their jihad against the atheistic Soviets in Afghanistan.

Sadat was not responsible for any of these developments except the treaty, but that agreement and his failure to curtail the streak of violence that was metastasizing within Egypt certainly contributed to the phenomenon. He had dismantled the heroic legacy of Nasser, jettisoned the dream of Arab solidarity, and retreated from state socialism, while failing to elevate any other collective idea in place of those. Historically, a vacuum such as that in any Muslim society has been filled by what is known as political Islam.

The Brotherhood Goes Public

By the time my *Washington Post* article appeared early that year, some young women, even professional women in Cairo and Alexandria, had resumed wearing the veil, which had been almost unknown under Nasser. Many gave up skirts and blouses for traditional full-length gowns and head scarves, signaling their piety. The most popular preacher in the country was a blind radical named Abdel Hamid Kishk, whose fiery sermons were circulated on audio cassettes. The Brotherhood itself was the opposite of clandestine: it was so visible and well organized that its posters appeared in the windows of Cairo buses and its thick, glossy magazine was on every newsstand.

One of the hundreds of Muslim Brothers released by Sadat in the early 1970s was Omar Tilmasani. At the time, few Egyptians knew who he was, but within a few years he was the public face of the organization, editor of its popular magazine *Al Dawa* (*The Call*, as in the muezzin's call to prayer), and a highly visible figure who worked openly in a decrepit Cairo office. When he died a few years later, more than half a million people attended his funeral.

In November 1977, two weeks before Sadat's trip to Jerusalem, by which time the United States was heavily invested in Sadat and his policies, Hermann F. Eilts, the U.S. ambassador, sent a long message to Washington headed "State of Muslim Brotherhood: The Ikhwan Today." Eilts reported that one of his political officers had engaged in a wide-ranging conversation with Tilmasani about the membership, influence, and objectives of the Brotherhood, and that Tilmasani had spoken proudly of the group's resurgence during Sadat's presidency.

"The Ikhwan, according to Talmasani, is concentrating its current efforts on religious education at [the] grass-roots level," Eilts wrote.

He maintained that Egypt's religious leaders, for too long, have been 'hiding in mosques' and have been unable to make religion relevant. Other than teaching people to pray and fast, they have been unable [to] inculcate principles of Islam in [the] general population. Talmasani argued people must know why they are carrying out religious acts if religion is to have [a] practical function. This is Ikhwan's goal, since [the] organization is convinced that 'one can find solutions for everything in Islam.' Talmasani ducked questions on how Ikhwan [is] organizing to carry out this campaign, beyond saying it [is] not confined to mosques and religious schools. He stated, however, that it is underway throughout [the] country and is achieving success [and] pointed to increased religious activity at universities with pride. Tilmasani said that many Arab governments had been opposed to the Brotherhood over many years, suspicious of its intentions, but he insisted those suspicions were unfounded. The group's message, he said, was one of tolerance: he maintained [the] true essence of Islam, as preached by Brotherhood, is 'work, love, and toleration.' [He] said Muslims have always welcomed Christians and Jews within their midst and have never practiced religious discrimination.

Tilmasani was probably correct about the Brotherhood's growing membership and political popularity, Eilts told the State Department, "but his description of Ikhwan as a benign, even benevolent, society is at variance with [the] historical record and is obviously self-serving. Arab governments, including Egypt, have opposed [the] organization since its inception because of its clandestine activities, including the use of violence."[21]

The dedication to organizing that Tilmasani described to Eilts paid off three decades later when the Brotherhood's candidate won Egypt's only free, popular election for president, easily outmaneuvering more sophisticated, Western-oriented candidates.

When I interviewed Tilmasani fourteen months after Eilts's report he was, as Eilts had noted, widely understood to be the Brotherhood's leader, or "Supreme Guide," but when I asked him who actually held that position, he replied coyly, "Sheikh al-Banna."

Nasser, he said, had been a "tyrant." Now that the Brothers were free to speak out under Sadat's friendlier regime, he said, "We are only expressing our point of view," which was that Islam "is a comprehensive system which regulates all aspects of human life. A Muslim can find his political, social, economic, and even family laws of conduct in our religion. Nobody can be a good Muslim who adopts some of the principles of Islam and not others." He insisted that members of the Brotherhood were "puritans" but were "never terrorists or fanatics," and said they were actually not opposed to the government. That is what the Brotherhood said for public consumption. The reality was less benign.

Eilts's cable had reported that "at 73, Talmasani gave appearance of being healthy and full of fight." When I met him, he came across as thoughtful and avuncular—the British journalist Edward Mortimer described him as "elderly, respectable, and harmless."[22] But his comments in our conversation, like the articles in *Al Dawa*, revealed the fundamentally intolerant and xenophobic outlook of the Brotherhood and its allies.

When he told me that "nobody can be a good Muslim who adopts some of the principles of Islam and not others," he was in effect condemning all the Egyptians who failed to pray five times a day, violated the Ramadan fast, gambled, smoked, or drank beer. He said "foreign hands, aimed at destroying the Islamic nation," were behind accusations of extremism. "East and West, the U.S. and the Russians are alike in that they don't want Egypt to flourish and rise to prosperity," he said, "because for both of them the Middle East is a favorite market. This has been true ever since the Crusades, which were not religious wars but an imperialist search for trade. . . . The Brotherhood wants Islam to be powerful so that nobody from either side can control us."[23]

This idea that Muslims are downtrodden and divided because of economic and strategic exploitation by outsiders is deeply entrenched in the Muslim world today. The Crusades, European colonialism, the longtime dominance of foreign companies in the Middle East oil business, real and imagined CIA interference in regional affairs, the U.S. invasion of Iraq, and of course unwavering American support for Israel are all seen as part of the same pattern and are all easy for Islamist ideologues to exploit in advancing their own agendas. Sadat was familiar with that pattern of thought but believed he could overcome it by delivering peace and prosperity. When the peace was seen as tainted and prosperity failed to arrive, the extremists found low-hanging fruit.

As time passed and life failed to improve except for the well-connected, even after the end of hostilities with Israel, Egyptians "were encouraged by the Islamic students and clerics [to believe] that if they just get unified and formed an Islamic state, then they would be able to cut back on corruption and do away with the fat cats who were living high on the hog and then there'd be more work for everybody," recalled H. Freeman Mathews Jr., at the time the second-ranking diplomat in the American embassy. "I think the fundamentalists profited from the disillusionment of the people that life, in fact, did not get better."[24]

Islamizing the Law

Beginning with the 1974 military academy attack and well into the 1980s under Sadat's successor, Hosni Mubarak, extremists within the

Islamist movement attracted the world's attention with episodes of violence—street riots, attacks on tourists, and assassinations, including of course the killing of Sadat himself. Each time, the Egyptian people as a whole ignored or rejected calls to rise en masse in support of whichever extremist group perpetrated the incident. The great majority did not endorse or support violence as a method of achieving the Islamization of society. Instead, nonviolent but determined activists concentrated on building goodwill through good works, on modifying social behavior, such as abolishing coeducation in the universities, and on reshaping Egyptian law to reflect Islamic ideals and the principles of sharia, or Islamic law.

According to Geneive Abdo's well-researched study, this legal evolution, which still shapes the Egyptian courts, "can be traced back to the mistakes and miscalculations of Egypt's secularist masters," a group in which she includes Sadat. "Chief among these was a 1971 decision by President Sadat to give in to demands from the Islamists, as part of the payoff for their devout anticommunism, for a constitutional amendment declaring Islamic holy law, the *sharia*, to be 'a principal source of legislation.'"[25] Nasser, a secularist and nationalist, had always resisted such a step.

In 1980, still under Sadat, a time when the Iranian revolution, the peace treaty with Israel, and the war in Afghanistan were stoking Islamist sentiment all across the community of believers, that constitutional provision was further strengthened to declare sharia to be the principal source of legislation, not just a principal source. As a result, forward-looking or modernist court rulings that Westerners might regard as progress, such as a decision limiting the practice of female genital mutilation, "were opened up to legal challenge by a growing corps of Islamist lawyers and magistrates," Abdo noted.[26] And the demand that this constitutional provision be fully implemented soon became a handy tool for Islamists seeking greater political power. Faculty and student groups that once discussed the Enlightenment in Europe now discussed arcane points of argument about religious law.[27]

Among pious Egyptians, which is to say most Egyptians, the change in the constitution was popular because of a belief that sharia, the legal embodiment of Islam, had long been subordinated to an alien legal code imported from a foreign culture. To them, reestablishing the Islamic foundations of the law represented a victory for cultural independence and pride, not a step backward in history. But as a practical matter, Sadat's acquiescence in this constitutional change inevitably created divisions and arguments that sometimes turned violent, because no community of Muslims in the modern world has been able to agree on what sharia actually requires. The many activities of modern life, and scientific advances that require new thinking about personal behavior, force Muslims to make decisions that cannot be guided by a holy book from the seventh century. What does sharia actually dictate about, for example, female genital mutilation, which is still widespread in Egypt? Is it really a manifestation of Islam, or a barbaric practice that drifted northward across Africa and became entrenched in custom? And what about alcoholic beverages? These are clearly banned by Islam, but Egypt is heavily dependent on tourism and thus not in a position to impose a total ban. Besides, Nasser nationalized the wineries and distilleries, so the government itself was in the booze business. Regardless of what sharia required, Sadat was not in a position to enforce its rules about alcohol because doing so would have thrown thousands of people out of work.

These contradictions are hardly unique to Egypt. Arguments about what sharia requires and how to implement it can be heard every day in many Muslim countries: Does the faith prohibit women from driving? Only in Saudi Arabia. Was there really a religious basis for the Taliban's prohibition of kite flying in Afghanistan? Is abortion permissible? Yes in some countries, no in others. May a woman initiate divorce proceedings? Yes in some countries, no in others. Should girls go to school? The Taliban say no; in Saudi Arabia, the government builds huge universities for women.

Once Sadat opened the door to arguments on such matters, he was never able to close it again. He pivoted back and forth in a vain attempt to please everyone.

Sometimes he followed what seemed to be a secular, modernist path, as when he appointed a liberal woman, Aisha Rateb, to be minister of social affairs, a position in which she campaigned to liberalize personal status laws, to the outrage of conservatives. On the other hand, he appointed Abdel Hamid Mahmoud, a strong supporter of Islamist groups and of full implementation of sharia, to be rector of al-Azhar University, the leading Islamic institution for a thousand years. Sadat made symbolic gestures to burnish his image of piety, such as referring to himself by his first name, Muhammad, not just Anwar, and adopting the title *al-rais al-mumin*, the believer president. When he staged a triumphal return to El Arish, an important town in the Sinai restored to Egyptian control after the peace treaty, immediately upon descending from his plane he knelt for prayers of thanksgiving led by the grand sheikh of al-Azhar—a public relations stunt intended to show all Arabs that he had the support of Islam's premier theological institution.

But he also permitted and endorsed activities that alienated believers, such as the annual summer migration of rich Gulf Arabs to Egypt, where they were known to purchase underage girls from poor families, and the publication of celebrity magazines featuring women in bikinis.[28] Sadat flaunted his close friendship with Osman Ahmed Osman, a construction tycoon affiliated with the Muslim Brotherhood, whose son married one of Sadat's daughters. While Osman nudged Sadat toward Islamist viewpoints in private, stirring up one kind of trouble, his Arab Contractors Company got the fattest contracts, stirring up another kind of trouble: popular anger about corruption. And Sadat encouraged cultural imports from the West, imports that were alien to the Egyptian masses, just as the Khedive Ismail's embrace of opera had been in the nineteenth century. Financial aid from Japan went to construction of a new opera house. More foreign films were shown. The Grateful Dead gave a concert at the Pyramids. Western-brand hotels operated gambling casinos at which only foreigners who possessed hard currency were permitted to play. Simultaneously, Sadat permitted the proliferation of mosques that were privately funded, not under government control, which became pulpits for the most radical and fiery of the new Islamist preachers. By 1979, only 5,600 of Egypt's 34,000 mosques were subject to state supervision.[29]

Sadat's successor, Mubarak, dealt with the Brotherhood and its Islamist allies by brutally suppressing them, stifling dissent and imposing what amounted to one-man rule. This had the effect of limiting violence and protecting the tourist industry, but the political and social seeds planted in Sadat's day continued to germinate.

In 1987 the scholar Yahya Sadowski, then at the Brookings Institution in Washington, wrote a provocative article titled "Egypt's Islamist Movement: A New Political and Economic Force," assessing the Brotherhood's impressive gains. Having spent time in Egypt myself that year, I found little to dispute in his conclusion: "The fundamentalists no longer whisper their message in clandestine cells; they have moved to the center of public life. Fundamentalists control many clubs and most student organizations at Egyptian colleges and secondary schools. They form an influential lobby in most professional organizations, including the national associations of doctors, lawyers, and engineers. They have forged links to the general public by building networks of schools, banks, and consumer cooperatives. Their message percolates out of radio shows [and] television broadcasts, and in several major newspapers. Most dramatically, in the past couple of years fundamentalists have emerged as the loudest (if not yet the most numerous) voices" in parliament.[30] Those were the forces that stormed into the political vacuum created by the overthrow of Mubarak in 2011. The Brotherhood's cadres did not engineer the downfall of Mubarak, but they were the only group well-enough organized and funded to win the presidential election that ensued.

Sadowski observed, as Geneive Abdo had, that one of the most effective tools at the Islamists' disposal was the legal system and the judiciary. Lawyers and judges sympathetic to the Brotherhood's objectives did not separate themselves from the legal system. Instead, as Sadowski put it, "they seek to transform such organizations into instruments for the propagation of Islam."[31] Thus they tried, with varying degrees of success, to enact laws embodying religious tenets, such as restricting the sale of alcoholic beverages, banning what they saw as blasphemous books, and issuing court rulings imposing limits on women's personal status. In their view, whatever problems Egyptians were facing, "Islam is the answer." It was analogous to a takeover of American law schools and courts by conservatives aligned with the tea party, creationists, and the right-to-life movement.

In a smaller, less consequential country, none of these developments might have mattered much except to the people involved. But Egypt and Egyptians exerted an outsize influence on the entire Muslim world. With the exception of Turkey and possibly Pakistan, it was the greatest military power among Muslim nations. Its population was by far the largest in the Arab world. Egyptian films and television programs were popular in many countries. The Egyptian news media were widely influential. Religious teachings and books emanating from al-Azhar had influenced Muslim thinking for centuries. Thus the rise of activist Islam under Sadat spread ripples far beyond Egypt's borders—just as the struggle between the Muslim Brotherhood and Egyptian secularists led by the army reverberates today in Tunisia, Syria, Iraq, Mali, and other Muslim countries.

Even while Sadat was still president, G. H. Jansen, in a study of the rise of Islamist movements, could perceive that the Muslim Brotherhood, while never formally legalized, "has become incontestably the single most powerful organization in Egypt outside the army."[32] The Ikhwan may not have endorsed violence themselves, at least not in public, but they fertilized the thinking of those who did.

As became apparent late in Sadat's tenure, and especially after his death when the credo of his assassins became known, the extremist bill of particulars against him was extensive and included matters both great and trivial. Among his offenses: He made peace with the Zionist occupiers of Jerusalem and prayed at the sacred al-Aqsa Mosque while it was under infidel control. He drank wine at a dinner with President Carter and allowed state-owned breweries and distillers to produce alcoholic beverages. He allowed his wife, Jehan, to travel around Egypt and the world preaching the doctrine of family planning and fewer children. He supported the Shah of Iran against a religious revolution and gave him refuge after he had been deposed. He kissed Rosalyn Carter in public. And to doctrinaire Muslims, Sadat's piety was suspect because he often spoke with pride about "Egypt's

7,000-year civilization," while they viewed all history before the birth of Muhammad in 570 as a time of pagan ignorance.

Sadat, the religious conservatives said, with considerable justification, lived in luxury while his people lived in poverty. He supported modernization of the status of women. He tolerated the production and sale of pork. (This commerce was conducted entirely by Christians but nevertheless it was unacceptable for the Islamist zealots to see pork, forbidden by their faith, sold openly in Egypt's big cities.) Sadat allowed Egypt to be drummed out of the worldwide fraternity of Muslim nations over the peace treaty. And he encouraged the spread of Western economic and cultural influence, such as the opera and foreign films. These actions and policies could not be squared with the image of Sadat the village boy with his forehead pressed to the dirt floor of a rural mosque.

Contrary to Islamic teaching, Sadat insisted on separating affairs of state from affairs of the pulpit: "No religion in politics, no politics in religion," he often said, although, as one scholar noted, that was true more in rhetoric than in practice because in Egypt, as in most Sunni Muslim countries, mosque and government are closely intertwined. Most religious leaders are employees of the state, and the state controls religious institutions such as charitable endowments funded by a tax on the population. Sadat could ban political parties with religious affiliations, but he could not get the state out of the religion business, and he would have been well advised to stop proclaiming that the two were separate.

In fairness to Sadat, and to his successors, it would be difficult for any leader of a majority-Muslim state today to chart a safe and popular course between modernization and engagement with the global economy and culture, on the one hand, and the strictures of Islamic tradition on the other. During Europe's Dark Ages, Muslim thinkers and scientists were the world's intellectual leaders, but by the eighteenth century the Muslim world had largely fallen into political and scholarly isolation. Napoleon's invasion of Egypt in 1798 and the establishment of British colonial power in India, Iraq, Palestine, and the Arabian Peninsula introduced to the Muslim masses Western ideas of politics, law, education, and social organization. Ever since, there has been a perpetual struggle between those who look to Islam for their political and cultural guidance and who wish to see the principles of Islam dominate public policy, and those who wish to live in more secular societies in which Muslims are free to worship but governmental systems and economic institutions reflect modern ideas of social organization, usually modeled on those of the West.

In general the former group prefers to limit social and political interaction with non-Muslims while those in the latter group welcome or at least accept it. There are extremists on both sides and in many countries where Muslims represent a majority of the population the response has been cyclical—the so-called modernists prevail for a decade or two, then there is a reaction in favor of the traditionalists. In Pakistan, the cycle has more or less been controlled by the inclinations of whatever ruler is in power. In Saudi Arabia, the ruling family has always identified itself and the country with the traditionalists, but there is also a new generation of Saudis more inclined to see value in external ideas and organizations. In Turkey, the secularists prevailed for decades under the system imposed by Mustafa Kemal Ataturk after the breakup of the Ottoman Empire, but the conservatives and traditionalists have gradually reasserted themselves over the past decade. Dubai is a wide-open international city on many levels, but signs in shopping malls still warn against public displays of affection.

Most of the time, a ruler can enforce one orientation or the other by the exercise of power, as Saddam Hussein did in his secular Iraq and as the al-Saud rulers do in religious Saudi Arabia. To find a balance that accommodates multiple viewpoints and permits free expression to all of them is close to impossible. In Egypt, Sadat tried to manage the cycle to his political advantage, but the result was to unleash forces of reaction that were difficult to control. In the end, Sadat failed this test, as did Mubarak after him.

Toward the end of Sadat's life, he came to regret his encouragement of the Brotherhood because the organization, overestimating public support for its agenda, overplayed its hand. For example, members of the Brotherhood seized the opportunity of the "bread riots" of January 1977, which Sadat denounced as "an uprising of thieves," to attack nightclubs and bars in tourist areas, threatening the livelihood of thousands. Some affiliated groups flaunted the money that was flowing to them from outside Egypt. And the Brotherhood infuriated Sadat by its strident opposition to his peace treaty with Israel. On the very night the treaty was signed, as Egyptians watched the ceremony in Washington on television, the National Union of Students, by then dominated by Brotherhood members and sympathizers, distributed leaflets attacking the agreement on religious grounds. These denounced Israel as a "usurper" state that sought to establish a Jewish kingdom from the Nile to the Euphrates. The Koran, they said, "imposes on every Muslim the duty to arise and struggle to regain every square meter" of Arab land. (Ironically, a small leftist party— the very sort of people against whom Sadat had set the Islamists in the first place—had distributed the same statement, word for word, the week before.)[33]

According to John Waterbury, a scholar who lived in Egypt during the Sadat years, the student groups became "the most active and potentially dangerous elements among the fundamentalists." Sadat sought to use the government's religious institutions such as al-Azhar to counter the students' angry denunciations of him, but "his efforts lacked credibility" because the students "seized upon the various humiliations inflicted upon Egypt by Menachem Begin's one-sided interpretation of the peace process."[34]

Many Islamist leaders were again jailed during what Mohamed Heikal called the "Autumn of Fury," the spasm of mass arrests that preceded Sadat's assassination by renegade members of the armed forces during a military parade on October 6, 1981, the anniversary of the October War.

Mubarak kept a tight lid on dissent in his three decades as president, including a relentless effort to control religious extremism, but it still flared up from time to time. In the most notable incident, in 1997, militants gunned down fifty-eight tourists and four Egyptians at the Temple of Hatshepsut in Luxor, one of Egypt's premier attractions. A violence-prone group known as al-Jamaa al-Islamiya asserted responsibility; one of its stated objectives was to force the government to release Omar Abdel Rahman, a fiery preacher who had been arrested as a suspect in the Sadat assassination plot, acquitted, then imprisoned on unrelated charges.

After Mubarak was brought down by a popular uprising and Egypt for the first time chose a president by popular vote, the Muslim Brotherhood again came out of the shadows to give victory to its candidate, Mohamed Morsi. That outcome demonstrated that the Brotherhood retained its wide popular appeal and that it had preserved its skill at organizing through the years in which Mubarak suppressed it. But Morsi soon learned the difficulty of governing in ways that would satisfy the diverse elements of the Muslim population and at the same time maintain peace with the Christians. Like the Brotherhood of the late 1970s, and like his predecessors in office, he failed the balance test. A year after taking office, he had so alienated Egypt's sophisticated urbanites that they clamored for the military to take him down, and celebrated when the army responded. The officers who took over once again declared the Brotherhood the enemy, labeled it a terrorist organization, and arrested not only its leaders but people outside the organization perceived as sympathizers.

Morsi may have been an incompetent politician, but even if he'd had the skill of a statesman, he and the Brotherhood would have confronted the insoluble problem that has plagued Islamist movements of all stripes since the Middle Ages: the lack of consensus within the faith about what form of government and society Islam requires. There is no central doctrinal authority in Islam, no Muslim Vatican. The Koran gives detailed instructions about certain aspects of life, such as how to distribute the spoils of war, but is silent about others, including, of course, activities that were unknown in the time of Muhammad.

In Egypt, under all presidents since the 1952 revolution other than Morsi, the state has generally conducted its affairs by standards and policies that seem reasonable and forward-looking—which was precisely the indictment delivered by the religious absolutists. The Napoleonic invasion of 1798 shockingly demonstrated the power of technology over tradition; since then, under every government, Egypt has embraced scientific knowledge, military skill, and development of the bureaucracy as the objectives of the state. Before Morsi, there was no religious path to secular power, which is why extremist groups such as Takfir w'al-Hijra went outside the law.

Since Morsi was shoved aside by the military after his turbulent year in office, religion has again been largely excluded from politics. Yet the balance is never fully settled; Islam by its nature does not accept exclusion from power. Moreover, a few months after Morsi was succeeded by his former defense minister, General Abdel Fattah al-Sisi, a *Foreign Affairs* article argued persuasively that Sisi was no secularist: while on active duty as an officer, he had been at the forefront of a religious movement within the armed forces that had originated under Sadat and has gathered strength ever since.[35] Yet even Sisi drew a clear line between Islamist politics and the murderous absolutism of the extremists, which he said was antagonizing the world and blackening the reputation of Islam. "It's inconceivable that the thinking that we hold most sacred should cause the entire [Islamic world] to be a source of anxiety, danger, killing and destruction for the rest of the world. Impossible!" he said.[36]

The credo of Hassan al-Banna, who founded the Muslim Brotherhood in 1928, declares that "Islam founds the state on the principles of justice, establishes government in terms of clearly defined rights, and allows each member of various classes in the nation his due, without frustration, misunderstanding, or injustice." Any Muslim would agree with that as a statement of ideals, but what does it mean in practice in the modern world? Al-Banna, like others who seek a religious foundation for the state, is clear about what not to do: adopt foreign, alien, or other non-Muslim systems of human organization. "Ever since the Oriental nations forsook the teachings of Islam and attempted to substitute others, which they believed would help solve their problems," he wrote, "they have been caught in a morass of uncertainty and have suffered bitter defeats; the price for deviation has been high, in dignity, morality, self-respect and administrative efficiency." In his view, the unhappy reality was that Muslims suffered from self-inflicted wounds because they embraced ideas and practices imported from other cultures: "The Muslims themselves are at war with their faith; they break their own sword and freely hand a dagger to those who would bring them down, by cooperating with those who seek to demolish the religion which is the very foundation of their regimes and the source of their strength."[37]

Perhaps, but again, what does that mean in practice? In modern life any government, of whatever form, has to deal with practical questions for which there are no specifically "Islamic" answers. Does Islam permit in-vitro fertilization, for example? What about life insurance, which until recently was banned in Saudi Arabia as a form of gambling with God? What forms of taxation other than the religious levy called *zakat* are legitimate? How can commerce be financed without interest on loans, which some theologians say is prohibited in Islam? Should boys and girls be in the same classroom? Is military alliance with non-Muslims ever permissible? May a Muslim be cremated? Is music sinful? Should a country even have a legislature, or is legislation unnecessary, as some believe, because all required law can be found in the Koran and the Hadith, the verified sayings of the Prophet?

Then there is the unresolved matter of the nature of the state, the form of government or social organization, and who is to run it. Should the head of government and the senior religious leader be the same person? The Koran and the Hadith do not provide the answer. Salafists, who aspire to return to some pure, if imaginary, form of Islam as it existed in the Prophet's Arabia, talk of restoring the caliphate, the system in which the head of state was also the leader of the religion. (Caliph, or *khalifa* in Arabic, means successor, as in the "rightly guided" caliphs, the first four successors of Muhammad.) For centuries the Ottoman sultan was also the caliph, even if his religious leadership was nominal. But the position of caliph itself was created by human beings, by the early believers who needed someone to be in charge after Muhammad died. Nothing in the Koran or the Hadith specifies who is to be in charge, or how he is to be selected. No one could credibly claim the title today, as was demonstrated when the leader of the so-called Islamic State in Iraq and Syria, widely known as ISIS, declared himself caliph in 2014. Hardly any Muslims beyond his band of extremists—a tiny fraction of worldwide Islam—accepted this self-appointment.

Hanging over all these questions is a still more troublesome one: Does the faith permit or require violence to resolve such matters? If a group of Muslims believes the state or its ruler is violating the rules of the faith as they understand them, are they permitted or even required to use force against the ruler, or is it sufficient to write and teach in opposition? Are non-Muslims to be tolerated, shunned, or killed? Many groups that fall under the rubric of Islamism share a vision of a more pure, faith-based society. The question is what that means and how to achieve it. For groups such as the Taliban in Afghanistan, the Takfir w'al Hijra, the Shebab in Somalia, Boko Haram in Nigeria, the self-styled Islamic State, and of course al-Qaeda, the answer is to impose their will by force. For other religion-based groups, the answer is to spurn violence and achieve their goals by example, by education, by preaching, and by legal activism. The same split existed and still exists within the Muslim Brotherhood itself.

Sadat never attempted to master these nuances within Islam. When he declared that there should be "no politics in religion, no religion in politics," he said it was because "religion was never a bond." He claimed to run a government based on "science and faith." Science, he said, "is the emancipation of the human mind to accomplish good and achieve progress," whereas faith "is a commitment to principles, values, and ethics upheld by religions which, before and after the advent of divine religions, have unceasingly toiled to liberate the human and entrench [his] dignity and freedom."[38] That sentence, which appeared to equate Islam with other monotheistic faiths and even with pagan creeds, presented a view that was anathema to the religious activists.

Sadat even preached that all three of the great monotheistic religions were at home in Egypt: Moses lived in Egypt, the Holy Family found refuge there, and Islam prospered in Egypt in its first great expansion beyond the Arabian Peninsula. He pledged that once Egypt had recovered all of Sinai, he would build, on the site of the Monastery of St. Catherine, "a mosque, a church, and a synagogue as a living witness to their belief in the same God, the God who was worshipped by Abraham, the father of monotheism."[39] It is true that Islam teaches that Muslims, Jews, and Christians worship the same God and derive from the same prophetic tradition, but it does not teach that the three faiths are equal in truth or merit.

To critics such as Mohamed Heikal, an erstwhile confidant who broke with Sadat over the peace treaty with Israel, Sadat's pronouncements on these subjects were sophistries masking policies that divided the country. Sadat, Heikal said, "became Mohamed Anwar el-Sadat, the pious, the leader of the faithful. He told the nation that sometimes, when confronted with a particularly difficult problem, he would go to sleep and wake up to discover that by some mysterious transcendental aid the solution to the problem had been given to him as he slept. But at the same time that he presented himself as the most devout of Moslem rulers, he was talking of harmonizing the worship and worshippers of the three religions of the book—Islam, Christianity and Judaism. It is not surprising that the freedom with which he used the term 'atheist' to abuse his political opponents should have encouraged others to apply the same term to himself."[40]

In *The October Working Paper*, the lengthy manifesto of his personal beliefs and his objectives for the country that he published after the 1973 war, Sadat said, "With the October War, we have embarked on a new stage in the life of this ancient people, the ten main tasks of which I sum up again as follows." The list he gave included "an open society which enjoys freedom," but omitted any mention of Islam.[41] And in a message to the Islamic World Festival in London in 1976, he declared that "Islam does not force anyone to adopt it, nor is it biased against those who have not embraced it; it does not conspire against those who have not adopted it as a faith, nor does it seize opportunities to discriminate against followers of other religions, because they all are, from the standpoint of Islam, people with legitimate rights, guaranteed freedoms, and safeguarded beliefs, free to worship, to practice their rites and observances."[42] These ideas sounded appealing in Europe and the United States but to the true believers they represented heresy and were among the reasons that the extremists turned against him and eventually killed him. Sadat sowed the seeds of religious conflict, and of his own destruction.

It may be true, as Omar Tilmasani said in our 1979 conversation, that the majority of Muslim Brothers are not "terrorists or fanatics." But it is also true, as all Egyptian presidents since the 1952 revolution have learned, that there exist within the Brotherhood groups and cells willing, even eager, to resort to violence to promote their agenda. In fact, this dichotomy exists not just inside the Brotherhood but in Islam itself. It has been reflected in centuries-long arguments about the nature of *jihad*: does it mean spiritual struggle or armed force?

Many scholars and historians have noted that the worldwide cause of Islamism is undercut by the absence of a unified program or platform. There is no single document, not even the Koran itself, which all groups accept as a platform for a unified political and social program. Muhammad is reported to have said, "Beware of newly invented matters, for every invented matter is an innovation and every innovation is a going astray and every going astray is in Hellfire." That injunction is relatively easy to follow on matters of doctrine, but defies application to modern government and society. There is no manifesto approved by all groups, overt or clandestine, violent or nonviolent, that says, here is how we will come to power and how we will rule once we are in charge.

The Islamic state (not the group claiming that name that appeared in Iraq in 2014 but the ideal Islamic community to which they all profess to aspire) has always defied definition because the Prophet never specified how the Muslim community was to conduct its affairs after his death and because Islam has no controlling doctrinal authority. It can even be questioned whether Muhammad intended to found a state at all, or only a community of believers within a state. Thus it is hard to imagine that extremist groups such as al-Qaeda could merge their tactics and objectives and live in political coexistence with those of better-established groups such as the Muslim Brotherhood, to say nothing of the modernizers and secularists.

Sadat cannot be blamed for the ambiguities of Islamic doctrine or for the existence of extremism within Islam, which predated him by centuries and is on the march today across the Muslim world. What he can be blamed for is giving credence to some of the extremists' views by his decisions while in office and by his personal conduct on the world stage. Not only did he turn the Brotherhood loose, in the Muslim worldview he validated many of its adherents' arguments.

Other modern-day rulers of Muslim countries, beginning with Ataturk, have espoused secular policies, but Sadat was uniquely positioned as Nasser's successor, a world figure, and president of a crucial and deeply religious country in which the Brotherhood had originated. Because of his prominence, and because of what now are widely perceived as his manifest failures, one principle on which all the Islamist groups can agree on today is that their country, their society, must not be run as Sadat ran Egypt. He thought he could manipulate the forces of religious devotion. Instead, he became an example of what pious Muslims oppose, wherever they are. If their countries are weak, divided, or backward, their perceived path to betterment lies across the familiar terrain of Islam, not across the terrain of American culture, secular philosophy, liberated women, religious tolerance, multicultural environments, or peace with the Zionists. Sadat could not have fathomed the power of a movement like the so-called Islamic State, whose fanatic warriors shot and beheaded their way to power across broad stretches of Iraq and Syria in 2014. It is safe to say that Saddam Hussein, a committed secularist, the iron-fisted ruler of Iraq whom the United States ousted, would not have made the same mistakes as Sadat, whose successors are confronting the power of the Muslim Brotherhood today.

8 The Tarnished Legacy

After the October War, Anwar Sadat was acclaimed throughout the Arab world. And when he returned from Jerusalem bringing the prospect of peace, he received a rapturous welcome home.

The time of adulation was brief. The Hero of the Crossing was not a hero for long.

Just four years after his address to the Knesset, Sadat was assassinated by members of his own army, who opened fire during a parade commemorating the war. He died unmourned in Egypt and widely reviled, just like his friend the Shah of Iran, to whom he had given refuge. He had squandered his popularity through grandiose pretension and pharaonic excess, increasingly autocratic politics, separation from the aspirations of the masses, and near-total failure to deliver the economic benefits that the Egyptians had expected to come with peace. In style and substance, he had severed himself from the Egyptian "family" he claimed to represent.

His assassins were religious extremists, but they were outliers only in that they resorted to violence, not in their sentiments about the president. "The forces which conspired against Sadat were just as much a part of the mainstream in Egyptian society as were the forces which overthrew the Shah from the mainstream in Iran," Sadat's erstwhile confidant Mohamed Heikal argued. Heikal wrote that those in the West who failed to understand this should ask themselves why it was that "a man who was mourned as a heroic and far-seeing statesman in the West found hardly any mourners among his fellow countrymen" and why "a man who had for so long filled the television screens and captured the headlines should so soon after his death be almost completely forgotten."[1]

The answers lay partly in the image of himself that Sadat projected on the international stage—the man of peace, the contemplative pipe smoker who was also bold and imaginative, the self-described farmer who was convivial and comfortable at state dinners and imperial banquets. That image was appealing in Washington and Paris, but it was not appealing in the slums of Cairo or the cotton fields of the Nile Delta. The Egyptians who lived and worked there did not wear thousand-dollar suits or dine with French women or allow their bare-headed wives to be kissed on the cheek by foreigners. To the Egyptian masses, Sadat sought to present himself as a pious Muslim of humble origins, but that image became increasingly hard for the people to accept as Sadat gained international fame, consorted more and more with foreigners, and embraced foreign culture. People knew that he had lavish residences all over Egypt, many of them palaces from the old days of the monarchy, whereas the revered Nasser had lived simply.

As vice president in the 1960s, Muhammad Anwar el-Sadat was the designated successor to Nasser, but he was little known to his countrymen and even less known to outsiders. The few who did know him took him lightly. Nasser had been admired as the greatest Arab leader of modern times, despite his profound military and economic failures and his autocratic rule; Sadat was Nasser's loyal sidekick but had no constituency of his own. He had been speaker of the People's Assembly, Nasser's rubber-stamp legislature, but that did not signify the approbation of Egyptian voters. It was a position he could have held only as an agent of Nasser's will. People called him "Nasser's donkey."

"Initially we did not have that high an opinion" of Sadat, recalled Marshall Wiley, a diplomat who was serving in the U.S. "Interests Section" in Cairo at the time of Nasser's death. (There was no embassy; diplomatic relations had been broken during the 1967 war.) "In fact, when I first went there, when Nasser was still alive, Sadat was sort of the designated anti-American. He was going around the country making speeches attacking the United States, I presume under orders from Nasser. Many of the things he was saying were outright lies."[2] No one foresaw the dramatic shift in Egypt's strategic alignment that Sadat would engineer.

Throughout the eleven years of his presidency, Sadat's impetuous style, lazy work habits, sometimes erratic personality, and theatrical behavior were the subject of speculation and analysis by diplomats and journalists. Even those who saw him often and knew him well found his true nature difficult to grasp. He never wavered in his determination to regain every square inch of the land Egypt had lost to Israel in 1967, but his tactics zigzagged with the moment and the setting, sometimes to the chagrin of his closest advisers.

An early CIA assessment of his personality concluded that "he has shown himself to be a very short-range thinker."[3] But Hermann Eilts, who became U.S. ambassador after diplomatic relations were restored and talked to Sadat often and at length, came to the opposite conclusion. He said Sadat "was a man who thought a great deal. He would sit for long periods of time in silence, smoking his pipe and thinking. His thoughts, I felt, were never very deep, and I don't say that in any pejorative sense, but he thought in strategic terms. He was a conceptualizer in the same sense that Henry Kissinger was."[4]

At one time or another, American diplomats who worked with him described him as "a great fuzzy puppy"; "a grand seigneur type person"; "a man of tremendous vision and courage"; "an unguided missile"; "a genuinely warm person"; "a statesman of the first order"; and "a bit naïve." In retrospect, he was a visionary, so single-minded and focused on one great goal that he neglected to turn around and see the wreckage he was leaving in his wake.

Sadat had visited the United States during the Nasser years, and understood America well enough to know that sentiment in Congress overwhelmingly favored Israel. He knew he would have to win over its members if they were to grant the economic and military aid Egypt needed. Diplomats who served in the U.S. embassy after the restoration of diplomatic relations recalled that Sadat never refused to receive any congressional delegation, no matter how obscure its members, and that he was always gracious. Even Clement Zablocki, a rough-edged, bulb-nosed pol from Milwaukee who showed up in a red-checked sports jacket that looked like a horse blanket, got a respectful reception. After all, he was chairman of the House Foreign Affairs Committee.

Robert S. Dillon, who became deputy chief of mission at the U.S. embassy in 1980, told a revealing story about escorting a delegation from Minnesota to visit Sadat at his residence in Giza. "Suddenly [Sadat's wife] Jihan appears, carrying a baby—a grandchild. She says, 'Oh, Anwar, I didn't know you had company.' And he says, 'My dear, I would like you to meet some friends of mine.' And they are charmed out of their socks, of course."

Later, back at the embassy, when Dillon described this episode to Eilts's successor, Alfred "Roy" Atherton, the ambassador was amused, Dillon said. "'Oh, yes, the old 'babe in arms' routine, he is very good at it,' Roy says. The fact is that Sadat and his family were very good at staging these 'impromptu' scenes. I am not saying this in a cynical way. Sadat was smart enough to know that given the American view of Arabs, they had to be humanized. There were many ways of doing it, but the domestic scene was part of the play. He and his family played their roles very very well. . . . I liked and admired his style. I did come to understand, however, why a lot of Egyptians became disenchanted with Sadat. He was awfully distant towards them. The charm seemed reserved for foreigners whom he was trying to influence."[5]

Sadat relished the company of celebrities, the comfort of his multiple grand homes, and the adulation of the world's media, but they were not ends in themselves, at least not until his vision gave way to paranoia and delusions of grandeur in the last two years of his presidency. They were tools that he wielded to persuade the world to take him seriously and respond to his initiatives. He understood the importance of world opinion, and especially American public opinion, to his quest for peace with Israel and alliance with the United States.

For that reason, he rivaled Henry Kissinger in his courtship and flattery of the press, and he was good at it. As part of his campaign to present himself as a visionary peacemaker and friend of the West, he made it a point to know the names of Cairo's resident foreign correspondents and to know something about every reporter who interviewed him and the publication or network he or she worked for. We found him equally at ease in banter or in policy discussion, comfortable before the camera, always ready with a joke or bromide, in good English, to fend off questions he did not want to answer. He knew that the lectern-pounding, brow-mopping style of his frequent three- or four-hour speeches to Egyptian audiences was not appropriate in talking to the foreign press, so he maintained an informal tone and kept the sessions with the foreign press low-key, in the style of a chat among friends.

At one meeting with reporters after his trip to Jerusalem, he strode into the room with a cheery "good morning" and greeted many of us by name, a flattering ego-booster. At the time, news outlets all around the world were clamoring for access to this suddenly renowned statesman, and he was showing our editors that we, the privileged ones, had it; it made us look good to the home office, and we appreciated it. He made sure a visiting correspondent from Israeli television got a front-row seat—another message to Israel, to the United States, and to his Arab critics.

This courtship of the press was more than a reflection of Sadat's vanity. He had an innate understanding of public relations. In terms of content, he could have given his Jerusalem speech at the United Nations or anywhere else, but few would have paid attention. That was why he gave interviews to all three major American networks during the flight to Israel and allowed a reporter from *Time* to accompany him on the plane. And that was why his speeches to parliament, tedious as they could be, were broadcast on Cairo Radio in simultaneous English translation, so that we whose knowledge of Arabic was limited would hear his message as he delivered it to the Egyptians.

Yet despite all those endless speeches, it was difficult for his countrymen to develop a clear understanding of who he really was, perhaps because his public statements shifted with events, perhaps because he did not really know himself—his autobiography was titled *In Search of Identity*, and he wrote in its epilogue, "So far the search has not ended—nor do I believe that it will ever end."[6] Was he the loyal acolyte of Nasser, or the leader who began to purge Nasser's legacy almost as soon as he took office? Was he the village lad, as he described himself, or the dapper statesman? Was he the canny nationalist plotter whose resentment of British domination led him to conspire even with Nazi Germany, or was he a friend of the West?

The British jailed Sadat twice for his activities during World War II, in the period when Egypt was nominally independent but the British remained in control. Sadat's daughter Camelia said he "saw himself as Zahran, as a true patriot." Zahran was a young peasant who joined other youths in a clash with the British in which a British soldier was killed. The young men were sentenced to death. While his compatriots walked submissively to the gallows, Zahran "walked with his head held high. As he went to his death he proclaimed, 'I am dying to free Egypt.'"[7]

Even Sadat's attire made it difficult for his compatriots to know who he really was, for he was a man of costume. He had dabbled in acting as a youth—he was so taken with Mahatma Gandhi that he doffed most of his clothes and strode around carrying a walking stick—and his critics said he never got over it. Even Ambassador Eilts, who admired him, called him "a consummate actor."[8]

Sadat loved theatrical moments and theatrical events, and always dressed for whatever part he was playing. The costume was the message: a peasant's loose *gallabeya* for the village and countryside, an absurd field marshal's uniform festooned with decorations for military occasions. In the 1977 edition of the annual military parade commemorating the start of the October War, he wore jodhpurs with boots and spurs, and carried a silver-knobbed swagger stick. For diplomatic settings he sported elegant Italian suits and polished ankle-high boots. The tailored suits and starched collars led an Italian magazine to list him among the world's best-dressed men.

In the opening line of his autobiography, Sadat described himself as "a peasant, born and brought up on the banks of the Nile." Sadat was indeed born in a farming village, but he was no peasant. His grandfather was literate, his father was an army clerk, and the family moved to Cairo when Anwar was seven years old. The more Egyptians saw of him as president years later, the less they were fooled by his claim to be a *fellah*, a son of the soil just like them. They were outraged when, during the peace negotiations, Sadat offered to build a canal that would supply water from the Nile to Israel. In the culture of agrarian Egypt, the great river is nearly sacred; it is not a bargaining chip. His rash offer was a sign of his distance from national sentiment.

David Hirst and Irene Beeson, British journalists who despised Sadat for what they saw as his sellout of the Arab cause, judged him to be "intemperate, demagogic, alternately abusive and obsequious." They concluded that "Sadat the man had certain shallow gifts. He was an actor. He had a gambler's flair. But above all he was the consummate opportunist. . . . He was constant only in his inconstancy."[9] That harsh verdict reflected the authors' political views, but there was no doubt that Sadat could be duplicitous when it suited his purposes. His erstwhile Soviet allies had discovered that, to their regret.

A CIA historical analysis some years afterward said what those of us who watched Sadat closely during the peace negotiations could easily see: the adulation heaped upon him by world leaders and the international news media after Jerusalem went to his head. "Sadat's already special view of himself was given a new boost," a CIA agency consultant wrote. "We initially characterized this personality reaction as 'the Barbara Walters syndrome,' but by the summer of 1978, as it grew exponentially, we designated it as Sadat's Nobel Prize complex. As we followed his behavior particularly closely over the next several months, one of the most interesting changes had to do with the sharp increase in the first person singular. The frequency of the word 'I' increased dramatically in Sadat's statements."[10] He talked of "my people" and "my army."

A backroom conspirator of flexible loyalty one day, he relished ceremony and the spotlight the next. In public he was what he thought people wanted him to be at the moment, stern and fatherly in one setting, gregarious and engaging in another. His childhood flair for acting served him well in presenting himself to the world, but in the end it failed him utterly in his standing among the Egyptian people.

An Obscure Lightweight

When Nasser died unexpectedly on September 28, 1970, at the age of fifty-two, it would never have occurred to anyone that the obscure lightweight who happened to be vice president would soon seize the world's imagination, confound the superpowers, defy all conventional wisdom, and alter the lives of millions.

Initially, Sadat did not even have full control of the Egyptian government. His first task as president was to assert his primacy and consolidate his grip on power by purging a pro-Soviet clique of Nasser loyalists who opposed him. He always referred to this early power struggle as the "Corrective Revolution," meaning that the ideals of the nationalist revolution of 1952 had been lost in the backwash of Soviet influence until he restored them.

With the purge accomplished and his rivals in prison, he was free to chart a new course for Egypt. He pursued four lines of policy aimed at rehabilitating a defeated, demoralized, and destitute country: (1) to jettison Nasser's state-controlled socialist economy, which had bankrupted the state, and promote private investment; (2) to transfer Egypt's international alignment away from the Soviet Union's sphere of influence into a new alliance with the United States; (3) to seek peace with Israel because Egypt could not afford to continue the struggle and because only by pursuing peace with Israel could Sadat ingratiate himself with the Americans; and (4) to dismantle Nasser's one-party police state.

In the abstract, those policies made sense. In reality, the domestic political goals were never realized because Sadat could not bring himself to permit unfettered democracy, and the economic goals were not achievable, by him or anyone. Egypt's giant factories were obsolete and hopelessly uncompetitive, but they could not be shuttered because they employed hundreds of thousands who would be put out of work. Nor could they be privatized, even if investors had been willing to buy them, because delivering state assets into private hands, especially foreign hands, would have ignited massive political resistance. Years of state control of industry, banks, utilities, and transportation had stripped Egypt of competitive managers who understood marketing, pricing, and quality control. The national currency, the pound, was worthless outside Egypt. The housing stock was decrepit; public utilities and services were crippled by years of neglect and lack of investment; public health conditions were appalling; and agricultural policy was skewed to favor the production of long-staple cotton, which could be exported to earn desperately needed hard currency but did not feed a fast-growing population that outstripped the country's resources. Mass riots in January 1977 forced the government to keep in place ruinous subsidies that were crippling state finances. Egypt needed new buses, hospitals, and electric generation plants. It needed trucks to replace the ubiquitous donkey carts, and vast new tracts of modern housing to replace the mud huts of the villages. It did not have the money for any of them.

Peace and the economic investment policy known as *infitah*, or "opening," brought materialism but not prosperity. It delivered some massive aid projects, brought in foreign banks, and presented opportunities for the well-connected, but it produced few jobs for ordinary citizens, whose numbers continued to proliferate.

Sadat's economic policies and his embrace of the West ushered Egypt into a time of what might be called cultural deracination. The economic "Open Door" of infitah was a door to corrupting Western influences but not to much Western investment. The new money that did come in fueled inflation; but because many taxes were set in fixed amounts, state revenue did not increase with prices, while the population continued to grow and with it the demand for subsidies and housing.

Sadat knew little about economics, but even if he had been a giant of economic thinking he could not have delivered on the fundamental promise of his presidency: that peace with Israel, however hard to swallow, would quickly bring a new era of prosperity, fueled by foreign investment, American aid, and cash support from the newly rich Arab oil states.

After Camp David, Sadat appeared on state television to predict that every citizen would enjoy prosperity and have a home with modern conveniences within three years. His inability to deliver on such rash promises undermined his standing among the people. They might have accepted Egypt's cultural drift and alienation from its Arab heritage if these trends had been accompanied by comfortable apartments and more cash income, but for the vast majority that was not the case.

The sudden appearance in new, privately owned, markets of imported consumer goods was welcomed by the foreign community and by the few Egyptians who could afford them, but for the masses these luxuries only fueled resentment. The Egyptian working man, whose basic lunch was a bean sandwich on coarse bread and perhaps a slice of watermelon, was not going to be buying Danish butter or French wine, to say nothing of German automobiles.

In Nasser's day it was illegal for Egyptians to possess foreign currency. Now in the mid-1970s it was theoretically legal, provided that those who had it could prove that they had obtained it through approved channels. But by and large, the only families that had access to dollars or other foreign currencies were those who had sons or brothers sending money home from jobs in the oil countries, and they were required to exchange it into Egyptian pounds at artificially low rates set by the Central Bank. A more favorable rate, naturally, was available to foreigners.

Sadat did dismantle the Arab Socialist Union, which under Nasser had been the only legal political party. Its handsome building overlooking the Nile in downtown Cairo was converted into offices for foreign banks. Ordinary Egyptians had no love for the ASU, but the presence of foreign banks, which Nasser had prohibited, was an uneasy reminder of the pre-Nasser era when Egypt was dominated by outsiders.

With the end of war, some components of the moribund economy did come back to life. The Suez Canal reopened, with hefty tolls that delivered hard currency to the government. Tourism resumed, to the point where Cairo suffered for years from an acute shortage of hotel rooms. Statistically, economic growth in the mid-1970s was impressive, but that growth was upward from a very low base.

Egypt became increasingly dependent on aid from other countries, and foreign aid did indeed flow in. Overall, from 1974 to 1980, Egypt received nonmilitary credits and grants totaling $17 billion.[11] As early as 1977, even before Camp David, the United States commitment exceeded $900 million a year, more than was allocated to the rest of Africa and Latin America combined.[12]

Within five years of Sadat's death, a detailed list of nonmilitary of projects in Egypt financed by U.S. taxpayers filled 103 pages. It covered every kind of activity—vehicle maintenance training, rural health clinics, agricultural research, computerization of industry, construction of grain silos, development of water and sewage treatment plants, modernization of the Port of Alexandria, installation of electric power distribution equipment, street paving, reconstruction of food markets, construction of a "tallow and fats storage facility," and updating of navigation charts for the Suez Canal. Buses built in Arkansas were brought in to upgrade Cairo's battered fleet. (Unhappily, the engines of the first batch of buses were so noisy that Egyptians referred to them mockingly as "The Voice of America.") In addition, the United States was providing $219 million annually in food aid and $110 million a year in cash because, as the U.S. Agency for International Development (USAID) noted, "Egypt lacks sufficient foreign exchange to repay its external debt and to import the goods and services needed to revitalize the economy."[13]

As the USAID's report indicated, the infusions of foreign aid stabilized the government balance sheet, but they did little to improve the lives of ordinary Egyptians because the growth in population outstripped industrial production and gains in agricultural productivity. Egypt was structurally and politically unable to lift itself out of the morass produced by years of war, misguided policies, and neglect of infrastructure.

A decade after infitah supposedly shifted Egypt's emphasis to private-sector development, the USAID report said that Egypt's lapse back into economic stagnation was largely a result of "excessive governmental control of the economy. The public-sector dominance of Egyptian industry and questionable economic policies, including inappropriate public pricing, stifle innovation and repress productivity. Many government owned and operated industrial plants, such as fertilizer and aluminum smelting, absorb large quantities of scarce resources in economically inefficient production."[14]

The United States in the late 1970s also replaced the Soviet Union as the principal supplier of weapons to the Egyptian armed forces, a transformation that pleased the military but did nothing to satisfy the needs of the general population.

Sadat never understood that a modern economy based on private investment and nongovernment employment could not exist in parallel with the old statist system. Even as he proclaimed infitah, the vast, bloated network of state-owned industry built up under Nasser, and a longstanding policy of guaranteeing a government job to every university graduate, ensured that every factory and office would be filled to overflowing with people who had little to do and little incentive to do well at what tasks they did have. The state-owned national airline, for example, had the highest ratio of employees to passengers of any airline in the world, but service at ticket counters and baggage claims was abysmal. These armies of workers could not just be sent away like Soviet military advisers; they hung on the economy like a mammoth anchor. Sadat ended the job guarantee for university graduates but at the same time he increased the number of universities, flooding a reduced job market with restless young people looking in vain for worthwhile employment.

A New Beirut?

Egypt should have been well-positioned to capitalize on the deterioration of Beirut, which because of Lebanon's civil war had lost its position as the Arab world's center of finance, commerce, and information. As the war devastated Beirut, Western banks, news media, consulting companies and other enterprises were forced to relocate to other capitals. Cairo should have been a logical choice, but it was woefully unprepared for such an influx, in infrastructure and in law. In theory Egypt was putting aside a collective fear of foreign economic domination that had its roots in the nineteenth century to welcome foreign investment, but investors who tested the waters found them chilly and murky.

In addition to the obstacles thrown up by a mammoth, self-interested bureaucracy in which inertia was dominant, the country was physically unable to accommodate the well-heeled potential newcomers who were looking for a new base after Beirut was lost. Egypt's decrepit national infrastructure—power plants, water supply, sewage treatment, telephone service, roads—had been neglected for years, to the point that potential foreign investors could not find adequate sites or services for new factories. Modern office space was virtually nonexistent. Outdated restrictions on foreign currency—which Sadat could have swept aside with the stroke of a pen, had he understood their pernicious effect—made it impossible to buy an airplane ticket at the airport; tickets could be bought only in downtown offices during regular business hours, at the official exchange rate. Foreign residents who decided to buy a low-quality Egyptian-made automobile rather than fight endless battles with customs officials over imports received priority on delivery if they paid with hard currency, but still had to face a daunting obstacle: they were required to prove that they had obtained their foreign currency legally. They were paid in foreign currency, of course, but that was insufficient qualification to satisfy the bureaucrats at government agencies.

Moreover, in an attempt to protect public-sector industries from competition, Egypt's new foreign investment law required that projects be self-sufficient in foreign currency, meaning that much of their output would have to be exported. Unfortunately, Egypt had a well-deserved reputation for poor quality and shoddy products, which undercut its ability to export. An executive of France's Michelin tire company for example, told reporters that he had decided to go elsewhere because Michelin would never try to sell tires in the world market that said "Made in Egypt," which would be a sure sign of poor quality. Foreign-sponsored projects were required to move their money through one of the moribund state-owned banks at unrealistic exchange rates. Those banks were models of inefficiency, operated by functionaries totally unfamiliar with the high-interest environment in which the industrialized countries were then operating. It was fitting that the clock on the tower of Egypt's Central Bank had no hands; the concept that "time is money" had not penetrated.[15] Even when foreign banks were allowed in, they were required to operate under many of the same outdated restrictions as the state-owned banks. Legal residents of Egypt such as myself were permitted to hold dollar-denominated accounts at Citibank when it finally opened in Cairo, but a check written on that account to anyone outside Egypt took months to clear.

Investors came and looked around, but like Michelin, they mostly went elsewhere. One that did stay, Xerox Corporation, placed advertisements in Cairo newspapers announcing the opening of a representative office, but the ads gave no telephone number. That was because Xerox, unwilling to pay bribes, could not obtain telephone service. That was a symptom of the corruption that pervaded every aspect of public life. At the top, cabinet ministers and department directors profited from dubious land deals and "commissions" on transactions. At the bottom, every clerk expected a few coins for performing some service. University professors gave higher grades to students who paid them for tutoring outside class. Everyone understood that Egypt was a *baksheesh* society. That was not Sadat's fault, because it was that way long before him, but he not only failed to correct it, he adopted economic and fiscal policies that encouraged it.

So pervasive and visible was the corruption that the U.S. embassy in early 1979 sent an alarmed warning about it to Washington, noting that the new flow of American aid money was contributing to it and that Sadat's style of governing made him incapable of dealing with it:

> In addition to a lack of real resources, the government's ability to address problems is limited by institutional weaknesses, including considerable corruption. The Egyptian bureaucracy has grown so large that in many cases it barely functions. Everyone dealing with it, Egyptian or American, is fast frustrated. Egypt's bureaucracy has been notably inefficient and venal on at least a petty scale throughout history; with the increased money available in

the economy this phenomenon is on the increase. This corruption is widely assumed to extend to the highest level of Egyptian society. Sadat's wife and his closest advisor are popularly believed to be involved, although hard evidence to support this charge is difficult to come by.

The government's ability to deal with major social and economic issues is further limited by Sadat's physical and psychological isolation. His peripatetic style of government makes it difficult for key officials to get decisions. Access to the President is strictly limited, and most who surround him are very reluctant to give Sadat bad news. He has few close associates. This would be less damaging if subordinate officials were willing to make independent decisions. Unfortunately, the nature of Egyptian society pushes almost all issues to the top for resolution. Until Sadat reaches a decision, all too often nothing happens. Frequently, little happens even after Sadat issues directives; there is little follow-up, and bureaucratic inertia is massive.[16]

That was all true, but by that time the United States was locked into its relationship with Sadat, as he had intended, and there was no alternative.

Crippling Subsidies, Devastating Riots

In economic terms, the seeds of the 2011 uprising that overthrew Sadat's successor, Hosni Mubarak, were planted and fertilized in the 1970s.

One obstacle to economic progress that proved insuperable during Sadat's tenure was the pervasive system of subsidies that had been established in the Nasser era. Egyptians were poor. Nasser wanted them to live better. He delivered electricity from the Aswan Dam to villages. His government built rural health clinics. And he established a nationwide network of government-run stores and depots where people could buy tea, sugar, cooking oil, bread, fuel, and other essentials at subsidized prices. Because Egypt consumed far more than it produced, many items had to be imported, which meant that the government had to pay for them in scarce foreign currency. Dollars and yen and pounds sterling that might otherwise have bought new hospitals, schools, and power plants were consumed at the dinner table.

The system, like every system in Egypt except the Suez Canal, was riddled with contradictions and corruption. Foreigners who were legal residents of Egypt were entitled to buy at the same prices as the local people, even if they had plenty of money. Bread was so cheap farmers were using it as cattle feed. Customers were allowed to buy a certain amount of meat without regard to quality, so they bribed grocers to give them the better cuts.

By the mid-1970s, as the population grew, these subsidies were bankrupting the state. In 1979, subsidies accounted for more than a third of a government budget deficit of 6.7 billion pounds, a figure that does not include the cost of indirect subsidies for electricity, bus fares, and other services.[17]

Under pressure from the International Monetary Fund, Egypt had little choice but to cut these subsidies. On the morning of January 18, 1977, Egyptians awoke to learn from the news media that the government had raised prices overnight by as much as 31 percent on flour, rice, soap, cigarettes, butane gas used for cooking and heating, and other basic commodities. Caught by surprise, they took to the streets in rage. For three days Egyptian cities were wracked by the biggest riots since the 1952 revolution; windows were smashed, roads were blocked, government buildings were assaulted, cars were stoned. Demonstrators attacked hotels, buses, streetcars, and police stations. In Alexandria, the home of Vice President Mubarak was pillaged. "Down with the Khedive," the mobs shouted, likening Sadat to the ruler who had fawned over European culture and led the country to bankruptcy a century earlier. "Your daughter is living in splendor while we are ten to a room!" In Cairo, the mobs seized Tahrir Square, in the heart of the city, just as other mobs would do in the "Arab Spring" protests against Mubarak's rule thirty-four years later.[18]

As violence spread, police fired tear gas; demonstrators showed reporters the "Made in USA" markings on the canisters. When the official death toll hit forty-three, the government deployed the army to restore order. A curfew was imposed on Cairo and Alexandria.

But the rioters got what they wanted. Mamdouh Salem, then prime minister, not only rescinded the price increases but left in place salary increases that had been intended to cushion them. Sadat and his government survived, but the memory of the riots has crippled economic decisionmaking in Egypt ever since.

Sadat had only himself to blame for the mob's outrage. The subsidies could have been decreased and prices raised gradually, to lessen the impact. The government could have conducted a public relations campaign to explain its economic plight and prepare people for what was coming. The president could have announced the decision himself, in a speech that first stressed the economic better times that were supposedly ahead. It was a measure of Sadat's isolation from the ordinary citizens he claimed to exemplify that he took no such measures to prepare them and forestall their wrath.

Thus the subsidies remained in place and Egypt's economic plight deepened. In April 1977, Sadat was in Washington to seek still more assistance. He was accompanied by his economy minister, Hamid Sayih, who told President Carter that in order to balance the budget, "We could cut investment, which in a country growing at [only] 2.6 percent a year is not feasible. Or we could cut on defense, but that involves our security and we can't take risks there. Or we could cut our foreign debt service payments, but then our creditors would lose confidence in us. Finally we could cut expenditures and cut subsidies," which by then was out of the question because of the riots. Egypt lacked the hard currency to make $2 billion to $3 billion in debt service payments coming due, Sayih said, and "will need more than $7 billion just to cover the foreign exchange costs" of planned development.[19]

At the time of the October War, Egypt had about eight hundred thousand men on active duty in its armed forces. Even after the security "risks" that Sayih was talking about had mostly been removed by the Sinai II troop disengagement agreement, Egypt was still required to pay, feed, and equip a very large military force because demobilization would have exacerbated the unemployment problem and could have been politically risky.

Given the conditions at the time, no leader could have brought prosperity in a single generation, and Sadat was reckless to promise that he would do so. He was indifferent to economic detail, but even if he were a technocrat and had come into office inclined to restructure the economy from top to bottom—which would have meant closing the white-elephant state industries and laying off tens of thousands of workers—he was permanently dissuaded from doing so by the bread riots.

The United States by the mid-1970s was fully committed to Sadat and prepared to be generous, but not to the extent that Sayih detailed for Carter. Saudi Arabia and other Arab oil states could have filled the gap, but their generosity would dry up as Sadat pursued peace with Israel. The result was that the economic distress of ordinary Egyptians remained largely as before, while a new class of what were known as "Fat Cats" was able to take advantage of the liberalized investment rules. This relatively tiny group flaunted its new wealth, with big imported cars, expansive new apartments overlooking the Nile, and lavish weddings at the best hotels. Their prosperity, often fueled by close ties with Sadat and his cronies, such as the contractor Osman Ahmed Osman, only increased the grumbling in the streets.

During one of Sadat's speeches, a well-known Nasserist politician interrupted him to challenge infitah, the Open Door foreign investment policy, saying it was a "policy of consumption" that did not serve the interests of farmers or workers and benefited mostly foreigners. Sadat responded with a forthright defense of the policy, insisting it would bring more jobs, more production, and modern technology. When he took office, Sadat said, Western economists told him the country was bankrupt, and he was shocked when his own finance minister confirmed it.[20] The old policies had left the Egyptian economy at "less than zero," he said. Both men were right: the country was destitute and it was necessary for Sadat to chart a new economic course, but the way he did it led to more conspicuous consumption than productive investment.

Egyptians had lived through years of privation when imported consumer goods were virtually absent and people made do with cheap locally made products of notoriously poor quality. Buyers were not fooled by cheap knock-offs of Western brands that carried such fake names as "Heimz." The Open Door policy unleashed pent-up demand, and consumers with money went on a spending spree, stimulating inflation and stirring resentment among the have-nots. No longer did the prosperous and the well-connected have to drink Egyptian wine, which was terrible, or wear Egyptian-made clothing. Almost overnight, Egyptians developed the attitude that everything imported was desirable and everything that was desirable must be imported. A political cartoon showed two men marveling over the Great Pyramid: "Fantastic, it must be imported."

Mohamed Heikal, one of the relatively few who had become wealthy in the Nasser era, owner of a spectacular apartment overlooking the Nile, wrote that "Egypt was being transformed from a planned, to a market, to a supermarket economy." At least the "old feudal class" that prevailed before the 1952 revolution was rich because of land ownership, which meant deep roots in the country, Heikal said, "but the new rich had no roots."[21] In Nasser's time, Heikal had been the voice of Egypt as presidential spokesman and as editor of the most influential newspaper, *Al-Ahram*. Heikal had also been close to Sadat and had been his minister of information, but Sadat dismissed him as editor of *Al-Ahram* because he was a visible reminder of the Nasser years. Heikal said he was not fired, he quit, but in any case their breach was never repaired. Heikal was free to talk to foreigners, but within Egypt he was silenced. His caustic comments on the economy were published only outside the country.

Political Failure

Sadat's other great domestic failure was political. He never found a formula that would balance the people's aspirations for liberty with his desire to maintain control. He wanted Egyptians to feel free, but he insisted that they behave in ways he found acceptable. He did mostly dismantle the police state that Nasser had imposed. He was justified in his boast that senior figures who had broken with him or fallen into disfavor (including Heikal and Ismail Fahmy, the foreign minister who quit over the Jerusalem trip) were not in jail, as they would have been in other Arab countries, but were visible at Cairo's best clubs and restaurants, enjoying the fruits of whatever connections they had made while in public life. But Sadat also insisted that people do what he told them to do. After all, Egypt was a "family," and he was the father.

Roy Atherton put it concisely: "Sadat's attitude, I think in genuine frustration, was, 'I know what's best for the country. Why don't they agree with me? I want democracy. I want a democratic society. But democracy does not mean the right to obstruct what I want to do.' He was always looking for some way to reconcile his authoritarian instincts with his intellectual commitment, I think, to the need to develop a democratic state. He could never quite reconcile the two."[22]

Had he been able to do so, he might well have spared Egypt the thirty years of repression and political stagnation that followed under Hosni Mubarak and the violence and turmoil that followed Mubarak's ouster in 2011.

A European or American who listened to Sadat's speeches would find that he always said the right things about liberty and democracy, about the rights of the people, and about establishing a "state of institutions" that would not be anchored in the personality of an individual. Sadat abolished the Arab Socialist Union and permitted the formation of a few political parties, but the government, meaning Sadat himself, retained the power to decide which parties would be allowed and which would not. Those deemed to be based on religion or funded by foreign governments were proscribed. Thus the Muslim Brotherhood was not permitted to form an overt political party, although candidates affiliated with the Brotherhood did win some seats in parliament by running on the tickets of nonsectarian parties.

"Democracy is my mission," Sadat said in one address to parliament, adding that he welcomed the formation of an opposition party because the country would benefit from a vigorous debate among well-intentioned, patriotic politicians. He said he might even change his mind about some issues if the opposition offered good arguments: "We want true and pure democracy based on opposing opinions."[23]

But in the eleven years of his presidency, he never permitted an election or held a referendum of which the outcome was in doubt. There were some genuine, hard-fought contests for individual seats in parliament, but progovernment slates always gained the majority. When Sadat made a show of democracy by putting a proposal before the public in a referendum, the announced result invariably was approval by more than 90 percent. For the peace treaty, it was 99.9 percent.

Sadat also took contradictory positions on the inflammatory subject of religion. He said publicly that religion should be separate from politics, and he preached tolerance and good will toward Egypt's substantial Christian minority; but he encouraged Muslim activism in universities and professional associations, and augmented the status of Islamic law in the constitution. He appointed a prominent feminist legal scholar, Aisha Rateb, to be minister of social affairs, the only woman in his cabinet, but quashed several of her proposed innovations. On the other hand, after first outraging liberals by rejecting legislation she proposed to enhance women's rights on personal status matters such as polygamy and underage marriage, he then signed it into law in 1979, infuriating conservatives and religious activists.

Sadat's glamorous, fashionably dressed wife, Jehan, traveled around the country promoting family planning, but the principal effect was to alienate a conservative population that believed children were gifts from God and did not appreciate the first lady's visible participation in public life. She was compared unfavorably to Nasser's wife, who had known her place and largely stayed out of sight.

Sadat had joined Nasser's Free Officers conspiracy in 1952 because he deeply resented British domination of Egypt's political life. But his memories of British humiliations did not stop him now from embracing all things Western, isolating himself from the people whose "father" he claimed to be. Beyond economics, the welcome Sadat extended to American and European culture and social attitudes unsettled the majority of Egyptians, who are culturally and socially conservative. They were baffled when the Grateful Dead performed at the Pyramids—tickets to that event cost four pounds, a week's wages for many Egyptians—and they were distressed that aid money from Japan was used for construction of a new opera house. Egyptians did not listen to Wagner or Puccini, they listened to Fayrouz and other Arab singers whose soulful lyrics spoke to them. Opera was European, an alien art form. People knew that the Khedive Ismail, the nineteenth-century ruler whose ruinous fiscal policies had delivered Egypt to foreign control, had spent a fortune to construct a grand opera house to mark the opening of the Suez Canal and later commissioned Verdi to write *Aida*. In the 1970s, construction of a new opera house was not on their wish list.

Outside the small urban elite, Egyptians were uncomfortable with the encroachment of materialism and of morally neutral ideas. To many of them, Western ideas and social standards were culturally corrupting. They wanted money and cars and television and refrigerators but they did not want religion excluded from classrooms, nor did they want drugs or extramarital sex for their children, or free choice in marriage, or miniskirts, or pornography on the newsstands, all of which were available by the late 1970s. The smashing of nightclubs on the road to the Pyramids and the destruction of their alcohol supplies during the 1977 riots were an early manifestation of the potential for popular backlash against the cultural drift.

The Short Life of Ismail Hakim

Those of us who lived among the Egyptians in that era could sense that the death of a young man named Ismail Hakim, in 1978, represented a symbolic moment, crystallizing what was going wrong. Hakim was thirty years old when he died. Newspapers said he died of liver disease, which is common in Egypt because of schistosomiasis, or bilharzia, but many people knew or suspected the truth: Hakim's liver disease was cirrhosis, caused by alcoholism.

His death was major news because he was the only son of a rich and famous father, Tawfiq Hakim, one of the most revered figures in Egypt, whose sharp features under an ever-present beret were recognized throughout the country. The elder Hakim was one of Egypt's most influential writers and playwrights of the twentieth century, a literary pioneer who celebrated the common man and often wrote in Egyptian dialect instead of classical Arabic.

Ismail Hakim was born when his father was fifty years old, and he took advantage of his rich, doting father to grow up in a most unconventional way. Not for him the traditional vocations of the upper classes, engineering or medicine or finance. He threw himself into rock music; he emulated the life of an American or British rock star, and his band, the Black Coats, was wildly popular in the blue-jean and discotheque society that was growing in Cairo and Alexandria.

By that time, emulation of American popular culture could be found everywhere in some highly visible segments of society. Pirated rock tapes were advertised for sale on campus bulletin boards. Cairo Radio, owned by the state, appealed to young listeners with an American-style dedication show, in English: "This one goes out to Sami from Hoda." Tape recordings of American rock music broadcasts, made by Egyptian students in the United States, were played on Egyptian radio, sometimes complete with their American commercials and station breaks. Suddenly there was an unbridgeable gap between university students who wore traditional clothing and attended religious meetings and those who wore jeans—men and women—and spent their time at discotheques with young friends their parents had not met. Egyptians at many levels were uncomfortable with the sudden emergence of Cairo as an international playground where gambling was legal—for foreigners—and where rich Arabs from the Gulf came to buy young Egyptian brides.

In that environment, the death of Ismail Hakim confirmed to the conservatives and the religious activists what they already believed: Sadat, with his embrace of the West, Italian suits, rich cronies, film festivals, and glamorous wife publicly promoting birth control, was leading Egypt into social and cultural anarchy. The life that young Ismail Hakim led had never been possible in the past; now that it was possible, Egyptians mostly found it abhorrent, and they blamed the person they held responsible, President Sadat.

In one episode, a university professor stirred up public outrage with a campaign of opposition to a government-approved golf course resort project near the Pyramids, sponsored by well-known rich friends of the president; it would have created what developers called "Palm Springs for the Arabs" next to the greatest monuments of Egyptian culture.[24] This was the rare case in which the outcry was so great it forced Sadat to back down and cancel the project; but when added to Sadat's peace treaty with the Zionists, his perceived abandonment of the Palestinians, and his forfeiture of Egypt's traditional position of leadership among the Arabs, his support for such a development alienated the same excitable masses who just a few years before had hailed him as *batal al-ubur*, the Hero of the Crossing. Now they chanted, *Feen al-futtur, ya batal al-ubur?* Where is our breakfast, Hero of the Crossing?

A Vacuum Unfilled

Thus Sadat never succeeded in establishing an ideological foundation for his presidency, other than the single-minded pursuit of peace with Israel, which by its nature produced another irreconcilable contradiction between his insistence that Egypt was the leader of all Arabs and his country's isolation from the rest of the Arab world. He never formulated a set of principles and ideals that would have filled the vacuum left by Nasserism, socialism, and pan-Arabism.

He endeavored to do that in his *October Working Paper*, the long 1974 blueprint for Egypt's political, economic, and social life as it rebuilt itself. In it he wrote, "Whereas the Revolution [of 1952] has accomplished so much in the field of social freedom, we must honestly concede that political freedom has not run the course people wanted." The people, he wrote, "are of full age and intelligent, requiring no stewardship from anyone." They are therefore entitled to justice, personal freedom, and government by institutions that "realize the sovereignty of the law . . . we must underline the significance of political freedom side by side with social freedom."[25] He often returned to those themes in his many speeches, but it is doubtful that many Egyptians actually read *The October Working Paper*, whereas everyone who was literate, it seemed, had read Nasser's *The Philosophy of the Revolution*. In general, Egyptians of Sadat's day were less interested in rhetoric about abstractions than they were in better living conditions, which for most of them Sadat failed to deliver.

Sadat freed political prisoners, curbed police excesses, and gave Egyptians more freedom to express themselves than they had under Nasser. One of his first decrees upon taking office was to abolish "sequestration," the term for state seizure of private property; his government eventually gave back many properties and businesses that had been nationalized under Nasser. He gave a modest measure of freedom to newspapers and magazines not controlled by the government. He lifted restrictions on religious activists that Nasser had imposed, and he appointed Coptic Christians and women to a few seats in parliament because they could not win them on their own. But he found that when he opened those doors people ran through them in directions he would not accept. The result was that after his death Egyptians lived for a generation in a state of political stagnation under Mubarak until all their resentments boiled over in 2011.

Removing the Sandbags

Under Nasser, Egyptians struggled for almost two decades in a state of war or of constant tension over the possibility of war. Under Sadat, once the Sinai II agreement had been signed in 1975, the threat of war receded and the tension subsided. Sandbags were removed from the entrances to public buildings. Large areas of the country that had been restricted to military use and closed to foreigners were reopened. Restrictions on photography in public places were eased. Most press censorship was lifted. Beneath this peaceful surface, however, political, economic, and religious discontent were on the rise. The "bread riots" of January 1977 had been only one symptom of a deeper problem.

"There is no question," the U.S. embassy in Cairo reported to Washington in August 1977, "that there is growing discontent on [the] part [of the] Egyptian public and military with Sadat's policies and performance. . . . The president has overexposed himself in public speeches. He has aroused great expectation, but has had no demonstrable success on any front. As a result, his policies, foreign and domestic, are being increasingly questioned not only by traditional anti-Sadat elements but also by moderates and middle class who have normally supported him."[26]

That was written three months before Sadat, well aware of the need to deliver something dramatic, went to Jerusalem. After that trip, the grumbling was overpowered for a while by peace euphoria; but the discontent gathered strength as peace failed to deliver on its economic promise and as the Egyptian people chafed at the conspicuous consumption of the newly wealthy and at their country's isolation from the Arab nation.

Ambassador Atherton, who wrote a perceptive retrospective analysis on this period, said the growing opposition to Sadat among Egypt's pious Muslim majority was by no means confined to the extremists. The malcontents included devout citizens across the social spectrum, from "the Egyptian civil servant who interrupts his daily work routine to observe the call to prayer at noon, to the lower-class laborer who is revolted by the government's periodic forays into birth control, to the peasant walking the streets of Cairo in search of work who is scandalized by the sight of women in halter tops and hot pants, to the ʿal-Takfir wʾal-Hijra member plotting the assassination of Egyptian officials to help usher in the 'new Islamic order.'" It was misleading, Atherton said, to equate "fundamentalists" with a penchant for violence. What most "fundamentalists" wanted, he said, was stricter observance of the call to prayer, and "a return to Islam for guidance in decisions on social life and possibly law, including the prohibition of alcohol, bans on dancing, and tough standards on what can be aired on television."[27]

Sadat, despite his protestations of piety, was not going to deliver on any of those aspirations. His fame and his "father knows best" approach to governance widened the gap between him and the great mass of Egyptians. As the discontent grew, Sadat adopted counterproductive tactics: he retreated from his pledge of democracy and became increasingly autocratic. Denouncing the political parties he had permitted to form as throwbacks to the time before the 1952 revolution, he created his own, the National Democratic Party. This was hardly a grass-roots organization. Its most influential members were "infi-tah millionaires and rural elites," as one scholar put it, but members of parliament and other prominent people rushed to join it anyway, to curry favor with Sadat.[28]

Sectarian Tension Surfaces

Popular dissatisfaction over political developments was compounded by increasing tension between Muslims and the minority Coptic Christians, whose leader, Pope Shenouda III, publicly opposed the peace treaty with Israel. Because Israel was cooperating with Christian militias that were fighting Muslims in the Lebanese civil war, rumors flew that Egypt's Christians were secretly arming themselves for a similar conflict. In a riot that erupted over an attempt by Muslims to build a mosque on land owned by Copts who were planning to build a church there, the death toll rose to thirty-five before police and troops restored order.

In fact it was inconceivable that the Copts of Egypt could play the role ascribed to them by Lawrence Durrell in *Justine*, the first volume of his *Alexandria Quartet*—that of a fifth column secretly working with Israel because they saw security for themselves in the establishment of sectarian enclaves. Egypt's Christians, unlike those in Lebanon, had no militia and controlled no territory, and the Israelis had no motivation for stirring them up. But they did live differently from Muslims, especially by operating butcher shops that sold pork, and on average were wealthier and better educated. Pope Shenouda had unrealistic political ambitions; he claimed that the Christian population was twice the size given in official figures, and he demanded that Sadat appoint a Christian as a second vice president.

Furious at the dissent mounting from all points on the political spectrum, Sadat in 1980 retreated from his promises of democracy and individual liberty and ordered parliament to pass what became known as "The Law of Shame."

Among the crimes prohibited by this draconian statute were misusing public funds, accepting bribes, endangering public property, "broadcasting or publishing gross or scurrilous words or pictures that could offend public sensibilities or undermine the dignity of the state," "allowing children or youth to go astray by advocating the repudiation of popular religious, moral, or national values, or by setting a bad example in a public place," and "advocating any doctrine that implies negation of divine teaching." Those judged to have violated this preposterous statute could be condemned to internal exile, prohibited from leaving Egypt, or barred from managing their own property or engaging in any economic activity. To no one's surprise, this law was approved in a referendum by an announced 98.56 percent of voters; but it failed to quell the dissent.[29]

By the summer of 1981, Sadat was beleaguered on many fronts. The religious tensions and the rising threat from Muslim extremists compounded his anger and his open dissatisfaction at Israel's refusal to deliver on the promise of Palestinian autonomy. Sadat's decision to give refuge to the Shah of Iran after he was driven from the Peacock Throne had angered nationalist and religious activists. The economy had not taken off. Saudi Arabia had cut off support and pulled out of an ambitious joint arms manufacturing venture. The new U.S. president, Ronald Reagan, was less of an admirer than Jimmy Carter had been. The Law of Shame was not silencing enough voices. Increasingly frustrated and suspicious, Sadat now concluded that any opposition, real or imagined, was no longer constructive.

The result was mass arrests, on September 3, 1981. This irrational and indiscriminate roundup corralled many of the most prominent people in Egypt, including Mohamed Heikal and Omar Tilmasani, the same Muslim Brotherhood leader whom Sadat had freed from prison a few years earlier. Government figures put the number arrested at 1,536; others said it was as many as 3,000. Newspaper editors, leaders of political parties other than Sadat's own, respected officials of professional syndicates, and popular religious leaders and preachers, Christians as well as Muslims, were among the detained. Pope Shenouda III was removed from his post and banished to a desert monastery.[30] Police and soldiers went to the homes and offices of the detainees and seized books, papers, and passports. The government shut down several publications and announced it would assume direct control of forty

thousand independent mosques, where some preachers had been giving fiery sermons denouncing the peace treaty and Coptic Christians.

Diplomats at the U.S. embassy concluded that with these arrests,
"After a decade's truce, marked by growing mutual distrust, Sadat
declared open war on Egypt's fundamentalist movement and reaf-
firmed in the clearest possible terms his concept of a secular political
system which demanded a rigid separation of religion and politics."[31]

Heikal, one of those detained, later noted that the effect of this
political crackdown was the opposite of what Sadat intended: it reinforced the trend toward religious activism. "As religion had become the
only channel open to dissent," he wrote, "this was hardly surprising,
but it meant that the delicate balance between religious and secular
which had been maintained in Egypt for so long, not always without
difficulty, was now tipped toward religion, and tipped in favor of elements which were at work underground, largely unseen and wholly
unacknowledged."[32] The crackdown actually benefited the Brotherhood politically because previously the government's tolerance had
made some people suspicious of the group's true motivations.

There was no conceivable logic behind these mass arrests of such
diverse individuals, and the roundup destroyed what remained of
Sadat's credibility. He insisted that all the arrested people were responsible in some way for fomenting the sectarian strife that was plagu-
ing the country, but given the diversity of prisoners, that was hard
to believe. At a news conference with foreign journalists a few days
later, Sadat dropped his usual friendly tone and denounced them for
likening him to the Shah of Iran. He said there was no comparison
between the situation in Egypt and what had happened in the Iranian revolution, and "I shall never permit this because this is not my
people, the Egyptian tradition, or the Egyptian conduct." He said he
"didn't do this [crackdown] because there was any danger against the
regime. On the contrary."[33]

It was true that except in the 1977 riots the people of Egypt never
took to the streets in a mass uprising against Sadat. And it was true
that the situation in Egypt in September 1981 bore little resemblance
to that in Iran before the departure of the Shah, when all of Iran was

paralyzed by strikes, shortages, and protests. But it was not true that there was no danger to Sadat and his regime. The extremist plot that would result in his assassination the following month was already brewing. Unfortunately for him, the plotters were not among those seized in the mass dragnet.

Violence-prone militants had infiltrated the military, apparently without being discovered by the security services. The most radical groups with agents in the army were plotting to get rid of Sadat; the annual military parade scheduled for October 6, 1981, presented an opportunity. An artillery unit that included a young lieutenant named Khaled Islambouli was assigned to take part. His anger at Sadat was compounded by a personal grievance: his brother had been among those seized in the mass arrests of September.

As always, the parade was an extravaganza, televised, and attended by most of Cairo's diplomats, journalists, and other prominent people. Sadat, in his medal-bedecked military uniform, was easy to spot, seated in his prime place on the reviewing stand.

When the truck carrying Islambouli and his colleagues reached Sadat's position, he put a gun to the driver's head—the driver was not part of the plot—and ordered him to stop. The driver fled. Islambouli and others emerged from the back of the truck, firing rifles and hurling grenades into the spectator seats.

A report to Washington from the U.S. embassy said that "Islambuli is believed to be the shadowy figure seen in most dramatic pictures of the assassination perching his rifle over the railing of the VIP podium and pumping bullet after bullet into persons seeking cover on the grandstand floor."[34] Sadat was dead before he reached a hospital. His secretary was also killed, and several prominent officials were wounded.

No convincing explanation has emerged for the security breach that enabled parade participants to carry live ammunition to the event. Some said it showed that there must have been a broader conspiracy within the army; others said it might have resulted from the assumption that the armed forces were all loyal and thus presented no risk to the president.

Investigations after the assassination revealed that Islambouli and his co-conspirators, adherents of a radical organization identified by the U.S. embassy as al-Jihad al-Jadid, the New Jihad, had expected to ignite a mass popular uprising against the regime; hence their simultaneous attacks on police stations by other participants in the plot. Takfir w'al Hijra, an ideologically similar radical group, of which Islambouli's arrested brother was a member, had harbored similar hopes when it had surfaced a few years earlier. But no such uprisings occurred either time. In the aggregate, the Egyptians were hostile to, or apathetic about, Sadat, but not to the point of insurrection or mass violence.

In a report to Washington six months afterward, titled *Reflections on October: The Sadat Assassination and Islamic Extremism*, Ambassador Atherton wrote, "What emerges is a picture of an overly ambitious but poorly organized conspiracy. Sadat's assassination was clearly the principal objective, but only a few members of the organization knew about this aspect of the plot beforehand. The actual assassins appear to have had it in mind to eliminate as many members of the [government of Egypt] hierarchy as possible, although this objective was clearly secondary to the killing of Sadat. In coordination with other elements of the organization, there may have been some planning to seize key government installations in Cairo and Upper Egypt in the vague hope of triggering a series of internal upheavals that would lead to a 'popular revolution' and set the stage" for the creation of an Islamic state. The plot failed, Atherton reported in this and other cables, because the extremists' penetration of the armed forces was shallow, and the conspirators overestimated their support among the general population.

"The extremists have no broad popular following and no common vision of what should lie beyond the present social order, once it is overthrown. Moreover, the general public views the extremists as a threat and supports the government's move to emasculate them," the ambassador wrote.[35]

Religious sentiment had surged in Egypt, encouraged by Sadat and his government, but in general the new activists were concerned more about Islamic law, justice, and social behavior than about violent insurrection. Most were not revolutionaries, although their ranks did include fiery preachers whose incendiary sermons could be interpreted as promoting or at least condoning violence in the name of Islam.

One of those was Omar Abdel Rahman, known as "the blind sheikh." He was arrested after Sadat's assassination, accused by the government of being the spiritual leader of the plotters, and tried along with Islambouli and the other suspects. Surprisingly, he was acquitted. He was later jailed again on other charges, but after his release he was admitted to the United States. He obtained a visa from the U.S. embassy in Khartoum, Sudan, and even after the State Department recognized its mistake and revoked the visa, the sheikh entered the United States unchallenged and received a green card. He is serving a life term in a U.S. federal prison after being convicted of conspiracy in an unsuccessful 1993 attempt to bring down the World Trade Center in New York—an attack that presaged the destruction of the Twin Towers on September 11, 2001.

Islambouli and four other suspects were executed in 1982 after a trial that journalists were permitted to observe. Five others were sentenced to life imprisonment, eight were sentenced to fifteen-year terms, and one to five years. During their trial, rather than defend themselves, they spent much of their time in court shouting their defiance and reciting prayers.

The Paradox of a Funeral

Sadat's funeral offered a living panorama of his standing in the world, among the other Arabs, and among Egyptians.

Dignitaries arrived from all cross the globe, including Menachem Begin and three former U.S. presidents, Richard Nixon, Gerald Ford, and Jimmy Carter. Henry Kissinger was also in the U.S. delegation. President Reagan did not attend because of security concerns, but he delivered an effusive statement: "President Sadat was a courageous man whose vision and wisdom brought nations and people together. In a world filled with hatred, he was a man of hope. In a world trapped in the animosities of the past, he was a man of foresight, a man who sought to improve a world tormented by malice and pettiness. As an Egyptian patriot, he helped create the revolutionary movement that freed his nation. As a political leader, he sought to free his people from hatred and war. And as a soldier, he was unafraid to fight. But most important, he was a humanitarian unafraid to make peace. . . . America has lost a close friend; the world has lost a great statesman; and mankind has lost a champion of peace."[36]

Congressman Zablocki, he of the red-checked jacket, attended the funeral as a member of the U.S. delegation. Afterward, he inserted into the *Congressional Record* a statement by Ambassador Sol Linowitz, whom Carter had appointed as a special representative to the Palestinian autonomy negotiations: "As a realist," Linowitz said, Sadat "knew that he lived in a world in which one force must be balanced against another, and he had the politician's sure instinct for the act or word that might create the effect he wanted. He played his role on the world stage with consummate skill, knowing that, when he was at center stage, his country would also be a focal point of attention and of world concern." Sadat had been, the statement said, "the irreplaceable man of our time."[37]

Those and similar encomiums were fair summaries of what statesmen and diplomats in the West thought about Sadat. The Arabs hardly shared their sentiments. Sudan, more African than Arab, was the only Arab League country represented at the funeral by its head of state. Somalia and Oman sent lower-level officials. All the others declined to attend. Begin's presence was sufficient to keep them away, but the radicals went further. Libya, Iraq, and Syria issued statements welcoming the death of "the traitor Sadat."

Sadat's place in Arab history, and in the sentiments of the Egyptian people, would have been different if Syria, Saudi Arabia, and Jordan had endorsed, or at least accepted, his peace treaty with Israel. But because it left the Palestinians stranded, and because of his impetuous tactics and headstrong style in negotiating it, that was not going to happen, as Sadat should have known. His insistence that the other Arabs would follow where Egypt led was divorced from reality. Syria's Assad thought Sadat had lied to him about his war aims in 1973 and misled him about peace negotiations. A few months after the Egypt-Israel treaty was signed, the rulers of Saudi Arabia were staggered by an armed takeover of Islam's holiest site, the great Mosque of Mecca, by Islamic extremists who accused the al-Saud regime of being culturally and politically tainted by the West and by their ties to the United States; the king and princes were in no position to compound their domestic challenges by accepting the legitimacy of Israel. As for Jordan, half its population was of Palestinian origin. King Hussein had undermined his standing with them by sending his army into battle against PLO guerrillas in the Black September conflict of 1971 and did not wish to alienate them further. Only in 1994, after Israel and the Palestine Liberation Organization had legitimized each other with the first Oslo autonomy agreement, did Jordan make full peace with Israel.

The people of Egypt were indifferent to Sadat's death. Unimpressed by the foreign dignitaries who appeared in Cairo for their funeral, they largely ignored the event. They went about their preparations for an upcoming religious holiday as if nothing important had happened. There could not have been a more stark contrast to the funeral of Nasser, eleven years earlier, when millions had poured into the streets to vent their grief and loss.

The Hero of the Crossing faded quickly from his compatriots' minds. I had left Egypt by the time of Sadat's assassination; when I returned a few years later, nobody I talked to mentioned him. In the mass popular uprisings of 2011 and 2012, Sadat's name was hardly heard, except as the man who had put the reviled Hosni Mubarak in power. His name was given to an industrial city northwest of Cairo, but is found in few other public places. His peace treaty remains; the man who forged it faded into Egyptian history.

Peace was a worthy and essential goal, and Sadat achieved it. His daring initiatives lifted Egypt from despair, restored its dignity, and regained all its lost land. Israel for the first time had accepted a permanent border that set a limit on its expansion, at least to its west. Egypt was better off and Egyptians were safer after Sadat's presidency than before. The Suez Canal, lifeline of global commerce and mainstay of the Egyptian economy, was reopened to ships of all nations. On the international front, Sadat and his policies changed the global economic balance through the oil revolution and tipped the balance in the Cold War by putting an end to Soviet aspirations for regional hegemony. Yet the people Sadat led were not grateful. For them, the price was too high. They could visit Israel now if they wished to do so, but few did. They relapsed into political apathy, which would stifle the country for the next thirty years. Rarely in modern times has a national leader squandered popular acclaim and international renown as did Mohammed Anwar el-Sadat, but his political failings cannot erase his indelible imprint on the Middle East and the wider world.

Notes

Thousands of previously classified U.S. government documents from the 1970s and early 1980s have now been declassified and made available to researchers. Other documents and records that were previously public have been compiled and annotated by scholars and independent researchers. These documents and records—some declassified by the government with the passage of time, some acquired through Freedom of Information Act proceedings—have been assembled by various organizations, and by the author, and are the source of much of the information in this book. Also available to researchers now are documents from Egypt, Israel, the Soviet Union, and other countries.

The sourcing of records is different in the Internet age from what it was in the days of paper copies. Documents placed online are sometimes unpaginated, or carry different titles or headlines from the original. In the reference notes, I have endeavored to provide enough information that those who wish to examine the material further can find it.

The principal collections cited in the reference notes are:

1. *Foreign Relations of the United States*: thick volumes of previously classified diplomatic and intelligence documents compiled and annotated by the State Department historian, listed by year and volume number, as in *Foreign Relations of the United States, 1977–1980*, volume 8, *Arab-Israeli Dispute*, January 1977–August

1978. Within each volume, documents are printed in chronological order. All are accessible online at http://history.state.gov/historical documents. Cited in the reference notes as FRUS, with year(s), volume number, and document number or page number, as in FRUS 1977–80, vol. 8, doc. 166.

2. *The October War and U.S. Policy*: key documents obtained from U.S. government agencies, compiled and annotated by William Burr and researchers at the National Security Archive, an independent organization based at George Washington University, Washington DC. This compilation is online at http://www2.gwu.edu/~nsarchiv/NSAEBB/NSAEBB98/. Cited in the notes as National Security Archive Compilation, with document number.

3. Henry A. Kissinger Telephone Transcripts: transcriptions of Kissinger's telephone conversations during and after the October War. Available on compact disc from www.paperlessarchives.com. Cited as HAK Transcripts.

4. State Department Electronic Telegrams 1973–74: diplomatic cables to and from U.S. embassies and consulates. Available on compact disc from www.paperlessarchives.com. Cited as State Department Telegrams.

5. *Cold War in the Middle East*: documents from the Soviet Union and Warsaw Pact countries compiled by the Cold War International History Project, Woodrow Wilson Center for Scholars, Washington DC. Online at http://www.wilsoncenter.org/digital-archive. Cited as Cold War History Project.

6. Gerald R. Ford Papers: archived at the Ford Presidential Library, Grand Rapids, Michigan. Online at www.thelibrarycollection.com/ford.html. Cited as Ford Papers. The library's collection includes the papers of Frank G. Zarb, White House "energy czar," cited as Zarb Papers.

7. *Intelligence and the Camp David Accords*: Central Intelligence Agency documents made public by the agency in November 2013. Online

at https://www.cia.gov/library/publications/historical-collection
-publications/president-carter-and-the-camp-david-accords/index
.html. Cited as CIA Camp David Files.

8. *President Nixon and the Role of Intelligence in the 1973 Arab-Israeli War*: documents made public by the CIA historian. Online at https://
www.cia.gov/library/publications/historical-collection-publications
/arab-israeli-war/index.html. Cited as CIA 1973 War File.

9. Documents at the Jimmy Carter Presidential Library, Atlanta,
Georgia: including Camp David history and papers and other files.
Online at http://www.ibiblio.org/sullivan/CampDavid-Accords-tour
.html. Cited as Carter Papers. Much of the Carter file has not yet
been digitized.

10. *Frontline Diplomacy*: a compilation of oral histories of U.S. diplomats overseas, sorted by country. Compiled by and available on
compact disc from the Academy for Diplomatic Studies and Training, Arlington, Virginia. Cited as ADST Oral Histories.

11. Anwar Sadat Archives, University of Maryland: speeches and writings by Sadat, and related documents. Online at http://sadat.umd
.edu/archives/index.htm. Cited as UM Sadat Archive.

12. National Archives of the United States, College Park, Maryland: sorted by records group, as in RG 59, General Records of the
Department of State. Cited as National Archives RG.

13. National Archives, Central Foreign Policy Files: a separate collection of declassified documents and files from the 1970s. Posted
online in 2013 at http://aad.archives.gov/aad/series-description.jsp?s
=4073. Cited as NA Central Foreign Policy Files.

14. Public Papers of the Presidents: volumes of statements, documents, and news conferences of the presidents; listed in chronological order. Published in bound volumes by the Government
Printing Office, Washington DC, and available online from the
University of California–Santa Barbara at http://www.presidency
.ucsb.edu. Cited as Public Papers.

Introduction

1. See part 3, section 2(b) of Hegel's *Reason in History*.

1. The War of Redemption

1. Kissinger, *Years of Upheaval*, 459.

2. See the introduction by William Burr to the National Security Archive Compilation.

3. Cable of October 12, 1973, State Department Telegrams, part 1.

4. *Arab News*, Jeddah, September 27, 2007.

5. Rogers memo to Nixon, May 1, 1972, na rg 59, central files 1970–73, Pol US-USSR, now declassified.

6. Remarks at Thirteenth Annual U.S.-Arab Policymakers Conference, Washington DC, September 13, 2004.

7. Kissinger, *Years of Upheaval*, 459.

8. Cline's paper is available at http://www2.gwu.edu/~nsarchiv/NSAEBB/NSA EBB415/docs/doc%201%2031MAY1973_INR_RAYCLINE(3).pdf.

9. Phone conversation, October 7, HAK Transcripts.

10. HAK Transcripts, October 8.

11. CIA 1973 War File.

12. Sadat, *In Search of Identity*, 242.

13. CIA 1973 War File.

14. Kissinger, *Years of Upheaval*, 460.

15. Seale, *Asad*, 195–98.

16. See chapter 6.

17. Speech to People's Assembly, November 26, 1977, UM Sadat Archive.

18. Sadat, "The Glorious Days of October," part 1 of *The October Working Paper*, published in English by the State Information Service, 1974, UM Sadat Archive.

19. HAK Transcripts, October 6, 6:40 a.m.

20. HAK Transcripts, October 6, 9:20 a.m.

21. National Security Archive Compilation, document 10.

22. HAK Transcripts, October 6, 10:35 a.m.

23. Burr, ed., *Kissinger Transcripts*, 343.

24. National Security Archive Compilation, document 15.

25. FRUS 1969–76, vol. 15, document 176.

26. CIA, *The 1973 Arab-Israeli War: Overview and Analysis of the Conflict*, http://www.foia.cia.gov/search-results?search_api_views_fulltext=The+1973+Arab-Israeli+War%3A+Overview&field_collection=.

27. Bar-Joseph, "The 'Special Means of Collection,'" 532. "CE" and "BCE" mean "Christian Era" and "Before Christian Era," terms adopted by academics who evidently believe the traditional BC and AD might offend someone.

28. Herzog, *War of Atonement*, 272.

29. CIA, *1973 Arab-Israeli War*, 16 (see note 26 above).

30. National Security Archive Compilation, notes to document 21B.

31. White House memorandum of conversation between Kissinger and other senior officials, October 14, 1973, document made available to the author by the National Security Archive. See also Insight Team of the *London Sunday Times*, *Yom Kippur War*, 280–82.

32. For details on the U.S. airlift, see the narrative at the Air Mobility Command Museum, http://amcmuseum.org/history/airlifts/operation_nickel_grass.php.

33. CIA, *1973 Arab-Israeli War*, 24.

34. Herzog, *War of Atonement*, 244.

35. National Security Archive Compilation, document 47.

36. National Security Archive Compilation, document 48.

37. Resolutions 242 and 338 are online at http://www.un.org/en/sc/documents/resolutions/index.shtml.

38. Kissinger Cable, November 2, 1973, State Department Telegrams.

39. National Security Archive Compilation, document 51.

40. CIA, *1973 Arab-Israeli War*, 24.

41. National Security Archive Compilation, document 60.

42. National Security Archive Compilation, document 62.

43. HAK Transcripts, October 24.

44. National Security Archive Compilation, document 67.

45. Kissinger, *Years of Upheaval*, 573. Italics in original.

46. National Security Archive Compilation, document 69.

47. National Security Archive Compilation, document 71. This is a translation of a letter dictated to Kissinger by Soviet Ambassador Anatoly Dobrynin under the pressure of the moment, which may account for some of the linguistic peculiarities.

48. Israelyan, *Inside the Kremlin*, 169.

49. Israelyan, *Inside the Kremlin*, 167

50. Kissinger, *Years of Upheaval*, 586. Were U.S. forces put on alert without the president's knowledge? See the CIA 1973 War File, note 13.

51. National Security Archive Compilation, document 73.

52. Kissinger, *Years of Upheaval*, 591.

53. Telephone conversation with Haig, October 25, 7:19 p.m., HAK Transcripts.

54. News conference, October 26, 1973, Public Papers.

55. HAK transcripts, October 26.

56. FRUS 1969–76, vol. 25, 771.

57. National Security Archive Compilation, document 85.

58. National Security Archive Compilation, documents 86 and 87.

59. Quoted in *New York Times*, October 29, 1973, 16.

60. National Security Archive Compilation, document 88B.

61. HAK Transcripts, October 30.

62. These extraordinary conversations are recorded in FRUS 1969–76, vol. 25, 807–36.

63. Sadat, *In Search of Identity*, 256.

64. FRUS 1977–80, vol. 8, document 17, p. 180.

65. Sorley, ed., *Press On! Selected Works of General Donn A. Starry*, vol. 1.

66. CIA, *1973 Arab-Israeli War*, 70.

67. Mike Sparks, "A Crisis of Confidence in Armor?" *Armor Magazine*, March–April 1998, 2.

68. Herzog, *War of Atonement*, 270.

69. CIA 1973 War File, 108.

70. Both sides deployed tanks in the eight-year war between Iran and Iraq, but in smaller numbers and often in static positions, where they functioned more like artillery.

71. Rabinovich, *Yom Kippur War*, 498–501.

72. National Security Archive Compilation, document 72.

73. National Security Archive Compilation, document 82.

74. National Security Archive Compilation, document 80.

75. UM Sadat Archive.

76. National Security Archive Compilation, document 82.

77. Sadat, "The Glorious Days of October," part 1, *The October Working Paper*, 25, UM Sadat Archive.

78. Kissinger, *Years of Upheaval*, 561

79. Parker, ed., *October War*, 248.

80. FRUS 1979–80, vol. 9, document 301.

81. Israelyan, *Inside the Kremlin*, 211–14.

2. The Eclipse of the Soviet Union

1. This account is at www.marxists.org/history/international/comintern/baku/foreword.htm.

2. *Current Digest of the Soviet Press* 7, no. 16 (June 1, 1955).

3. Campbell, *Defense of the Middle East*, 211. For a detailed account of this Soviet policy shift, see Allison, *Soviet Union and the Strategy of Non-Alignment*, 8.

4. Kanet, "Superpower Quest for Empire," 331–52.

5. Text of this letter at Israel Ministry of Foreign Affairs website, http://mfa.gov.il/MFA/ForeignPolicy/MFADocuments/Yearbook1/Pages/7%20Exchange%20of%20Letters-%20Bulganin-%20Ben-Gurion-%205%20and.aspx.

6. Minutes of the Communist Party of the Soviet Union Central Committee plenum, June 24, 1957, Cold War International History Project, http://digitalarchive.wilsoncenter.org/document/110459.

7. "Text of Khrushchev Interview on Wide Range of Issues between East and West," *New York Times*, October 10, 1957.

8. Adeed Dawisha, "Soviet Union in the Arab World," 10.

9. Testimony before the Senate Foreign Relations Committee, March 27, 1980.

10. Copeland, *Game of Nations*, 62.

11. "Probable Developments in the Arab States," National Intelligence Estimate no. 36–54, September 7, 1954.

12. Nasser, "Morrow of Independence," 77.

13. Stephens, *Nasser*, 160–61.

14. Barrett, *Greater Middle East and the Cold War*, 33.

15. Heikal, *Autumn of Fury*, 86.

16. Hashim, "From the Ottomans Through Sadat," 71.

17. See the discussion section in Alterman, *Sadat and His Legacy*, 63.

18. Parker, ed., *October War*, 45.

19. Primakov, *Russia and the Arabs*, 69.

20. Primakov, *Russia and the Arabs*, 307.

21. Interview with *Al-Siyassa* (Kuwait), November3, 1978.

22. Vassiliev, *King Faisal*, 354–55; Lacey, *The Kingdom*, 392–94.

23. Quoted in Lippman, *Egypt After Nasser*, 16.

24. Heikal, *Sphinx and the Commissar*, 222.

25. Sadat, *In Search of Identity*, 278.

26. Speech to People's Assembly, November 26 1977, UM Sadat Archive.

27. Primakov, *Russia and the Arabs*, 133.

28. ADST Oral Histories.

29. Bergus's messages to Rogers are online in the UM Sadat Archive. Like many diplomatic cables, they are written in truncated prose that omits definite articles.

30. Heikal, *Sphinx and the Commissar*, 232.

31. Sadat, *In Search of Identity*, 227; Heikal, *Sphinx and the Commissar*, 233–37.

32. Text online at http://www.washingtonpost.com/wp-srv/inatl/longterm/summit/archive/com1972-1.htm.

33. Sadat, *In Search of Identity*, 229–30.

34. Sadat, *In Search of Identity*, 230. For an extensive review of these events see Daigle, "The Russians are Going." Daigle argues that Sadat wanted an interim peace agreement with Israel to justify a decision to expel the Soviet advisers. But when no agreement was forthcoming, the only option was war, to which the Soviet advisers were, in Sadat's view, an obstacle.

35. FRUS 1969–76, vol. 15, document 16.

36. Letter quoted in Heikal, *Sphinx and the Commissar*, 244–46.

37. This letter is reproduced as appendix 1 to Sadat, *In Search of Identity*.

38. Parker, *October War*, 45.

39. Parker, *October War*, 115.

40. Hirst and Beeson, *Sadat*, 139.

41. FRUS 1969–76, vol. 15, document 25.

42. Heikal, *Sphinx and the Commissar*, 253–54.

43. *Policy of the Soviet Union in the Arab World*, 187–88.

44. Sadat, *In Search of Identity*, 238.

45. Heikal, *Sphinx and the Commissar*, 256.

46. ADST Oral Histories.

47. Primakov, *Russia and the Arabs*, 386.

48. Andrew and Mitrokhin, *World Was Going Our Way*, 14.

49. Thomas W. Lippman, "Iraq Displays a Jew Who Returned," *Washington Post*, July 27, 1976, A9.

50. Marr, *Modern History of Iraq*, 146.

51. Seale, *Asad of Syria*, 48.

52. Heikal, *Sphinx and the Commissar*, 283–85.

53. Meeting with oil executives, March 29, 1974, in FRUS 1976, vol. 36, document 345.

54. ADST Oral Histories.

55. National Archives RG 59, Records of Henry Kissinger, 1973–77, box 5, Nodis Memcons, November 1974, folder 1.

56. Hirst and Beeson, *Sadat*, 189–91.

57. See Beattie, *Egypt During the Sadat Years*, 178–79.

58. Text online at the website of the Knesset, http://www.knesset.gov.il/process/docs/egypt_interim_eng.htm.

59. What Egypt would do if, on the other hand, Israel attacked other Arabs remained a separate issue in the peace treaty negotiations of 1978. See chapter 5.

60. Memorandum of conversation, Salzburg, June 1, 1975, UM Sadat Archive.

61. UM Sadat Archive, speeches. Technically, Sadat asked the parliament to abrogate the treaty, but the parliament's response was not in doubt.

62. Kissinger meeting with Golda Meir, Jerusalem, January 15, 1974, UM Sadat Archive.

63. Thomas W. Lippman, "Chinese Taking Over Egypt's Center Stage," *Washington Post*, April 24, 1976, A10.

64. Thomas W. Lippman, "Cairo Press Denounces Soviets for Accusation," *Washington Post*, April 29, 1977, A24

65. Andrew and Mitrokhin, *World Was Going Our Way*, 167.

66. Conversations with Landrum Bolling, September 9–12, 1977, FRUS 1977, vol. 8, document 103, tab B.

67. CIA Camp David Files.

68. CIA Camp David Files.

69. Cable of July 21, 1973, State Department Telegrams.

70. Cable of December 1, 1973, State Department Telegrams.

71. Primakov, *Russia and the Arabs*, 307; see also Marr, *Modern History of Iraq*, 168–69.

72. Fukuyama, *Soviet Union and Iraq*, v–vii.

73. FRUS 1969–76, vol. 21, document 166.

74. Fukuyama, *Soviet Union and Iraq*, vi.

75. Cold War History Project, 114537.

76. CIA, Directorate of Intelligence, *Soviet Policy Toward the Middle East*, p. 21. Undated but based on events through 1986. Available at http://www.foia.cia.gov/sites /default/files/document_conversions/89801/DOC_0000499549.pdf. This study is a useful summary of the Soviet Union's relations with the Arabs from 1950 to the mid-1980s.

77. Telhami, *World Through Arab Eyes*, 174–75.

3. Oil Goes to War

1. BP *Statistical Review of World Energy 2010*, http://www.bp.com/statisticalreview. Throughout this chapter, the price refers to the so-called posted, or official, price— the baseline price for one barrel of a benchmark oil such as Saudi Arabian light or West Texas intermediate. (A barrel is forty-two gallons.) The actual price varied with the quality of the oil and the shipping distance.

2. Frank Verrastro and Guy Caruso, *The Arab Oil Embargo–40 Years Later*, Center for Strategic and International Studies, October 16, 2013, http://csis.org/publication/arab -oil-embargo-40-years-later.

3. Data compiled by Energy Information Administration, http://www.eia.gov/dnav /pet/hist/LeafHandler.ashx?n=PET&s=MCRIMUS1&f=A.

4. Kissinger, *Years of Upheaval*, 887.

5. Public Papers.

6. Yergin, *The Prize*, 464.

7. On the CIA's role, see Takeyh, "What Really Happened in Iran," 2, and Sick, *All Fall Down*, 6–7. The argument about the extent of U.S. involvement grows only murkier as more information becomes available.

8. For a detailed history of this development, see Terzian, OPEC: *The Inside Story*, chapter 2.

9. Yergin, *The Prize*, 583.

10. Quoted in Yergin, *The Prize*, 584.

11. For detailed narratives, see Yergin, *The Prize*, part 5, and Terzian, OPEC: *The Inside Story*, chapters 7–9. On Saudi Arabia and Aramco, see Nawwab, *Saudi Aramco and Its World*, 223, 228.

12. Memorandum of conversation of meeting between Kissinger, Yamani, and Prince Saud al-Faisal, then deputy oil minister, April 17, 1973, made available to author by researchers at National Security Archive, Washington DC.

13. ADST Oral Histories.

14. Terzian, OPEC: *The Inside Story*, 165.

15. Address to Thirteenth Annual U.S.-Arab Policymakers Conference, Washington DC, October 14, 2004.

16. See, for example, interview with *Newsweek*, September 10, 1973, 12.

17. Author's interview, June 19, 2013.

18. *Washington Post*, September 2, 1973, A1.

19. In this document and in diplomatic correspondence throughout the oil crisis, U.S. officials used the word *boycott*, which is a refusal to buy, when the correct word was *embargo*, a refusal to sell.

20. Nixon Presidential Library, National Security Council files, http://www.nixon library.gov/virtuallibrary/documents/nationalsecuritymemoranda.php.

21. Cooper, *Oil Kings*, 110.

22. National Security Archive Compilation, document 36A.

23. Akins's cable is reproduced as appendix 3 in Kechichian, *Faysal*.

24. Jungers's comments are on p. 134 of *American Perspectives of Aramco, the Saudi Arabian Oil-Producing Company, 1930s to 1980s*, an oral history compilation by the Regional Oral History Office, Bancroft Library, University of California, Berkeley, 1995.

25. Kissinger, *Years of Upheaval*, 885

26. Cooper, *Oil Kings*, 146.

27. Quoted in Stork, *Middle East Oil*, 284.

28. ADST Oral Histories.

29. Akins, "This Time the Wolf Is Here."

30. Memorandum of conversation with other senior officials, November 29, 1973, FRUS 1969–76, vol. 25, document 363.

31. HAK Transcripts, October 10, 1973.

32. HAK Transcripts, October 27, 1973.

33. Memorandum of conversation with other senior officials, November 29, 1973, FRUS 1969–76, vol. 25, document 363.

34. CIA, "The Arab Oil Cutback and Higher Prices: Implications and Reactions," October 19, 1973, http://www.foia.cia/gov/collection/president-nixon-and-role -intelligence-1973-arab-israeli-war.

35. National Security Archive Compilation, document 52.

36. National Security Archive Compilation, document 80.

37. Correspondence and memoranda about these negotiations are in Zarb Papers, box 8. See also Yergin, *The Prize*, 643–44.

38. Morse, "New Political Economy of Oil?"

39. Public Papers.

40. http://www.independent.co.uk/news/obituaries/tom-christian-island-leader-who
-connected-pitcairn-with-the-world-8786660.html; see also *New York Times*, obituary
of Tom Pitcairn, August 24, 2013, A-17.

41. Frank Zarb, oral history interview, http://www.nixonlibrary.gov/virtuallibrary.

42. For more details see *Time*, September 19, 1974, 35; and *Newsweek*, September 30, 1974, 38.

43. *Time*, September 22, 1974, 83

44. "Special Economic Report," *Newsweek*, September 30, 1974, 62.

45. Sadat, *In Search of Identity*, 304.

46. CIA, "The Arab Oil Cutback and Higher Prices: Implications and Reactions," October 19, 1973, http://www.foia.cia/gov/collection/president-nixon-and
-role-intelligence-1973-arab-israeli-war.

47. Terzian, OPEC: *The Inside Story*, 184.

48. CIA, "International Economic Impact of Increased Oil Prices in 1974," in FRUS 1969–76, vol. 36, document 277.

49. ADST Oral Histories.

50. See, for example, letter from Nixon to Sadat of December 28 1973, in UM Sadat Archive.

51. FRUS 1969–76, vol. 36, document 849.

52. FRUS 1969–76, vol. 36, document 309.

53. Faisal letter to Nixon, February 7, 1974, FRUS 1969–76, vol. 36, document 874.

54. State Department memorandum of conversation, Kissinger-Faisal meeting, October 13, 1974. A copy of this memcon was made available to the author by the National Security Archive.

55. U.S. General Accounting Office report to Congress, *Critical Factors Affecting Saudi Arabia's Oil Decisions*, May 12, 1978, 45.

56. The fullest account of JECOR's work, including an interview with Schotta, is in Lippman, *Inside the Mirage*, 167–78.

57. Zarb Papers.

58. *National Energy Outlook 1976*, xxiii (copy in Ford Library).

59. FRUS 1969–76, vol. 36, 762.

60. On IEA (International Energy Agency) website at http://www.iea.org/media
/aboutus/history/decisionofthecouncil.pdf.

61. FRUS 1969–76, vol. 36, 822.

62. *Washington Post*, November 26, 1993.

63. U.S. Energy Information Administration, *International Energy Outlook 2013*, http://www.eia.gov/oiaf/aeo/tablebrowser/#release=0-IEO2013&subject=0-IEO2013
&table=2-IEO2013&region=0-0&cases=Reference-d041117.

64. Energy Information Administration (EIA), *25th Anniversary of the 1973 Oil Embargo: Energy Trends Since the First Major U.S. Energy Crisis*, http://www.eia.gov/press
room/archive/speeches/25thann/sld001.htm.

65. See Priddy, "United States Synthetic Fuels Corporation."

66. "Address to the Nation on Energy and Economic Problems," January 13, 1975, Public Papers.

67. EIA, *25th Anniversary of the 1973 Oil Embargo: Energy Trends Since the First Major U.S. Energy Crisis*, http://www.eia.gov/pressroom/archive/speeches/25thann/sld
001.htm, slide 8.

68. Stanislaw and Yergin, "Oil: Reopening the Door."

69. Address to U.S.-Saudi Business Forum, Chicago, April 28, 2010.

4. Stranger in a Strange Land

1. This narrative is from the website of the Knesset at http://knesset.gov.il/lexicon/eng/geneva_eng.htm.

2. Text at https://www.jewishvirtuallibrary.org/jsource/Peace/syr1974.html.

3. Text at http://unispal.un.org/unispal.nsf/0/7FB7C26FCBE80A31852560C500 65F878.

4. Text at http://unispal.un.org/unispal.nsf/0/7D35E1F729DF491C85256EE700686136.

5. See *Historical Dictionary of Israel*, at http://israel_history.enacademic.com/915/Sinai _II_Accords.

6. FRUS 1977–80, vol. 8, document 63.

7. FRUS 1977–80, vol. 8, document 18.

8. Quandt, *Camp David*, 109.

9. FRUS 1969–76, vol. 36, document 345, p. 954.

10. Thomas W. Lippman, "Sadat Assails Carter View on Borders," *Washington Post*, March 13, 1977, A1.

11. FRUS 1977–80, vol. 8, document 9.

12. FRUS 1977–80, vol. 8, document 10.

13. Public Papers.

14. Quandt, *Camp David*, 44.

15. From the biography posted by the Israeli Ministry of Foreign Affairs at http://www.mfa.gov.il/mfa/aboutisrael/state/pages/menachem%20begin.aspx.

16. Shlaim, *Iron Wall*, 350–53.

17. FRUS 1969–76, vol. 36, p. 1037n6.

18. Text in Laqueur and Rubin, eds., *Israeli-Arab Reader*, 206.

19. FRUS 1969–76, vol. 36, document 52.

20. Quandt, *Camp David*, 61.

21. Quandt, *Camp David*, 67.

22. Dayan, *Breakthrough*, 59–60.

23. FRUS 1977–80, vol. 9, document 138.

24. FRUS 1969–76, vol. 36, document 64.

25. FRUS 1969–76, vol. 36, document 100.

26. FRUS 1969–76, vol. 36, document 103.

27. FRUS 1969–76, vol. 36, document 107.

28. Quandt, *Camp David*, 110.

29. The text is printed as appendix B of Quandt's *Camp David*. It was also published in the *New York Times* on October 2, 1977.

30. FRUS 1969–76, vol. 36, document 124.

31. Dayan, *Breakthrough*, 68–69.

32. Text of letter at http://www.jimmycarterlibrary.gov/documents/campdavid25/CDA04.pdf.

33. FRUS 1969–76, vol. 36, document 141.

34. FRUS 1969–76, vol. 36, document142.

35. Speech of November 9, 1977, UM Sadat Archive.

36. FRUS 1969–76, vol. 36, document 145.

37. Texts of interviews at http://news.google.com/newspapers?nid=1913&dat=197 71115&id=26VGAAAAIBAJ&sjid=fvMMAAAAIBAJ&pg=1147,2246537.

38. State Department Telegrams.

39. State Department Telegrams.

40. An English text is available at UM Sadat Archive or from the Washington Institute for Near East Policy at https://www.washingtoninstitute.org/uploads/Documents /pubs/SadatandHisLegacy.pdf.pdf.

5. The Separate Peace

1. Text in Alterman, ed., *Sadat and His Legacy*, 203.

2. Schlaim, *Iron Wall*, 361–69.

3. NA Central Foreign Policy Files, no. 1393793187935.

4. FRUS 1977–80, vol. 8, document 158.

5. *Face the Nation* (CBS) and *Issues and Answers* (ABC), November 27, 1977.

6. Dayan, *Breakthrough*, 100.

7. FRUS 1977–80, vol. 9, document 139.

8. FRUS 1977–80, vol. 9, document 141.

9. NA, Central Foreign Policy Files.

10. FRUS 1977–80, vol. 8, document 177.

11. Vance, *Hard Choices*, 198–99.

12. See Eilts report on this meeting at http://static.history.state.gov/frus/frus1977 -80v08/pdf/frus1977-80v08.pdf.

13. Texts in *New York Times*, December 27, 1977, 16.

14. FRUS 1977–80, vol. 8, document 181.

15. FRUS 1977–80, vol. 8 document 184.

16. UM Sadat Archive.

17. FRUS 1977–80, vol. 8, document 189.

18. FRUS 1977–80, vol. 8, document 190.

19. FRUS 1977–80, vol. 8, document 198.

20. Available on the ministry's website at http://mfa.gov.il/MFA/ForeignPolicy/MFA Documents/Yearbook3/Pages/111%20Israel%20Government%20statement%20 following%20breakdow.aspx.

21. FRUS 1977–80, vol. 8, document 207.

22. Quandt, *Camp David*, 176–77.

23. FRUS 1977–80, vol. 8, document 218.

24. National Archives RG 59, Central Foreign Policy File, P850036–2366.

25. Cold War History Project, document 114537.

26. Vance, *Hard Choices*, 211.

27. William E. Farrell, "Israel Turns Down Appeal from Egypt for Friendly Move," *New York Times*, July 24, 1978, A1.

28. 1977–80, vol. 8, document 263.

29. 1977–80, vol. 8, document 276.

30. This was Sadat's position, but there was no basis for it. The text of Sinai II specified that it would remain in effect "until superseded by a new agreement." The expiration date applied to the mandate of the UN truce observer force.

31. Public Papers.

32. Peck and Lowrie, ADST oral histories.

33. FRUS 1977–80, vol. 9, document 21.

34. This and other Carter quotations in this chapter are from his memoir, *Keeping Faith*. The electronic edition, cited here, is unpaginated. See the chapters titled "Thirteen Days" and "After Camp David."

35. FRUS 1977–80, vol. 9, document 13.

36. William Quandt memorandum for the record, FRUS 1977–80, vol. 9, document 173.

37. Carter, *Keeping Faith*, "Thirteen Days" chapter.

38. ADST Oral Histories.

39. Public Papers.

40. Carter, *Keeping Faith*, note 35.

41. Statement at White House appearance with Carter and Sadat, September 17, 1978.

42. Vance, *Hard Choices*, 221–24.

43. Vance, *Hard Choices*, 221–24.

44. Carter, *Keeping Faith*, see note 35.

45. See report by Foundation for Middle East Peace at http://www.fmep.org/reports/special-reports/special-report-jerusalem/u.s.-policy-on-jerusalem.

46. Vance, *Hard Choices*, 225–26; Dayan, *Breakthrough*, 177–79; Quandt, *Camp David*, 233–34; Carter, *Keeping Faith*. Text of agreement and side letters in Quandt, appendix F.

47. Vance, *Hard Choices*, 227.

48. Speech at Ismailia University, November 5, 1978, and interview with Egyptian state television, December 25, 1978.

49. Memo to Carter, "Worst-Case Scenarios in the Middle East," November 24, 1978, CIA Camp David Files.

50. Author's interview, November 6, 2008.

51. Carter's account of this period is in the "No More War" chapter of *Keeping Faith*.

52. Vance, *Hard Choices*, 232–37.

53. FRUS 1977–80, vol. 8, document 133.

54. Carter, *Keeping Faith*.

55. Public Papers.

56. Carter, *Keeping Faith*.

57. Dayan, *Breakthrough*, 273; FRUS 1977–80, vol. 9, document 198.

58. FRUS 1977–80, vol. 9, document 185.

59. Remarks upon Sadat's departure from the United States, February 8, 1978.

60. Treaty and related documents in Quandt, *Camp David*, appendix H.

61. Italics in original. This paper is at http://www.ibiblio.org/sullivan/CampDavid-Legacy.html.

62. ADST Oral Histories.

63. ADST Oral Histories.

64. FRUS 1977–80, vol. 9, document 185.

65. FRUS 1977–80, vol. 9, document 345.

66. FRUS 1977–80, vol. 9, document 388.

67. UN Security Council Resolution 487, June 19, 1981.

68. For a full account of this episode, see Schlaim, *Iron Wall*, 384–88; See also Beattie, *Egypt During the Sadat Years*, 267.

69. FRUS 1977–80, vol. 9, document 258, note 3.

70. FRUS 1977–80, vol. 9, document 135.

71. FRUS 1977–80, vol. 9, document 404.

72. Dayan, *Breakthrough*, 82.

6. The End of Arab Nationalism

1. "Glorious Days of October," part 1 of *The October Working Paper*, 9–10, at UM Sadat Archive.

2. FRUS 1977–80, vol. 9, document 58.

3. Christopher S. Wren, "Hussein Appears to Oppose Israel-Egypt Dealings," *New York Times*, January 12, 1979, A2.

4. The text of the Arab League peace plan is at http://www.al-bab.com/arab/docs/league /peace02.htm.

5. Hourani, *History of the Arab Peoples*, 391–92.

6. Masadi, "Idea of Arab Nationalitarianism," 146.

7. Quoted in Andelman, *Shattered Peace*, 65. See also Rogan, *The Arabs*, 156–57.

8. Kramer, "Arab Nationalism: Mistaken Identity," 171–206. Kramer's article is a very useful survey of the concept of Arab nationalism and its historical development.

9. Carré, "Pouvoir et Idéologie Dans L'Egypte de Nasser et de Sadat," 259.

10. Aflaq, "Arab Unity Above Socialism," 148.

11. See Cook, *Struggle for Egypt*, 122; and Beattie, *Egypt During the Sadat Years*, 59–60.

12. Thomas W. Lippman, "Egypt-Libya Clash: Little Impact on Arab-Israeli Struggle," *Washington Post*, July 26, 1977, A11.

13. Thomas W. Lippman, "Syria and Egypt Will Take Steps Toward a Union," *Washington Post*, December 21, 1976, A1.

14. Speech to People's Assembly, November 9, 1977, in UM Sadat Archive.

15. FRUS 1977–80, vol. 8, document 166.

16. CIA "Situation Report," October 8, 1973. A redacted version of this document was made available to the author by researchers at the National Security Archive, Washington DC.

17. Message dated November 9, 1973, State Department Telegrams.

18. Ajami, *Arab Predicament*, 5–6.

19. Bureau of Intelligence and Research, intelligence summary, December 13, 1977, http://www2.gwu.edu/~nsarchiv/NSAEBB/NSAEBB463/docs/doc%202C%20 intsum.pdf.

20. FRUS 1977–80, vol. 9, document 100.

21. The author was among the journalists present at this event.

22. FRUS 1977–80, vol. 9, document 206.

23. ADST Oral Histories.

24. Quandt, *Camp David*, 140.

25. Author's interview, Damascus, March 1, 1976.

26. Report dated December 7, 1977, from "Intelligence and the Camp David Accords," https://www.cia.gov/library/publications/historical-collection-publications /president-carter-and-the-camp-david-accords/index.html.

27. Thomas W. Lippman, "Split Deepens Between Egypt, Other Arab States," *Washington Post*, November 7, 1978, A12.

28. Thomas W. Lippman, "Assad Charges Sadat 'Defected to Enemy' in Camp David Talks," *Washington Post*, September 21, 1978, A11.

29. Thomas W. Lippman, "Sadat Promises Peace to Cheering Egyptians," *Washington Post*, December 9, 1977 A1; Christopher S. Wren, "Sadat Awaits Calm in Storm," *New York Times*, April 10, 1979, A13.

30. Interview with *Al-Siyassa*, Kuwait, November 9, 1978.

31. Speech at Ismailia University, November 15, 1978. Sadat speeches and interviews that are not included in the UM Sadat Archive are available in bound volumes published by the State Information Service, Cairo.

32. Interview with Egyptian television, December 25, 1978.

33. Speech at Suez National Day ceremonies, October 24, 1978.

34. William E. Farrell, "Sadat Accuses Syrians of 'Hooliganism,'" *New York Times*, May 3, 1981.

35. Interview with *Al-Siyassa*, November 9, 1978.

36. Sadat, *In Search of Identity*, 312.

37. Quoted in Lippman, *Egypt After Nasser*, 261–62.

38. ADST Oral Histories.

39. State Department Bureau of Intelligence and Research, intelligence summary, December 2, 1977, NA Central Foreign Policy Files.

40. Christopher S. Wren, "Saudis' Leadership Attacked by Sadat," *New York Times*, May 25, 1979, A11.

41. FRUS 1977–80, vol. 9, document 192.

42. FRUS 1977–80, vol. 9, document 214.

43. *The October Working Paper*, part 1, p. 9; see also note 1 of this chapter.

44. Dayan, *Breakthrough*, 254.

45. Heikal, *Autumn of Fury*, 285.

7. The Rise of the Islamists

1. ADST Oral Histories.

2. Sadat, *In Search of Identity*, 234.

3. Beattie, *Egypt During the Sadat Years*, 15.

4. Abdo, *No God but God*, 52.

5. Sadat, *In Search of Identity*, 22.

6. CIA, "The Consequences of the Partition of Palestine," at http://www.foia.cia/browse_docs_full.asp?doc_no=0000256628.

7. Charles J. Adams, foreword to J. J. G. Jansen, *Neglected Duty*, xiii.

8. Heikal, *Autumn of Fury*, 138.

9. Heikal, *Autumn of Fury*, 143.

10. Ibrahim comments in Alterman, ed., *Sadat and His Legacy*, 103.

11. Davidson, "Political Violence in Egypt," 127.

12. Ayubi, "The Political Revival of Islam," 481–99.

13. Youssef, *Revolt Against Modernity*, 76.

14. CIA Camp David Files.

15. Academy for Diplomatic Studies and Training, "Moments in U.S. Diplomatic History: The Assassination of Anwar Sadat," part 1. This is a separate collection of oral histories from those cited as ADST Oral Histories elsewhere in this book. These are available online at http://adst.org/2013/09/the-assassination-of-anwar-sadat-part-i.

16. ADST Oral Histories.

17. Heikal, *Road to Ramadan*, 235–36.

18. Hinnebusch, *Egyptian Politics Under Sadat*, 199.

19. Hinnebusch, *Egyptian Politics Under Sadat*, 205.

20. Abdo, *No God but God*, 122–23.

21. NA, Central Foreign Policy files, November 4, 1977.

22. Mortimer, *Faith and Power*, 288.

23. Author's interview, January 1979.

24. ADST Oral Histories.

25. Abdo, *No God but God*, 165.

26. Abdo, *No God but God*, 165.

27. English text of constitution at sis.gov.eg.

28. Beattie, *Egypt During the Sadat Years*, 161–63.

29. Abdo, *No God but God*, 28.

30. Sadowski, "Egypt's Islamist Movement," 37.

31. Sadowski, "Egypt's Islamist Movement," 40–41.

32. G. H. Jansen, *Militant Islam*, 150.

33. *Washington Post*, March 27, 1979.

34. Waterbury, *Egypt of Nasser and Sadat*, 362.

35. Wenig, "Egypt's Army of God."

36. Speech at al-Azhar, January 1, 2015.

37. Al-Banna, "Credo of the Muslim Brotherhood," 45–47.

38. From Sadat, "The Egyptian Man," part 4 of *The October Working Paper*, pp. 100–101, UM Sadat Archive.

39. Speech at Alexandria University, July 26, 1978.

40. Heikal, *Autumn of Fury*, 286.

41. From Sadat, "The Egyptian Man," part 4 of *The October Working Paper*, pp. 100–101, UM Sadat Archive.

42. Message of April 5, 1976, text in UM Sadat Archive.

8. The Tarnished Legacy

1. Heikal, *Autumn of Fury*, 6.

2. ADST Oral Histories.

3. FRUS 1969–76, vol. 25, document 10.

4. ADST Oral Histories.

5. ADST Oral Histories.

6. Sadat, *In Search of Identity*, 314.

7. Camelia Anwar Sadat, "Sadat and His Vision," 3.

8. FRUS 1977–80, vol. 9, document 131.

9. Hirst and Beeson, *Sadat*, 354.

10. Assessment by Dr. Jerrold R. Post in CIA Camp David Files.

11. Waterbury, *Egypt of Nasser and Sadat*, 408.

12. Thomas W. Lippman, "Massive U.S. Aid Flowing to Egypt," *Washington Post*, June 20, 1977, A1.

13. U.S. Agency for International Development (USAID), *Status Report of United States Economic Assistance to Egypt as of April 1986*, delivered to Congress in 1987.

14. USAID, *Status Report of United States Economic Assistance to Egypt as of April 1986*, delivered to Congress in 1987.

15. On the failings of the foreign investment program, see Waterbury, *Egypt of Nasser and Sadat*, 129. For a comprehensive analysis of the Egyptian economy in this period, see Ikram, *Egypt: Economic Management in a Period of Transition*.

16. FRUS 1977–80, vol. 9, document 241.

17. Lippman, *Egypt After Nasser*, 115.

18. The author witnessed the riots.

19. FRUS 1977–80, vol. 8, document 17.

20. Reported in a cable to Washington by the U.S. embassy, NA Central Foreign Policy Files, document 1393798191028.

21. Heikal, *Autumn of Fury*, 94–95.

22. ADST Oral Histories.

23. Speech to parliament, November 4, 1978.

24. Thomas W. Lippman, "Pyramids Loom off the 18th Green," *Washington Post*, May 1, 1978, A1.

25. From Sadat, "Milestones Along the Way," part 2 of *The October Working Paper*, pp. 38–39, UM Sadat Archive.

26. Cable of August 27, 1977, State Dept Telegrams.

27. Atherton's report was made available to the author by researchers at the National Security Archive.

28. Beattie, *Egypt During the Sadat Years*, 237.

29. See *A Country Study: Egypt*, one of a series issued by the Federal Research Division, Library of Congress, at http://lcweb2.loc.gov/frd/cs/egtoc.html.

30. The best account of this event is in part 6, chapter 1, of Heikal, *Autumn of Fury*.

31. *Islam in Egypt, Part I: The Growth and Challenge of Islamic Fundamentalism and Extremism*, report to State Department, October 21, 1982. This document was made available to the author by researchers at the National Security Archive, and reprinted in *Middle East Policy* 21, no. 4 (Winter 2014).

32. Heikal, *Autumn of Fury*, 226.

33. David B. Ottaway, "Sadat Attacks Western Media, Denies Any Parallel to Shah," *Washington Post*, September 10, 1981, A19.

34. This report was among several cables related to the assassination plot made available to the author by researchers at the National Security Archive.

35. Atherton's report was made available to the author by the National Security Archive.

36. Public Papers.

37. *Congressional Record*, October 20, 1981.

Bibliography

Abdel-Malek, Anouar, ed. *Contemporary Arab Political Thought*. London: Zed Books, 1983.

Abdo, Geneive. *No God but God: Egypt and the Triumph of Islam*. New York: Oxford University Press, 2000.

Aflaq, Michel. "Arab Unity Above Socialism." In *Contemporary Arab Political Thought*, edited by Anouar Abdel-Malek. London: Zed Books, 1983.

Ajami, Fouad. *The Arab Predicament: Arab Political Thought and Practice Since 1967*. Cambridge UK: Cambridge University Press, 1981.

Akins, James E. "This Time the Wolf Is Here." *Foreign Affairs*, April 1973. http://www.foreignaffairs.com/articles/24416/james-e-akins/the-oil-crisis-this-time-the-wolf-is-here.

Allison, Roy. *The Soviet Union and the Strategy of Non-Alignment in the Third World*. Cambridge UK: Cambridge University Press, 1989.

Alterman, Jon B., ed. *Sadat and His Legacy*. Washington DC: Washington Institute for Near East Policy, 1998.

Andelman, David A. *A Shattered Peace: Versailles 1919 and the Price We Pay Today*. Hoboken NJ: Wiley, 2008.

Andrew, Christopher, and Vasili Mitrokhin, *The World Was Going Our Way: The KGB and the Battle for the Third World*. New York: Basic Books, 2005.

Ayubi, Nazih N. M. "The Political Revival of Islam: The Case of Egypt." *International Journal of Middle East Studies* 12, no. 4 (1980): 481–99.

Banna, Hassan al-. "The Credo of the Muslim Brotherhood." In *Contemporary Arab Political Thought*, edited by Anouar Abdel-Malek. London: Zed Books, 1983.

Bar-Joseph, Uri. "The 'Special Means of Collection': The Missing Link in the Surprise of the Yom Kippur War." *Middle East Journal* 67, no. 4 (Autumn 2013).

Barrett, Roby C. *The Greater Middle East and the Cold War: US Foreign Policy Under Eisenhower and Kennedy*. London: I. B. Tauris, 2007.

Beattie, Kirk J. *Egypt During the Sadat Years*. New York: Palgrave, 2000.

Berger, Morroe. *Islam in Egypt Today*. New York: Cambridge University Press, 1970.

Brzezinski, Zbigniew. *Power and Principle: Memoirs of the National Security Adviser 1977–1981*. New York: Farrar Straus and Giroux, 1983.

Burr, William, ed., *The Kissinger Transcripts: The Top Secret Talks With Beijing and Moscow*. New York: New Press, 1999.

Campbell, John C. *Defense of the Middle East: Problems of American Policy*. 2nd ed. New York: Praeger, 1960.

Carré, Olivier. "Pouvoir et Idéologie Dans L'Egypte de Nasser et de Sadat." In *L'Egypte d'Aujourd'hui.*, edited by R. Mantran. Paris: Editions du Centre National de la Récherche Scientifique, 1977.

Carrère d'Encausse, Hélène. *La Politique Soviètique au Moyen-orient*. Paris: Editions de Sciences Po, 1975.

Carter, Jimmy. *Keeping Faith*. New York: Bantam, 1982. Republished in paperback by the University of Arkansas Press in 2005.

Cook, Steven A. *The Struggle for Egypt: From Nasser to Tahrir Square*. New York: Oxford University Press, 2012.

Cooper, Andrew Scott. *The Oil Kings: How the US, Iran, and Saudi Arabia Changed the Balance of Power in the Middle East*. New York: Simon and Schuster, 2011.

Copeland, Miles. *The Game of Nations*. London: Weidenfeld and Nicolson, 1969.

Daigle, Craig A. "The Russians are Going: Sadat, Nixon, and the Soviet Presence in Egypt 1970–1971." *Middle East Review of International Affairs* 8, no.1 (March 2004).

Davidson, Charles R. "Political Violence in Egypt: A Case Study of the Islamist Insurgency 1992–1997." PhD diss., Tufts University, 2005.

Dawisha, Adeed. "The Soviet Union in the Arab World." In *The Soviet Union in the Middle East*, edited by Adeed Dawisha and Karen Dawisha. London: Heinemann, 1982.

Dawisha, Adeed, and Karen Dawisha, eds. *The Soviet Union in the Middle East*. London: Heinemann, 1982.

Dayan, Moshe. *Breakthrough: A Personal Account of the Egypt-Israel Peace Negotiations*. New York: Knopf, 1981.

Dekmejian, R. Hrair. *Islam in Revolution: Fundamentalism in the Arab World*. Syracuse NY: Syracuse University Press, 1995.

Fukuyama, Francis. *The Soviet Union and Iraq Since 1968*. Santa Monica CA: RAND Corporation, 1980.

Golan, Galia. *Soviet Policies in the Middle East: From World War II to Gorbachev*. Cambridge UK: Cambridge University Press, 1990.

Hashim, Ahmed. "From the Ottomans Through Sadat." *Middle East Policy* 18, no.3 (Fall 2011).

Hegel, Georg W. F. *Reason in History: A General Introduction to the Philosophy of History*, translated by Robert S. Hartman. New York: Bobbs-Merrill, 1953.

Heikal, Mohamed. *Autumn of Fury: The Assassination of Sadat*. Paperback ed. London: Corgi Books, 1984.

———. *The Road to Ramadan*. London: William Collins and Sons, 1975.

———. *The Sphinx and the Commissar: The Rise and Fall of Soviet Influence in the Middle East*. New York: Harper and Row, 1978.

Herzog, Chaim. *The War of Atonement*. Jerusalem: Steimatzky, 1975.

Hinnebusch, Raymond. *Egyptian Politics Under Sadat*. Cambridge UK: Cambridge University Press, 1985.

Hirst, David, and Irene Beeson. *Sadat*. London: Faber and Faber 1981.

Hourani, Albert. *A History of the Arab Peoples*. Cambridge MA: Belknap Press, 1991.

Ikram, Khalid. *Egypt: Economic Management in a Period of Transition*. A World Bank Country Economic Report. Baltimore: Johns Hopkins University Press, 1980.

Insight Team of the *London Sunday Times*. *The Yom Kippur War*. Garden City NY: Doubleday, 1974.

Israelyan, Viktor. *Inside the Kremlin During the Yom Kippur War*. University Park: Pennsylvania State University Press, 1995.

Jansen, G. H. *Militant Islam*. New York: Harper and Row, 1979.

Jansen, Johannes J. G. *The Neglected Duty: The Creed of Sadat's Assassins and Islamic Resurgence in the Middle East*. New York: Macmillan, 1986.

Kanet, Robert E. "The Superpower Quest for Empire: The Cold War and Soviet Support for 'Wars of National Liberation.'" *Cold War History* 6, no. 3 (August 2006).

Kechichian, Joseph A. *Faysal: Saudi Arabia's King for All Seasons*. Gainesville: University Press of Florida, 2008.

Kissinger, Henry A. *Years of Upheaval*. Boston: Little, Brown, 1982.

Kramer, Martin. "Arab Nationalism: Mistaken Identity." *Daedalus*, Summer 1993.

Lacey, Robert. *The Kingdom*. New York: Harcourt Brace Jovanovich, 1981.

Laqueur, Walter, and Barry Rubin, eds. *The Arab-Israeli Reader: A Documentary History of the Middle East Conflict*. Rev. ed. New York: Penguin Books, 2008.

Lenczowski, George. *Soviet Advances in the Middle East*. Washington DC: AEI Press, 1972.

Lippman, Thomas W. *Egypt After Nasser: Sadat, Peace, and the Mirage of Prosperity*. New York: Paragon House, 1989.

———. *Inside the Mirage: America's Fragile Partnership With Saudi Arabia*. Boulder CO: Westview, 2004.

Marr, Phebe. *The Modern History of Iraq*. 3rd ed. Boulder CO: Westview, 2012.

Masadi, Mahmoud. "The Idea of Arab Nationalitarianism." In *Contemporary Arab Political Thought*, edited by Anouar Abdel-Malek. London: Zed Books, 1983.

Morse, Edward L. "A New Political Economy of Oil?" *Journal of International Affairs* 53, no. 1 (Fall 1999).

Mortimer, Edward. *Faith and Power: The Politics of Islam*. New York: Random House, 1982.

Nasser, Gamal Abdel. "The Morrow of Independence." In *Contemporary Arab Political Thought*, edited by Anouar Abdel-Malek. London: Zed Books, 1983.

Nawwab, Ismail I. *Saudi Aramco and Its World: Arabia and the Middle East*. Dhahran, Saudi Arabia: Saudi Aramco, 1995.

Parker, Richard B., ed. *The October War: A Retrospective*. Gainesville: University Press of Florida, 2001.

The Policy of the Soviet Union in the Arab World: A Short Collection of Foreign Policy Documents. Moscow, Russia: Progress Publishers, 1975.

Priddy, Hervey A. "United States Synthetic Fuels Corporation: Its Rise and Demise." PhD diss., University of Texas, 2013. Available online at http://repositories.lib.utexas.edu/handle/2152/21978.

Primakov, Yevgeny. *Russia and the Arabs*. New York: Basic Books, 2009.

Quandt, William B. *Camp David: Peacemaking and Politics*. Washington DC: Brookings Institution, 1986.

Rabinovich, Abraham. *The Yom Kippur War: The War That Transformed the Middle East*. New York: Schocken Books, 2004.

Rogan, Eugene. *The Arabs: A History*. New York: Basic Books, 2009.

Rubinstein, Alvin. *Red Star on the Nile*. Princeton NJ: Princeton University Press, 1977.

Sadat, Anwar. *In Search of Identity*. New York: Harper and Row, 1977.

Sadat, Camelia Anwar. "Sadat and His Vision." In *Sadat and His Legacy: Egypt and the World, 1977–1997*, edited by Jon B. Alterman. Washington DC: Washington Institute for Near East Policy, 1998.

Sadowski, Yahya. "Egypt's Islamist Movement: A New Political and Economic Force." *Middle East Insight* 5 (November–December 1987).

Sayigh, Yezid, and Avi Shlaim, eds. *The Cold War and the Middle East*. New York: Oxford University Press, 1997.

Seale, Patrick. *Asad of Syria: The Struggle for the Middle East*. Berkeley: University of California Press, 1989.

Shlaim, Avi. *The Iron Wall: Israel and the Arab World*. New York: W.W. Norton, 2000.

Sick, Gary. *All Fall Down: America's Tragic Encounter With Iran*. New York: Random House, 1987.

Sorley, Lewis, ed. *Press On! Selected Works of General Donn A. Starry*. 2 vols. Fort Levenworth KS: Combat Studies Institute Press, 2009. Available online at http://usacac.army.mil/cac2/cgsc/carl/download/csipubs/PressOnI.pdf.

Stanislaw, Joseph, and Daniel Yergin. "Oil: Reopening the Door." *Foreign Affairs*, September/October 1993. Available online at http://www.foreignaffairs.com/articles /49205/joseph-stanislaw-and-daniel-tergin/oil-reopening-the-door.

Stephens, Robert. *Nasser*. London: Pelican Books, 1973.

Stork, Joe. *Middle East Oil and the Energy Crisis*. New York: Monthly Review Press, 1975.

Takeyh, Ray. "What Really Happened in Iran." *Foreign Affairs* 93, no. 4 (July–August 2014).

Telhami, Shibley. *The World Through Arab Eyes: Public Opinion and the Reshaping of the Middle East*. New York: Basic Books, 2013.

Terzian, Pierre. *OPEC: The Inside Story*. London: Zed Books, 1985.

Vance, Cyrus. *Hard Choices: Critical Years in America's Foreign Policy*. New York: Simon and Schuster, 1983.

Vassiliev, Alexei. *King Faisal of Saudi Arabia*. London: Saqi Books, 2012.

Vatikiotis, P. J. *The History of Egypt, From Muhammad Ali to Mubarak*. 3rd ed. Baltimore: Johns Hopkins University Press, 1985.

Waterbury, John. *The Egypt of Nasser and Sadat: The Political Economy of Two Regimes*. Princeton NJ: Princeton University Press, 1983.

Wenig, Gilad. "Egypt's Army of God." *Foreign Affairs*, October 31, 2014. Available online at http://www.foreignaffairs.com/articles/142327/gilad-wenig/egypts-army-of-god.

Yergin, Daniel. *The Prize: The Epic Quest for Oil, Money, and Power*. New York: Simon and Schuster, 1991.

Youssef, Michael. *Revolt Against Modernity: Islamic Zealots and the West*. Leiden, Netherlands: E. J. Brill, 1985.

Index

Sayih, Hamid, 261–62
"Saturday Night Massacre" (Watergate scandal), 20
Schlesinger, James, 13, 26, 97
Schotta, Charles, 107
Schultz, George P., 100, 107
Seale, Patrick, 8, 67
Shamir, Yitzhak, 183
Sharon, Ariel, 19, 183
Sidki, Aziz, 62, 64–65
Simon, William E., 70, 107
Sinai Peninsula: el-Arish (town), 162, 177, 232; Egypt's assault on, 14–15; Israeli settlements in, 152–55, 161–62, 168; Third Army trapped in, 22–25, 27, 28–32. See also "land for peace" formula
Sinai II disengagement agreement, 73–74, 122–23, 269–71; Baghdad boycott and, 203
Sisi, Abdel Fattah al-, 239
Six-Day War (1967), 11; Israel's borders and, 14–20, 32, 80, 93, 96, 119; oil embargo and, 93, 96, 104–5; UN Security Resolution 242 and, 121–22, 125, 151, 153. See also "Judea and Samaria"; "land for peace"
Soviet Union: aid to Egypt, 49–51, 57; anger toward Israel, 22, 26; anticolonialism and, 41–46; Baghdad Pact (1955) and, 42–43, 44; Baku international congress (1920, Azerbaijan), 42; competition with U.S. or influence, 37, 46–47, 49, 98–99; comprehensive regional resolution and, 124–25; Czech arms deal, 44, 48–49; decline in influence on Arabs, 75–81; foreign policy failure in Egypt, 76; foreign policy objectives, 41, 46, 52, 67–68; ideological gap, 65, 66–68; influence on Egypt, 51–53, 55; role in Egypt, 39–40, 75–81, 149; strategic defeat of, 37; weapons to Egypt, 55–56, 59–66, 75
Soviet-U.S. détente, 11–14, 19, 23, 27–28, 98, 125
Soviet-U.S. joint statement for Middle East negotiations, 136; Israel's rejection of, 136–37

Stalin, Joseph, 41–42
Stanislaw, Joseph, 114
"Steadfastness and Liberation Front," 204
Sterner, Michael, 57, 230
Sudan: coup attempt in, 58–59; Khartoum Summit, 188, 194
Suez Canal 22, 44–45; Egypt's crossing of, 14–15; nationalization of, 48, 86; reopening of, 106, 254
Sykes-Picot Agreement (1916), 42, 191
SYNFUELS Corporation, 113, 115
Syria: cease-fire and, 22; disengagement of forces and, 104–5; merger with Egypt, 193; October War and, 8–11, 34; peace talks and, 117–24, 133–35; Soviet Union and, 43, 45, 50, 52, 66–67, 77. See also Assad, Hafez al-; Baath Party; United Arab Republic

Takfir w'al Hijra, 221–22, 239, 241, 275. See also extremists, Muslim; Muslim Brotherhood
Telhami, Shibley, 81,
"Three No's Policy" toward Israel, 188, 194
Tilmasani, Omar, 226–28, 243, 272
Trans-Alaska Pipeline, 102
Treaty of Friendship and Cooperation (Egypt-Soviet), 54–55, 56, 57, 58

United Arab Republic, 193. See also Egypt; Syria
United Nations, Geneva peace conference. See peace conference (Geneva)
United Nations Security Council Resolution 242 (1967), 21–22, 59, 121–23, 125, 151–52; Israel's annexation of Golan Heights and, 184; Israel's settlements in territory obtained in 1967 and, 155–57. See also "land for peace"
United Nations Security Council Resolution 338 (1973), 21–22, 118–19, 121–23; Soviet-U.S. enforcement of Arab-Israeli cease-fire and, 25, 27–28. See also October War: cease-fire
United States: competition with Soviets for influence, 37, 46–47, 49, 98–99; "containment" strategy, 46; intelligence

Other works by Thomas W. Lippman

Understanding Islam: An Introduction to the Muslim World

Egypt After Nasser: Sadat, Peace, and the Mirage of Prosperity

Madeline Albright and the New American Diplomacy

Inside the Mirage: America's Fragile Partnership with Saudi Arabia

Saudi Arabia on the Edge: The Uncertain Future of an American Ally

Arabian Knight: Colonel Bill Eddy USMC and the Rise of American Power in the Middle East